Anonymus

Handbook of the Sudan

Anonymus

Handbook of the Sudan

ISBN/EAN: 9783742899552

Manufactured in Europe, USA, Canada, Australia, Japa

Cover: Foto ©Andreas Hilbeck / pixelio.de

Manufactured and distributed by brebook publishing software (www.brebook.com)

Anonymus

Handbook of the Sudan

[*All Rights Reserved.*

HANDBOOK

OF THE

SUDAN.

PART I.—GEOGRAPHICAL.

THE SUDAN, SOUTH OF OMDURMAN; FROM WADAI TO ABYSSINIA, AND FROM KHARTUM TO THE ALBERT NYANZA.

PART II.—HISTORICAL.

SKETCH OF THE HISTORY OF THE SUDAN TO DATE.

COMPILED IN THE INTELLIGENCE DIVISION, WAR OFFICE,

BY

CAPTAIN COUNT GLEICHEN,
Grenadier Guards, D.A.A.G.

1898.

LONDON:
PRINTED FOR HER MAJESTY'S STATIONERY OFFICE,
BY HARRISON AND SONS, ST. MARTIN'S LANE,
PRINTERS IN ORDINARY TO HER MAJESTY.

And to be purchased, either directly or through any Bookseller, from
EYRE & SPOTTISWOODE, EAST HARDING STREET, FLEET STREET, E.C.; or
JOHN MENZIES & Co., 12, HANOVER STREET, EDINBURGH, and
90, WEST NILE STREET, GLASGOW; or
HODGES, FIGGIS, & Co., Limited, 104, GRAFTON STREET, DUBLIN.

Price Two Shillings.

INTRODUCTORY NOTE.

With the exception of a portion of the Bahr el Ghazal country and parts of the Nile south of Lado, no part of the regions treated of in the following pages has been traversed by Europeans since the Hicks' Disaster in 1883.

Many changes have doubtless occurred since the spreading of the Mahdist rebellion over these vast territories; but these changes are mainly historical, affecting the condition, lives, and numbers of the population.

As regards topography, the rivers may have altered their course to some extent, much ground must have gone out of cultivation, and we know that many towns and villages have ceased to exist, whilst wild animal and vegetable life has been on the increase. But it can hardly be expected that important changes can have taken place in the territorial aspect of the countries dealt with.

It is, therefore, to be hoped that the following account of the geographical aspect of the Sudan, compiled from the works of responsible travellers, will be found to be accurate.

[In Part I, nearly half of Chapters III and IV, and almost the whole of Chapter V, has been taken from the "Report on the Egyptian Provinces of the Sudan," Intell. Branch, W.O., 1884. To the same source is due most of the history (Part II) from 1837 to 1882.]

J. C. ARDAGH,
Major-General, D.M.I

15th *July*, 1898.

CONTENTS.

PART I.—TOPOGRAPHICAL.

CHAPTER I.

THE WHITE NILE FROM KHARTUM TO THE ALBERT NYANZA.

	PAGE
General Description (downstream)	1
Junction of the Niles at Khartum	2
Navigability (upstream)	2
Landing Places	6
Climate	7
Distances (in miles)	8
The Nile above Khartum (detailed description)	9

CHAPTER II.

TRIBUTARIES OF THE WHITE NILE.

		PAGE
(a)	The Blue Nile :—	
	General Description	21
	Detailed Description	22
(b)	The Sobât	26
(c)	The Bahr ez Zeraf	27
(d)	The Bahr el Ghazal	28
(e)	The Bahr el Arab	35
(f)	Southern Affluents of the Buhûr el Ghazal and el Arab	36

CHAPTER III.

COUNTRY ON THE LEFT BANKS OF THE WHITE NILE AND BAHR EL ARAB.

		PAGE
(a)	Kordofan :—	
	General Description	38
	Means of Transport	41

	PAGE
Route I—Omdurman to El Obeid:—	
(i) Omdurman to Abu Kurat *via* Tira el Hadra	42
(ii) Khartum to Abu Kurat *via* Woad Shelai	44
(iii) El Getaineh to Abu Kurat	45
(iv) Abu Kurat to El Obeid	45
Water Supply	48
Population and Tribes	51
Towns and Localities (El Obeid, &c.)	56
Produce	57
Animals	60
Climate	61
(b) Darfur:—	
General Description	64
Inhabitants (v. also p. 54)	67
Produce	69
Towns (El Fasher, &c.)	71
Route II—El Obeid to El Fasher	72
" (i) *via* Guradi	73
" (ii) *via* Foga (telegraph route)	77
Southern Darfur, between Dara and Hofrat en Nahas	78
Route III—Dara to Hofrat en Nahas	79
(c) Dar Nuba:—	
Description	82
Population	83
(d) Shilluk District:—	
Description and Population	84

CHAPTER IV.

COUNTRY TO THE EAST OF THE WHITE NILE.

(i) *Country between the White and Blue Niles.*

(a) Sennar:—	
General Description	87
History	88
Topography	88
Inhabitants	90
Animals and Climate	93
Route IV—Sennar Town to Kawa	94
(b) Dar el Fungi:—	
Description	95
(c) Beni Shangul:—	
Description	96

(ii) *Country East of the Blue Nile.*	PAGE
General Description	97
(d) Gedaref:—	
Description..	98
Gedaref to Gallabat Country	99
(e) Gallabat:—	
Description..	99
Inhabitants..	100
(f) Country between the Blue Nile and Gallabat:—	
Description..	100
Rahad and Dinder Rivers..	101
(iii) *Country East of the Bahr el Jebel.*	
General Description	101
Former Stations and Communications..	102
Inhabitants	105
Produce	107

CHAPTER V.

BAHR EL GHAZAL COUNTRY.

General Description of Southern Provinces	110
(a) Bahr el Ghazal (old Mudirieh)	111
Topography and Villages..	112
Bongo Country and Inhabitants..	114
Dinka Country and Inhabitants..	119
Nuer, Jur, and other Tribes	121
Krej and Dar Fertit Country	125
(b) Lado (old Mudirieh)..	126
(c) Rohl (old Mudirieh):—	
Topography and Villages..	127
(d) Mâkaraká (old Mudirieh):—	
Description..	129
Tribes	130
Topography..	131

PART II.—HISTORICAL.

CHAPTER I.
HISTORY UP TO 1882.

	PAGE
Early History	139
Conquest by Mehemet Ali	143
Upper Nile Explorations and Developments	147
Conquest of Darfur	151
Relations with Abyssinia and Harrar (1874–1879)	153
Gordon's Operations	159
Campaigns against Slave Traders	164
Rise of Mahdism	170

CHAPTER II.
EVENTS ON NILE FROM 1882 ONWARDS.

1883 and the Hicks' Expedition	174
Arrival of Gordon at Khartum	175
Nile Expedition Starts	176
Fall of Khartum and Death of Gordon	178
Gianis	179
Egyptian Army	180
Toski and Frontier Fighting	181
Dongola, 1896	183

CHAPTER III.
DARFUR AND KORDOFAN FROM 1882 ONWARDS.

Sketch of Events	185

CHAPTER IV.
EASTERN SUDAN FROM 1882 ONWARDS.

Suakin Expedition, 1884	188
" " 1885	189
Abyssinians Attack Dervishes; Battle of Matamma	191
Recapture of Tokar	192
Battle of Agordat and Recapture of Kassala	193

CHAPTER V.
BAHR EL GHAZAL AND EQUATORIA FROM 1882 ONWARDS.

Lupton and the Rebellion	195
Emin and the Rebellion	196
Relations with Congo Free State	200
Capture of Regaf	205

APPENDICES.

	PAGE
APPENDIX I—THE SUDD	207
,, II—GLOSSARY OF SOME SUDANESE TERMS	214
,, III—BONCHAMP'S JOURNEY TO THE UPPER SOBÂT, 1897–98	216

LIST OF AUTHORITIES CONSULTED.

*Perennial Irrigation (Willcocks), 1894.
*Report on Egyptian Provinces of Sudan, Red Sea, and Equator, 1884.
Incidents of a Journey through Nubia and Darfoor (Ensor), 1875-76.
Uganda and the Egyptian Soudan (Felkin), 1879-80. 2 vols.
Petermann's Mittheilungen, 1875, 1877, 1879, 1880, 1881, 1883, 1888.
General·Report on the Province of Kordofan (Prout), 1877.
Northern and Central Kordofan (Colston), 1878.
The Cradle of the Blue Nile (de Cosson), 1873. 2 vols.
Travels in Africa (Junker), 1875-86. 3 vols.
Voyage aux deux Nils (Lejean), 1860-61, and Atlas.
The Nile Tributaries of Abyssinia (Baker), 1861-62.
Survey of the White Nile (Logbook by Lieut. Watson), 1874-75.
Emin Pasha and the Rebellion at the Equator (Jephson), 1887-88.
Reisen in Nubien, &c. (Russegger), 1838.
*Report on the Soudan (Lieut.-Col. Stewart), 1883 (Blue Book, Egypt, No. 11, 1883).
Reisen im Gebiete des Nil (Marno), 1869-73.
With Hicks Pasha in the Soudan (Colborne), 1883.
Reise in der Egyptischen Äquatorial Provinz und in Kordofan, 1875 (Marno).
Campaigning on the Upper Nile and Niger (Vandeleur), 1897.
Bulletins de la Société Khédiviale de Géographie, 1876-93.
Proceedings of the Royal Geographical Society, 1884, 1887.
Mahdism and the Egyptian Sudan (Wingate), 1891.
Ten Years Captivity in the Mahdi's Camp (Ohrwalder), 1892.
Colonel Gordon in Central Africa (Hill), 1884.
Mittheilungen der Geog. Gesellschaft in Wien, 1870.
Ten Years in Equatoria (Casati), 1880-89. 2 vols.

---

* Government Publications.

LIST OF AUTHORITIES CONSULTED—*continued.*

Fire and Sword in the Sudan (Slatin), 1895.
Heart of Africa (Schweinfurth), 1868–71. 2 vols.
Travels in Central Africa (Petherick), 1862. 2 vols.
Ismailia (Baker), 1869–73. 2 vols.
*Eritrea (Major Barker), 1894.
*Eritrea and Abyssinia (Col. Slade), 1896.
Zeitschrift für Allgemeine Erdkunde, 1879.
*History of the Sudan Campaign (Colvile), 1889. 2 vols.
*Intelligence Reports, Egypt, 1891–98.
Emin Pascha (Schweitzer), 1898.
Albert Nyanza (Baker), 1867. 2 vols.
Journal of the Discovery of the Source of the Nile (Speke), 1863.
Sette Anni nel Sudan Egiziano (Gessi), 1891.
L'Afrique explorée et Civilisée, 1881–85.
A Walk Across Africa (Grant), 1864.
      And numerous other Periodicals and Newspapers.

* Government Publications.

PART I.—TOPOGRAPHICAL.

CHAPTER I.

THE WHITE NILE FROM OMDURMAN TO THE ALBERT NYANZA.

GENERAL DESCRIPTION (DOWNSTREAM).

AFTER leaving the Albert Nyanza, the White Nile (or, as it is called up there, the Bahr el Jebel) flows for 135 miles in a deep broad arm with scarcely any slope or velocity to Dufile, and then, after a short and troubled course, tosses over the Fola Falls in a channel only 50 yards broad. From here it continues as a torrent to about Regaf.

Here the river is 7 feet deep at low Nile and 15 feet in flood time, discharging between 500 and 1,600 tons (18,000 to 60,000 cubic feet) per second. The regulating effects of the great lakes are well felt here. It is here at its lowest in winter, begins to rise about the 15th April, with a maximum about the end of August.

From Regaf to Bor, 112 miles, the river is in one channel, with a rapid fall.

From Bor to the junction of the Bahr el Ghazal, 316 miles, the river meanders in numerous marshy channels, with a very feeble slope. The main channel, always used, is the Bahr el Jebel. In this reach are the sudds, dams of living vegetation, at times capable of barring the surface and completely blocking navigation (*v.* p. 3 and Appendix I for details of the *sudd*).

At the junction of the Bahr el Ghazal and the Nile is a lake called No, or Mogren el Buhûr, varying in size according to the season, but in the summer about 60 square miles. At that time of year the lake and swampy surroundings act as an evaporating basin, and the loss of water is consequently considerable. The waters here also become polluted with decaying green vegetable matter.

The Bahr el Ghazal has a feeble discharge in summer, but occasionally exceeds the Bahr el Jebel when in flood.

In the stretch between the Bahr el Ghazal and the Sobat, 80 miles, the current is slow, and the channel is occasionally blocked by sudd.

During flood the Sobat has a discharge nearly equal to that of the Bahr el Jebel above the junction. In summer the discharge from the Sobat is feeble, and the river is occasionally quite dry. The soil brought down by the Sobat is light and friable.

Here the river changes its name* and now becomes the Bahr el Abiad, or White Nile. From this point down to Omdurman, 505 miles, it receives no more affluents, except occasional tributes in very rainy seasons from several small khors on the east bank. The breadth of the river in this stretch varies considerably at different points, but averages about a mile at high Nile, and the depth ranges from 15 feet at low Nile to 23 feet in flood time.

The current is sluggish, and its action is nearly throughout on the right bank, owing to the prevailing north-west winds. Bottom sandy in parts, but mostly mud.

JUNCTION OF THE NILES AT KHARTUM.

At Khartum half Nile usually occurs about the middle of July; high Nile at the end of August or beginning of September, lasting about a month. Half Nile end of November; lowest Nile in April.

Maximum Blue Nile flood about 25th August. Its mean discharge at high Nile at Khartum is 8,000 tons (280,000 cubic feet) per second.

In flood the discharges of the two Niles are nearly equal, but from November to March the White Nile is the main source of supply.

The average difference here between low and high Nile is 22 feet ($17\frac{1}{2}$ to 26 feet).

The Blue Nile branch east of Tuti Island is sometimes dry at low Nile.

---

* According to some, the change takes place at Lake No.

NAVIGABILITY (UPSTREAM).

From Omdurman upstream to Lado, practically 1,000 miles, the only obstacles to navigation at any time of the year are :—

    1. Scarcity of fuel (for steamers).
    2. The *sudd*.
    3. Sandbanks.

1. In 1875 Gordon wrote :—" Navigation from Lado to Khartum is almost impossible; firewood is scarce and becomes more so every year; there are numerous sandbanks." Fuel.

All travellers concur in the difficulties of procuring sufficient fuel for the steamers, especially in the *sudd* districts, where trees are scarce, and the difficulties in getting at them are very great.

The only method would appear to be to institute numerous wood stations along the banks from which to replenish the steamers or the fuel-nuggers which they tow, and to moor floating wood stations at intervals in the *sudd* reaches.

2. The *sudd* is formed as follows :— *Sudd.*

The Bahr ez Zeraf, the lower course of the Bahr el Jebel, and the Bahr el Ghazal, are all liable to become choked with masses of vegetation or grass barriers formed by floating islands of weeds, &c. The river bed then assumes the appearance of a vast marsh, which, if neglected, becomes impracticable for navigation.

As Colonel Gordon states, below Regaf the Nile spreads out into lakes; on the edge of these an aquatic plant with roots 5 feet long flourishes.

The natives burn the tops when dry, the ashes form a mould, fresh grasses grow till it becomes like *terra firma*. The Nile rises and floats out these masses; they come down to a curve in the river, and then stop, and so the river becomes at length blocked. These barriers have been cut away many times; Sir S. Baker cut his way through 80 miles of sudd, but unless the river is kept open by constant navigation, it is always liable to reform. In September, 1880, Gessi Pasha suffered great hardships on the Bahr el Ghazal during his voyage back to Khartum. He found a grass barrier in front, and a strong wind drove other floating islands down upon him in rear, thus blocking him up for weeks.

In September, 1879, Mr. Felkin was unable to proceed from Lado to Khartum by water on account of the *sudd*, which Mr. Lupton had been trying for nearly a year to open up. At that time, 26 miles of grass had been removed. In 1881 Mr. Felkin reported the Nile as clear again.

The Nile when it flows into Lake No (Mogren el Buhûr, or Mouth of the Streams), appears to be a channel varying from 100 yards to a mile in breadth, but, from the masthead of a steamer, it would be seen that there is a sea of grass on either side of this water channel, and that the real banks of the river are 4, 8, or even 12 miles distant on either side. Under all this grass is water, which is slowly making its way down to fill up the void caused by the absorption of the water by sand and sun. The grass which floats on the top of the water is so thick that it is possible to walk on it; and, were it not for this covering, the evaporation over such a vast area would greatly diminish the supply of water to Lower Egypt.

A considerable part of the Nuer tribe actually live on the floating mass of vegetation, fish and the stalks of a waterlily forming their only food. The surface of the water is covered by a dense tangled mass of papyrus, ambach, and other water plants, which in places grow to a height of from 15 to 30 feet.

At the rise and fall of the Nile, quantities of the grass get torn away and floated down stream. If the season is unusually wet, the stream increases in bulk and rapidity, and innumerable large masses of the grass are sent floating down.

The channel of the river (not its true banks) is very tortuous, and at Lake No, where the Bahr el Ghazal flows into the Nile, there is a sharp turn to the east. If the water contributed simultaneously by the Bahr el Ghazal happens to be insignificant and incapable of sweeping away the floating masses, a block is the result.

The Nile was blocked by the *sudd* from 1870 to 1874, from 1878 to 1881, in 1884, and in 1895. Since 1896 it is believed to be open.

For full details and methods of dealing with the *sudd*, *v.* Appendix I (p. 207).

Navigation above Sobat.

3. Sandbanks are of course more of an obstacle at low **Sandbanks.** Nile than at high Nile, and shift about every year; but, judging from the accounts of numerous travellers, they do not appear to form any considerable obstacle.

Steamers used to take 20 to 40 days up stream from Khartum to Regaf, and 15 to 30 days down stream; a good deal depended on the *sudd* and the season.

The navigation of the river up to the mouth of the **Navigation** Sobat is at all times easy, occasional islands and sandbanks forming the only difficulties. The deepest channels lie usually towards the eastern bank.

From the Sobat to Lado the navigation of the river is not in itself difficult, but a perfect and recent knowledge of the route is required, in order not to deviate into one of the lateral branches that are frequently met with, and which, varying from year to year, are chiefly in evidence during and after the rainy season. There are also many sandbanks on this stretch.

Above Lado (according to Colonel Gordon):—

"The River Nile is navigable for boats at all seasons from Lado to Bedden, and during three parts of the year it is navigable for steamers of moderate draught to a point within 3 miles of Bedden, but in the dry season steamers cannot proceed higher than Gondokoro.

"The road by land from Lado to Regaf, and from Regaf to Bedden, is through well cultivated undulating country.

"From Bedden the river is navigable for boats to Kiri, but the rapids at Bedden necessitate a transhipment at that station. The road between these two points by land is through an open country, sloping gently down to the river. Two considerable streams are crossed, one of which, the Lima, is generally knee-deep, but after storms is impassable. It has a steady current. The second, the Kya, is a torrential stream, and always dangerous to cross.

"After passing the Kya, the country becomes more rugged, and this continues on both sides of the Nile, until near Kiri, where it opens out again, and continues open to near Labore.

"The river from Kiri to Labore cannot be termed impassable. There are some awkward rapids in it, but they would soon become known, and the river might be utilised to a great extent. The land road is good and through cultivated country.

"At Labore the country comes down more abruptly to the river on both sides. The river continues of much the same character as between Kiri and Labore up to the junction of the Asua with it, when a series of more serious rapids occur, which terminate in a steep rapid, with a fall of about 1 in 6, known as the Fola Rapids. For about $2\frac{1}{2}$ miles beyond this the river is free from any obstacle up to Dufile and even to Lake Albert. The land road passes along the river's edge, the chain of mountains on the west bank coming down close to the edge, and leaving a small plain at their base. This continues nearly up to the point of junction of the Asua, where the country ends in a steepish cliff on the river bank. The road crosses the River Tyoo, a considerable stream 9 miles from Labore. Eight miles further on it leaves the river bank, and, crossing several torrent beds, it follows the foot of the hills to near Dufile. This part of the country is a wilderness.

"The only real difficulty in the navigation of the Nile is the Fola Rapid. The abruptness of the land on each side of the rapid prevents any hope of towing a boat or steamer through it.

"Just above these rapids the country opens out into a vast plain, bounded on the west by the Kookoo Mountains.

"The Nile from Dufile to Lake Albert is very sluggish, and papyrus isles abound in it. The west bank is well cultivated, but the east bank is generally deserted."

It need perhaps hardly be remarked that the channel, and even bed, of the Nile varies from year to year, and that therefore even the most accurate surveys (such as Lieut. Watson's in 1874) do not hold good, as regards details, for any length of time. Emin Pasha, writing in 1878, found many variations from the above-mentioned survey, and still more would there be 20 years later.

LANDING PLACES.

As for landing places on the White Nile, Gordon states that in the stretch between Fashoda and 100 miles north of it, "people do land, but it is over your knees in the rainy season." The only other landing places between Fashoda and Regaf are at the junction of the Sobat, then nothing except Shambeh and Keniseh for 360 miles till Bor; then one halfway between Bor and Lado, the remainder being at Lado, Gondokoro, and Regaf. Above Regaf one can land anywhere up to the Fola Rapids. Between Dufile and Magunga there are five landing places.

CLIMATE.

The rains on the Upper Nile in the "Equatorial" regions from the Albert Nyanza to the Bahr el Ghazal fall mainly from February to April. As one proceeds northwards the heavy rains become later, the *kherif* or rainy season between the Sobat and Khartum being, as a rule, from the end of June to the end of August. Rains.

Colonel Stewart states (1883) :—

" At Gondokoro (near Regaf) the rainy season begins in April and lasts till September. The rains are very heavy, lasting sometimes for 10 or 12 hours. From Gondokoro south to the Equator the rainy seasons increase in length till on the Equator it may be said that rain and sunshine succeed each other in rapid succession all the year round. January, February, and March are, however, the wettest months."

Heavy thunderstorms and rains occur at intervals during the rest of the year, especially from October to January, in the hilly region round Regaf and the *sudd* district to the north of it.

During the late autumn, winds are very variable, blowing from all points of the compass. East and southeast winds perhaps predominate, especially in the upper reaches. Winds.

The temperature from August to December does not range high, and rarely exceeds 92°. In the *sudd* region the maximum averages about 85°, but owing to the dampness of the district, fevers are rife, and the heat and mosquitoes are difficult to bear with equanimity. Temperature.

Distances* along the Nile above Omdurman.

Bank.	Name of Place.	Miles. Intermediate.	Miles. From Omdurman.
R.	El Getaineh	49	49
R.	El Kuraza (Kordofan road leaves river opposite here)	12	61
L.	J. Arashkol	34	95
R.	El Kawi (Koweh, Kawa)	25	120
—	Abba Island (N. point, extends 18 miles)	34	154
R.	Gebelèn (Jebel Ain)	61	215
R.	J. Ahmed Aga	111	326
L.	Kaka	54	380
L.	Fashoda (on island † at high Nile)	64	444
R.	Mouth of Sobat river	61	505
R.	„ Bahr ez Zeraf	25	530
L.	Lake No (Mogren el Buhûr)	45	575
L.	Mouth of Bahr el Ghazal	9	584
L.	Hellet Nuer	116	700
L.	Shambeh	100	800
R.	Bor (up backwater)	100	900
L.	Lado (in ruins)	94	994
R.	Gondokoro (in ruins)	6	1,000
L.	Regaf	12	1,012
L.	Bedden	13	1,025
L.	Kiri (foot of cataract, "Fola Rapids")	26	1,051
L.	Muggi	11	1,062
L.	Laborc	15	1,077
L.	Dufile (head of cataract)	34	1,111
L.	Wadelai	89	1,200
—	Lake Albert Nyanza	45	1,245
—	Murchison Falls	32	1,277
—	Ripon Falls and Victoria Nyanza	255	1,532

* Taken off Lieut. Watson and Chippendall's Survey of the White Nile, 1874.
† There is some doubt on this point.

The Nile above Omdurman.

(For routes along the banks, *v.* pp. 42 to 45.)

Based on Lieut. C. M. Watson's, R.E., Survey and Log-Book, October to December, 1874.—High Nile. Other Authorities:—Marno, Prout, Vandeleur, Felkin, Colborne, Chippendall, Gordon, Baker, Junker, Schweinfurth.

R. = Right Bank—East; L. = Left Bank—West; W.C. = Water Channel.

Place.	Miles.		Description.
	Intermediate.	From Omdurman.	
	5	5	Current opposite Omdurman 1·6 knots (October). For the first 175 miles, as far as the south end of Abba Island, the course taken (by Lieut. Watson's 4-knot steamer) hugs the east bank. After this point it is mostly in mid-channel. W.C. 2 miles broad, both banks low and flooded, and heavily wooded. Low sandy hills on R.
J. Ardah ..	7	12	Low range of hills L. Channel narrows.
	13	25	Volcanic bluff L. Auli hill R., a little further on.
	10	35	W.C. 3 miles.
Mahmudieh ..	3	38	Mahmudieh R. Village.
Abu Hagr ..	7	45	Bank rises slowly. W.C. 1¾ miles. Kordofan road leaves river gradually from Abu Hagr L.

Place.	Miles.		Description.
	Intermediate.	From Omdurman.	
J. Arab Musa ..	2	47	Arab Musa hills on L, 4 miles from bank.
El Ketaineh (Geteina, Ketena).	2	49	El Ketaineh R. L. covered with trees. A small neatly-built town on the high right bank of the river. Landing place for goods and slaves. Large herds of camels, goats, and oxen. Dhura, maize, and sugar-cane grow luxuriously. River 600 yards broad, strong current. Two camels and eight men to a ferry boat load here.
Es Salahieh ..	2	51	Es Salahieh L. (or R.?) Cultivation and sand-hills R. For the next 30 miles W.C. 2 miles, L. much flooded, and many trees.
Wad Sheli ..	17	68	Wad Sheli (Woad Shelai or Shelahait).
	3	71	Wood. Fine sand R.
Feki Ibrahim ..	2	73	Feki Ibrahim R. Woods. Distant hill 30 miles west.
	9	82	J. Arashkol range becomes visible in S.S.W.
Gezireh Manir ..	8	90	Manir Island.
Jebel Arashkol ..	4	94	J. Arashkol, 10 miles from L., apparently volcanic. Country between here and Nile termed Tura el Khadra.
Ed Duêm ..	6	100	W.C. ¼ mile. Ed Duêm village L. Both banks wooded. A ferry, Meshra Tura el Khadra, close above Duêm. Action here 23.8.83. Small Egyptian garrison repulsed Mahdists. Formerly fortified camp; dirty and unhealthy. Many islands now for the next 20 miles—Shebeslieh, Hegasi, Hassaniyeh, Mabileh, Om Lebben, &c.

Arab Musa—Gebelên.

Kaweh (or Kawa)..	20	120	Kaweh (or Hellet ed Danagla) R. Formerly a good-sized town; houses chiefly unburnt bricks, conical roofs; mimosas. W.C. 250 yards. Karanek village L. Thick woods L. District known as Ellahawin. Formerly depôt of grain for White Nile. Kawa village in ruins 1883. Square fort facing the river, built 800 yards from village by Hussein Pasha in this year; surrounded by a ditch. Caravan road to Sennâr town, v. p. 94.
	18	138	Hill R. 4½ miles.
El Munga ..	4	142	El Munga village L. Grass land. W.C. opens out to
Abba Island (north end).	12	154	1 mile at the north end of Island of Abba. A few huts and a little cultivation and many trees R. District called Manageh. Take eastern channel.
Marabieh ..	3	157	Marabieh R. Action 29.4.83. Hicks Pasha defeated the Dervishes. Western channel unknown. Very few trees on Abba (other accounts say "the finest timber in the Sudan"); gradually becoming quite bare; ditto R.
Abba Island (south end).	15	172	Eastern channel 400 to 700 yards. Many birds and monkeys. There is a ford (between Sennaar and Kordofan) at the south end of the island close to
Abu Zehr ..	6	178	Abu Zehr or Zeir village L. Shilluk and Bagara Selim country begins. Also serût fly.*
	22	200	W.C. ¾ mile. Low L., high grass. Jebel Ain on R. A rocky reddish double-peaked hill running east and west. Little wood.
J. Ain (Gebelên = two hills).	15	215	Massacre of Egyptian troops here by Mahdists 1882. Marsh on L. with trees beyond. Rate of current 1·25 knots. Distant peak E.S.E. 40 miles. Hicks Pasha's victorious expedition to Sennaar reached Gebelên in summer 1883.

* A fly with sharp sting, drawing blood; very persistent; orange coloured; size of small wasp; black and white wings; most frequent during and after rains.

White Nile.

Place.	Miles.		Description.
	Intermediate.	From Omdurman.	
	12	227	Marsh both banks. Hippopotami and numerous birds.
	23	250	Reeds extend for 400 yards R. Wood behind. W.C. 300 yards. From Jebel Ain up to Fashoda, *i.e.*, for about 230 miles, both banks are very marshy, rendering it difficult to land. The marshes extend from 10 yards to 400 yards from the water, and in rear of them are usually to be found belts of trees. Current 1 to 1·4 knots. Width of W.C. perpetually alters.
Gagamudi	20	270	Gagamudi. Reed fringe 20 yards. Wood. No inhabitants. Both banks thickly wooded, large trees, fringed with thick swamp.
J. Ahmed Aga ..	56	326	Jebel Ahmed Aga R. 400 feet high, volcanic; a few small trees to the summit. A small stream, often dry, Bahr el Dinka, flows into the river just north of the hill. Marsh penetrable here and wood obtainable.
Matenieh Island ..	4	330	Matenieh Island : navigable channel L. 10 miles long. Shilluk country and numerous huts L. No inhabitants R. Both banks marshy, grass and *ambach*.* No trees.
Kaka	50	380	Kaka, Shilluk town L. 400 yards from river. Wood. River takes a turn here. District called Ghrab el Esh.
El Ghrab	7	387	El Ghrab L. Marshy banks, few trees.

Fashoda	..	56	443	Fashoda is situated on the left bank (an island at high Nile) in N. lat. 9° 52′ 16″. E. long. 32° 19′ 7″, 443 miles by river from Khartum. It completely commands the river, and was formerly fortified by a wall and flanking towers. It was formerly a Government convict settlement, with a garrison of 800 men and 3,500 native inhabitants. A considerable amount of land was under cultivation—cotton (150 tons in 1873), maize, sugar, &c. It is now (1898) believed to be garrisoned by only a few Dervishes, who use it as a post from whence to raid grain for Omdurman, and to collect revenue from the river boats, and taxes from the neighbouring Shilluks and Dinkas. East channel navigable. For the next 50 miles the banks are low; a few trees L. at first, then grass both banks, villages only L.; subsequently scattered trees R.
Sobat River	..	62	505	Junction of Sobat (or the Bahr el Asfar = Yellow Nile); 150 yards wide, quite full (25th October), current 2 knots. The meeting of the Sobat and Nile is very marked, the former being yellowish and the latter a blackish green. The Sobat water is far superior to that of the Nile (for further description, v. p. 26). There was formerly an Egyptian station (Sobat) and small garrison here L. bank. (N. lat. 9° 23′ 50″; E. long. 31° 48′ 36″.) Healthy; wood station 3 miles up stream. From this point the Nile flows west and east for the next 80 miles. Some travellers state that a northerly branch of the White Nile, the Lōlle, joins the Nile opposite Sobat. Island in Nile opposite junction of Sobat, with Shilluk village, Nau, on L. bank. Quantities of fish and birds. Natives use light *ambach** rafts curved up in front to a point; have to be dried as water soaks in. On leaving Sobat the Nile, now termed the Bahr el Jebel, is about

* A thick cane-plant, lighter than cork.

Place.	Miles. Intermediate.	Miles. From Omdurman.	Description.
	15	520	1,200 yards wide for a short distance and then becomes hemmed in with high marsh of tall grass and *ambach*. Many floating islands (October).
			On R. marsh only 10 yards wide, trees close to stream. Many villages L. W.C. 160 yards.
Giraffe River (Bahr ez Zeraf).	10	530	Mouth of the Bahr ez Zeraf on R. Clear W.C. 20-25 yards, probably closed up now. (For further description, v. p. 27.) From here onwards, both banks are mostly invisible, being concealed by high grass and other marsh. W.C. only 40 to 80 yards wide.
Bahr el Ghazal	54	584	Junction reached of Bahr el Ghazal and White Nile. According to some, it is only from this point upwards that the latter is termed the Bahr el Jebel.
			The junction of the Bahr el Ghazal with the Bahr el Jebel presents the appearance of a lake (Lake No, or Mogren el Buhâr) about 3 miles in length and 1 in width, varying according to the season. There is but little appreciable stream from the Bahr el Ghazal, and it bears rather the character of a backwater.
			The river has a current of about 1¼ miles per hour as it sweeps round the angle, and its breadth here does not exceed 130 yards.
			The depth of the lake varies from 7 to 9 feet. The surrounding country is a vast flat with slight depressions. In the wet season extensive lakes are formed, and sodden marshes during the dry weather. At low water

			the lake is divided into two sections connected by a channel over half a mile long.
			The Bahr el Ghazal is navigable as far as Meshra er Rek (*v.* p. 28).
			The passage leading to the Bahr el Ghazal from the White Nile is so choked up with masses of floating papyrus and weed that the stream is scarcely perceptible.
			A multiplicity of backwaters, and waters remaining in old river beds, adjoin it; but an enormous volume of water is carried through this channel to the Nile.
			There is always great difficulty in navigating the mass of floating weed, and it was while so engaged that Gessi, shut in for weeks by the grassy barrier (or *sudd*), suffered such hardships.
			Entrance channel of Bahr el Jebel only 15-20 yards. On turning south the marsh becomes much higher; principally *ambach*; W.C. 40-60 yards; floating *sudd*; no animals; a few birds. River very curly; no banks visible; current 1·8 knots. Papyrus both sides and floating marsh.
Hellet Nuer	..	51	635	A few trees R.
		65	700	Some scattered Nuer villages L., about 2 miles from stream. Many floating islands, necessitating constant change of course.
Maiet Hurshid	..	10	710	Maiet Hurshid lagoon depression R.; apparent R. 6 miles distant, and L. 10 miles; 2-knot current; channel varies from 20 to 60 yards, swelling occasionally into small lakes (*maiet*) on either hand.
		40	750	A few trees R.
		20	770	Large *maiets*.
Bahr ez Zeraf	..	27	777	South mouth of Bahr ez Zeraf channel; no current; 20 yards wide; probably closed now.
Shambeh	..	23	800	Shambeh. Former wood station L. Lies 2 miles up a broad backwater, with slight current; therefore a small river possibly flows in here. Huts L. at mouth of backwater.
				On regaining the main channel the river winds very much; many

Place.	Miles.		Description.
	Inter-mediate.	From Omdurman.	
Kika	10	810	*maiets*; marsh much lower; firm ground, and trees visible in many places a mile or two off. Kika village L.
Meraba Sidera ..	7	817	Village L. Dry land. W.C. 150 yards. Channel R., said to join the Bahr ez Zeraf.
Abu Kika	13	830	District on R.
Kenisseh ("Church")	10	840	Former Missionary Station L. Old garden 1½ miles up the river. Forest 200 yards from L. Plenty of wood. River 461 feet broad here. Current 1·9 knots.
Tugu	3	843	Village R. on island (?). Less marsh; *ambach* and papyrus disappeared; banks very flat. A few fishing villages.
Aliab	27	870	Aliab district L.
Bor	30	900	Bor, "an inconvenient wood station." Established as an Egyptian post by Gordon in 1874. The Dervish forces, beaten at Regaf by Chaltin (February, 1897), are reported to have retired to Bor, and to be there still (1898). Numbers reported variously from 5,000 to 15,000 altogether, probably exaggerated. Bor lies on the R. bank about ¼ mile up a backwater at right angles to the Nile, on the far bank of a channel running parallel to the main stream. Latter breadth 552 feet, current 1·9 knots. Another possible wood station 1 mile up stream. On leaving Bor, the L. bank is a flat plain to the horizon; R. firm ground, 7 feet high, with forest in process of denudation. W.C. 60–120 yards.

Shambeh—Regaf.

	20	920	R. high and wooded; L. marshy. Fishing villages.
	6	926	Sharp turn, strong current.
	4	930	Banks exchange character. L. 5 to 15 feet above water, woode 1. R. flat, a foot or two above water. Shir district on R. Many huts and much cattle both banks, chiefly on R.
	6	936	Follow west channel of stream; less current.
	4	940	Village; friendly natives.
	3	943	A mile south of junction of two channels, a third channel visible on R. bank, reported to join the Sobat. Gebel Lado visible to S.S.W. 47 miles off.
	15	958	Cultivated ground L. Both banks firm ground.
	7	965	Numerous islands. W.C. 350 yards. Strong current and awkward turns. Many huts and villages both banks. Banks become higher and well wooded in parts.
Lado	28	993	Lado L. bank. Station formed by Gordon in 1874. Headquarters of Emin's Province; in his time a well built town, brick buildings, fortifications, gardens, promenades, &c. Now (1898) in ruins.
Gondokoro	7	1,000	Gondokoro, formerly Austrian Mission Station. R. bank. A Headquarters Stations was built here by Sir S. Baker and called Ismailia, in May, 1871. Now in ruins. N. lat. 4° 54′ 25″; E. long. 31° 43′ 46″. Both banks now begin to rise. Many islands.
Regaf (Rejaf)	12	1,012	Regaf, on L. bank. Post established by Gordon in November, 1874. Taken by Dervishes, October, 1888. Headquarters of Dervishes in the Equatorial Province, 1888–1897. Driven out by Chaltin, 17.2.97. N. lat. 4° 44′ 32″; E. long. 31° 39′ 24″. River 560 yards wide. Chaltin reports (1897) earthquakes as common here. [From the R. bank opposite, a track leads, parallel to the river and about 12 miles distant from it, to Duflé, and thence to a point opposite Wadelai.] Bari tribe both banks. The banks now rise higher, and the country becomes hilly; fine scenery; many large trees. Past wooded islands; slow current at first, 1¼ knots; subsequently

White Nile.

Place.	Miles. Intermediate.	Miles. From Omdurman.	Description.
Beddén	13	1,025	very rapid at Beddén; boats have to be towed, and generally goods have to be transhipped at Beddén, a former Egyptian station on an island. Width of river 100 yards. Dr. Felkin took 11 hours from Regaf up the rapids to Beddén in November, 1878—towed in nuggar by natives—and 1½ hours on return journey. The Congo forces under Chaltin struck the Nile here in February, 1897, and drove the advanced Dervish post back. For the next 25 miles the banks are about 8 feet high (November) and well wooded.
Kiri	25	1,050	Kiri. - Former Egyptian post on L. From here onwards to Dufile the Nile is mostly unnavigable on account of rapids. Height a.s.l, 1,819 feet.
	5	1,055	5 miles beyond Kiri are the Guji Rapids.
	5	1,060	Yerbora Rapids.
Muggi	2	1,062	Muggi L. at foot of Neri Hills, 1,500 feet, scattered hills on R. Old Egyptian post.
	6	1,068	The river channel only 60 yards wide. Series of rapids to
Labore	9	1,077	Labore L. Former Egyptian post. Above Labore the river makes a bend to the east occasioned by the Kuku and Meto Hills on the L. bank. Series of rapids.
Asua River	19	1,096	Mouth of Asua River, R. bank.
Fola Cataract	4	1,100	Fola Rapids or Cataract, in narrow gorge. The name of Fola Rapids is often given to the whole series of rapids between Kiri and Dufile. Quite unnavigable. W.C. 50 yards broad. 2½ miles south of the cataract

Regaf—Mgerenin.

Unyama River	..	7	1,107	the river is free from obstacles, but navigation again does not begin till the mouth of the Unyama River, R. bank.
Karas	..	3	1,110	Karas, a village L.
Duflé	..	3	1,113	Dufile on the L. bank. Height a.s.l., 2,053 feet. Formerly an Egyptian post. The old fort is situated close to the water's edge at a bend in the river; grass and reeds 10 feet high all round; parapet, ditch, and mud-brick walls of houses still left, behind these some lemon and cotton trees are the only sign of the Egyptian occupation (1895). It was finally evacuated by Emin's troops 5.1.89 and taken possession of by the Dervishes. High ground L. Jebel Ellingoa (900 feet) just behind Duflé. British flag hoisted here (14.1.95) by Major Cunningham and Lieut. Vandeleur. N. lat. 3° 34′ 21″; E. long. 32° 2′ 00′ (Vandeleur). For the next 25 miles the banks are well populated; country not inviting; a few trees scattered about; villages hidden away among high rocks and boulders on small hills close to the river. A certain amount of mtama and dhurra cultivated, but very few sheep or goats.
Umia	..	11	1,124	Village L. bank; Debolan village behind it.
Kogora	..	5	1,129	Village L. bank.
Ungwe	..	8	1,137	Village R. bank—chief's name Abu Suma. Somo grain. Country to the east becomes open and flat, with high grass. River broadens; large quantities of sudd met with; few landing places; marshy.
	..	7	1,144	Range of hills begins on R. bank, parallel to river, and 2 miles from it. Landing place west bank; clouds of mosquitos. River becomes about 1½ miles broad, but the W.C. through the sudd is only about 500 yards.
Bora	..	24	1,168	Bora, an old Egyptian fort on the R. bank; deserted. Emin's last steamer sank here, through old age. Stream fairly strong; large floating islands; care necessary in navigation.
Mgerenin	..	10	1,178	Village L. bank. Rhinoceros, elephant, antelope.

White Nile.

Place.	Miles. Intermediate.	Miles. From Omdurman.	Description.
Towara	10	1,188	A Madi village. Strong current. Many mosquitos at night.
Wadelai Fort	12	1,200	Old fort on L. bank; completely grass-grown (1895). N. lat. 2° 43' 11''; E. long. 31° 28' 00'' (Vandeleur). Former Egyptian post. Occupied by Owen and relinquished by Thruston in 1894.
Fachora	1	1,201	Very strong stream; river narrows considerably. Very large village R, on rising ground overlooking rapid. A few miles above Fachora the river opens out into a small lake; much papyrus and floating vegetation. Lur (or Alur) tribe both banks.
Ayara	16	1,217	Village of important chief L. bank—friendly. Country barren and dried up. Bend in river; 150 yards broad; strong stream.
Amat	4	1,221	Village on R. (?) bank; river 600 yards. From here onwards the L. bank is thickly wooded and luxuriant, with a few clearings and poor fishermen's huts and canoes. Shuli tribe R. bank. River gradually widens, until almost imperceptibly one finds oneself on the Albert Nyanza.
	24	1,245	

CHAPTER II.

TRIBUTARIES OF THE WHITE NILE.

(a) BLUE NILE.
(b) SOBÂT.
(c) BAHR EZ ZERAF.
(d) BAHR EL GHAZAL.
(e) TRIBUTARIES OF BAHR EL GHAZAL.
(f) SOUTHERN AFFLUENTS OF THE BUHUR EL GHAZAL AND EL ARAB.

(a) THE BLUE NILE.

General Description.

THE Blue Nile (or Bahr el Azrek) has its sources in the mountains of Abyssinia, *i.e.*, in the third great reservoir of the Nile, Lake Tsana. This lake has an area of 1,160 square miles and is 5,800 feet above sea level.

The river is 846 miles long. It is comparatively clear in summer, but during flood, from the beginning of June to the end of October, it is of a reddish-brown colour, highly charged with alluvium.

The Blue Nile flood swells fitfully in May, begins to rise steadily in June, and is at its maximum about the 25th August. It falls rapidly after the middle of September.

During the dry season the Blue Nile is so reduced that there is sometimes not sufficient water for the small vessels engaged in transporting produce from Sennâr to Omdurman. In this season the water is beautifully clear, whence the name of the Bahr el Azrek. It is much superior in quality to the White Nile water.

Detailed Description.
(Marno, February to August, 1870, and others.)

The usual limit of navigation for nuggers on the Blue Nile upstream of Omdurman is Karkoj, and this portion of the river is traversed by them mostly in the dry season, *i.e.*, from about the end of October to the end of May. Between June and October the flood, coupled with strong south winds, is sometimes too much for loaded nuggers. On the other hand, during the dry season there is often not enough water for navigation.

The country on the banks of the river above Khartum is for the first 100 miles or so uninteresting. The banks are steep and high (February) and in places bare and sandy. Numerous villages, mostly on the left bank, and chiefly composed of tukls. Cultivation of cotton, dhura, &c., alongside the river. For journeys by land the left bank is generally used.

Place.	Miles.		Description.
	Inter-mediate.	From Khartum.	
Soba	25	25	Old Soba L. bank, New Soba R. bank. Formerly the capital of a flourishing kingdom.
El Fun, Efun, or Eilafun	6	31	Large village R. bank.
Beshagra	10	66	Village R. bank. Reported Dervish grain depôt and powder factory.
Kamlin	14	80	(In ruins in 1871.) Large village L. bank, much cultivation (*v.* also "Report on Nile and Country between Dongola, &c.," Part III, Route VIII (iii)).
Rufaa	26	106	Village R. bank. Grain stores, 1897.
Messalamieh ..	14	120	Large village—8,000 inhabitants; 3 or 4 miles from L. bank. Large area of cultivation almost to the White Nile—exports quantities of corn.
Abu Haraz (Rahad River)	20	140	Near the junction of the Rahad River (dry in dry season), on R. bank (*v.* p. 101). Road to Gedaref and Kassala branches off here. Banks wooded.
Wod Medani ..	2	142	Wod Medani (Woad Medineh or Wold Medina). Crossing-place from east bank. Large market, ruinous village, former Egyptian garrison.
River Dinder ..	18	160	Mouth of the Dinder River, R. bank; dry in dry season (*v.* p. 101).
Sennâr	70	230	Sennâr. Large village L. bank; 6,000 inhabitants in 1863. Formerly important. Route from here west to Abba Island (*v.* Pruyssenaere, p. 94). Market Mondays and Thursdays. Climate changeable and unhealthy. North winds too strong in winter, and dampness after rainy season breeds fevers. Formerly Egyptian post

Blue Nile.

Place.	Miles.		Description.
	Intermediate.	From Khartum.	
Karkoj ..	50	280	under a Mamur. Many animals, from elephants to parrots, in the vicinity. In January, '63, the Nile here was 550 yards broad and 9 feet deep. High Nile is 21 feet and Low Nile 6 feet deep. An important trading centre in the old days for gum arabic, tamarinds, cattle, cotton, coffee (from Abyssinia), vegetables, &c. This is the last place where one can lay in stores for further travel. The river here is at High Nile 470 yards broad, average depth 23 feet, current 5 miles per hour; at Low Nile the figures are 330 yards, 8 feet, and 1¼ miles respectively. Surroundings bare. Woods, chiefly acacia, &c., begin at some distance off. (Marno took 25 days in a nugger from Khartum to this point, in February.) The Upper Sennâr negro race, the Hammeg, now begin to populate both banks; a dirty, indolent race. From Karkoj upwards both banks are highly cultivated and fertile, but only on the narrow strip which is liable to inundation in flood time. Camels become gradually replaced by donkeys and oxen. Too damp for horses; many mosquitos and poisonous flies (surréta*). Much rough cloth woven. Track on R. bank lies through cultivation and occasional thick woods.
Bedos ..	56	336	A village on high hilly ground, just south of the large Hamda Wood. Many lions in the neighbourhood. R. bank.
Rogeires ..	12	348	Roseires (1,621 feet above sea level), a straggling town of tukuls surrounded by zoribas. Numerous tribes, old Egyptian post. Two markets a week.

			Remarks.
"Seventh Cataract"	..		Hilly ground, thick dom palms along river banks; mimosa woods to the east. Plenty of game. Many rocks in the river, the so-called "7th Cataract" for the next 40 miles. Navigation very difficult.
Kharaba	..	25	373	A village with many water-holes. Guinea fowl, &c., in abundance. R. Ground rises and becomes stonier. Thick forests, many khors.
Eivan	..	18	391	A large tukul village at the south foot of J. Maaba, a hill 400 feet above the river. R. Baobab trees. Kafala trees begin (strange-looking trees, with the bark hanging in strips). The track leaves the river and passes over stony ground and through many villages and woods cut up by khors.
J. Madalik	..	35	426	Jebel Madalik on L. bank. Track approaches river.
Tumat River	..	1	427	Junction of Tumat River on L. bank. Woods gradually leave the river and disclose beautiful scenery of hills and valleys. Uneven hill, J. Fámaka, stretches S.E.
Famaka	..	5	432	Famaka, R. bank, situated opposite the massive Gebel Fazokl, on L. bank. The river here is narrow and very deep, and flows through rocky banks. A deep khor joins the river here from the S.E. The village was founded by Mehemet Ali in 1840, and surrounded by a wall of boulders, of which little remains, and that chiefly on the east side. Tukls and formerly some tiled houses. The southernmost Egyptian post after its incorporation in the Sennár Province by Said Pasha in 1856. Before this date, and after 1873, there were posts in the gold country of Dar Berént and Beni Shangul to the south.† Magnificent view from Gebel Fazokl, which lies 2,659 feet above sea level and 897 feet above the river, and lies due north and south. In 1897 an Abyssinian post was reported to be holding Famaka. Beyond Famaka the Blue Nile becomes the "Abai", and its wanderings through Abyssinian territory hardly come within the scope of this work.

* V. p. 11. † V. p. 96.

(b) THE SOBÂT.

General Description.

The mouth of the Sobât (sometimes called Bahr el Habesh or Bahr el Asfar) is about 505 miles south of Khartum by river. In January, 1863, Baker reports it as being bank-full, with a powerful current and a depth of from 26 to 28 feet. The water is far superior to that of the White Nile, but is yellowish in colour and colours the Nile for a great distance. The force of the stream is so superior to that of the White Nile that it banks up the waters of the latter as it joins them. This has the effect of heading back the floating vegetation.

The breadth of the mouth is given variously, from 60 to 140 yards, and the depth from 18 to 30 feet, evidently varying according to the season. The channel is very winding, and in the rainy season (May to October) is reported navigable up to three days' journey beyond Nasser. In the dry season, however, it appears occasionally to dry up altogether in parts.

The sources of the river are so far undiscovered, but they must evidently lie in the mountainous regions of Southern Abyssinia, for the water is coloured by earthy volcanic matter. Four hours' steam above Nasser the river is said to be divided in four branches, named, from north to south, Adura, Nikwar, Gelo, and Abual, whose banks are inhabited by tribes rich in ivory and camels. The Jibbe (Juba?) River is said to be the main branch higher up.

Bóttego's expedition in 1896 penetrated from Lake Rudolf to the upper reaches of the Sobât and followed the course of the "Juba" River (not to be confused with the other Juba which flows into the Indian Ocean), which appears to be the main source of the Sobât. [On his way he came across two affluents on the right bank, the Gelo and Upeno; he turned up the latter towards Abyssinia and was shortly afterwards killed by the natives, only two of his party (Vannutelli and Citerni) escaping.]

Theories in Abyssinia and elsewhere point to the Omo River as being the upper course of the Sobât. This has been denied by several travellers, but the question has not been finally set at rest (*v.* Appendix III for latest information).

Ascent of the Sobât.

For the first 60 miles the country on both banks is flat prairie and marsh, with a few low forests and huge grasses. Nuer tribe, numerous villages, harmless people. Many crocodiles and hippopotamus. Birds and game, ostrich, antelope, and lion numerous. Deleb palms; floating vegetation occasionally met with. Banks, 12 to 18 feet high, left bank highest; slow current; no trees right bank. Villages :—

Alual	55th mile	—	Nuer tribe.
Angog	67th „		„ „
Agot	72nd „		Bonjak tribe.
Gêl	92nd „		„ „
Geziret el Habeshi	105th „		Reported occupied by Abyssinian post, 1897. Doubtful.
Amol	118th „		Falang tribe. Country now becomes more wooded.
Ajak	158th „		
Nasser	170th „		

All the above villages on the left bank.

Nasser (Nâzir), a former Egyptian post, lies low on a bend in the river; marked by a large dôm palm. Large village of Deng opposite. Much cattle and elephants. Nyuak tribe, friendly.

Exploration ends about here, though some travellers (*e.g.*, Debono in 1855) appear to have gone higher up.

(c) Bahr ez Zeraf.

Thirty-eight miles (five hours' steam) west of the mouth of the Sobât is the mouth of the Bahr ez Zeraf (Giraffe River). This is not, strictly speaking, a river: it is a lateral channel of the Bahr el Jebel, which issues from this river 23 miles north of Shambeh.

It is very winding, about 19 feet deep at the mouth, and with a water channel of varying width, occasionally broadening out into small lakes. It flows through a perfectly flat prairie country diversified with forest. This prairie is sometimes dry in the winter, but is flooded during the rainy season and is cut up in every direction with marshy channels.

Baker in 1870, owing to the *sudd* near Lake No, tried a short cut *viâ* the Bahr ez Zeraf to the upper Bahr el Jebel, but was stopped by the accumulation of grass and swamp. The following year he tried again, and after being left high and dry in parts by the sinking of the waters, he succeeded after immense difficulties in cutting his way out through 80 miles of *sudd* and mud in two and a half months (January to March, 1871).

Marno in 1872 penetrated to within 28 miles of the Bahr el Jebel, but was obliged, by shallows and obstructions, to turn back; and Gordon in 1874, after going a certain distance, had to do the same; he described it as a "ditch."

The district is sparsely inhabited by the Nuer tribe.

Up to Zeriba Kawer, a former station of the Chief Kutchuk Ali, about halfway, 80 miles, up the river, the latter is navigable, but beyond this it rapidly gets shallow (January and February). Reeds very cutting. Boats have to be hauled along here by main force. Marshy, stinking banks and water; millions of mosquitos, black, biting ants, and damp heat; monotonous outlook. River gradually becomes a bankless swamp. Occasional raised dry bits of land, called "dabba." Only one outlet from this into the Bahr el Jebel and the channel very difficult to find, being narrow, though deep, and often blocked with floating vegetation. Rainy season, April to July.

In 1874 the Bahr ez Zeraf was blocked up, and it is very probable that it is not now navigable.

(*d*) BAHR EL GHAZAL.

The Bahr el Ghazal is navigable as far as Meshra er Rek. It flows into the White Nile through a narrow channel and through Lake No (*v.* p. 14).

The river becomes wider above the mouth, but the breadth is frequently only sufficient for a single vessel, while the depth is 30 feet or more. During the rains, the surrounding country becomes like a vast lake.

Passing through the Nuer land, the river wends its way through a finely wooded country to the mouth of the Bahr el Arab; here it has a width of 1,000 feet, but narrows immediately on passing this affluent.

The depth now falls to about 15 feet, showing that the Bahr el Arab is the main contributor to the lower portion of the river.

The current in the Bahr el Ghazal becomes hardly perceptible as it passes through the Dinka country, and the spreading waters give the appearance of lakes.

The river towards Meshra er Rek varies in depth from 8 to 15 feet, and is covered with floating grass islands.

The following description by Dr. Junker of the Bahr el Ghazal is the most complete, accurate, and recent account of that river. It is therefore given in his own words:—

"We started (in a paddle steamer) up the Bahr el Ghazal on the 21st February, 1880, and I began at once to record the angle measurements of the fluvial channel, and to sketch any salient features in the course of the river and its immediate vicinity. During the rainy season the whole region of the Moqren el Bahür forms an extensive lake, whereas at low water it is divided into two sections, which communicate through a channel a little over half a mile long. Even after entering the river properly so called, the observer seeks in vain for any conspicuous object, or even a mere bush, from which to take his bearings. On both sides extensive tracts are permanently flooded, but the river gradually narrows, apparently, to half or even a third of the lacustrine depression; nevertheless, it still for some hours of steam navigation maintains a clear waterway at least 50 yards wide. Throughout this stretch nothing was visible except a dry patch on the right side, occupied by a wretched fishing hamlet whose Nuer inhabitants led a sort of amphibious existence.

"A little higher up there came into view, also on the right side, the Maiyeh bita Komundári (the Keilak of the older maps), branching off like a river far into the interior. A second backwater followed, still on the right side, and soon after the Maiyeh bita er Rêq, on the left. Smaller channels of like formation, and communicating with the main stream, also occur for a long way on both banks; but they are so little conspicuous that it is often difficult to say whether they are the mouths of tributaries or merely backwaters.

"An apparently endless uniformity is the prevailing feature of the landscape, the low grassy mere scarcely broken by a few tall papyrus stalks. An open expanse which I noticed, penetrating far into the grassy steppe, our *reïs* told me was the Khor Deleb. Half an hour beyond it we sighted another wretched Nuer fishing village. With the field-glass I could descry some ten huts, on which about 30 of the natives had swarmed, the better to observe our steamer. In the immediate vicinity the main stream is joined by an important affluent, which would appear to be a northern branch of the Khor el Arab.

"Shortly before noon we passed two Deleb palms (*Borassus flabelliformis*), forming on the left side a distinct landmark near the mouth of the already-mentioned Khor Deleb. Some scrub and a few old termite hills, rising above the grass on the distant horizon, indicate the locality where this dreary watery region begins to merge in more solid higher ground.

"In the course of an hour we passed the third Nuer hamlet in this region—a group of some 20 mud huts with straw roofs peeping up above the grass. The stream, which had hitherto presented a free surface at least 50 yards wide, now assumed a sudden and surprising change. The navigable open track seemed to trend sharply round to the right; hence my astonishment when we made straight for a narrow opening in the grass, which would have escaped any but a sharp eye familiar with the locality. We thus suddenly passed from a broad waterway to a narrow channel, where the steamer's paddle-boxes grazed the herbage on both banks. This was the continuation of the Bahr el Ghazal, whereas the apparent main stream turned out to be only the Bahr bita el Arab branch.

"The open current was only 15, or in the broadest places at most 50 yards wide, and pond-like expanses were but rarely met. Nor was it often possible to detect the true river banks, or distinguish the parting-line between land and water. The higher grounds, rising like islands above the grassy plains, were indicated more by their scanty brushwood and ant-hills than by their actual elevation; while the region exposed to inundation stretched in many places far into the dreary waste.

"In the midst of this oppressive monotony it was a relief for the eye to rest on a few clumps of trees away to the south-west. The trip itself had hitherto been made, if slowly, at all events without any interruption. Now, however, began our troubles, floating grass getting entangled between the paddles, which had every now and then to be cleared, or else the whole waterway becoming obstructed by floating masses which required more or less effort either to break through or remove. Hence the rate of progress varied greatly, thus considerably increasing the difficulties of my survey.

"About three o'clock we met the first real grass barrier, which, however, was surmounted in the course of twenty minutes, during which the ropes of the boats in tow snapped several times. Later followed other loose accumulations, which, though easily removed, still caused much delay; one more compact mass especially took fully an hour to be mastered. At sunset we cast anchor, to give the *Embába* time to overhaul us.

"Early next day, the 22nd February, I resumed my observations, while the puffing and snorting engine continued its struggles with the grassy obstructions. Now, for the first time, we noticed a stretch of woodlands near the left bank, followed later by another on the same side, while on the opposite bank two solitary trees served as clear landmarks for my calculations. Beyond the Ghaba Jer Dekka, a little grove close to the river, the stream meanders incessantly through the monotonous plains, nowhere relieved by a single conspicuous object. Here the floating obstructions thickened; but towards noon we unexpectedly reached a good broad waterway, and after another sharp bend a large Maiyeh (backwater) was passed on the right, soon followed on the left by a large tree, grouped round which were a few Negro huts.

"Our experienced pilot now drew my attention to the new barriers which had been formed since his last trip, and which required considerable efforts to set aside. Those, on the other hand, which have once been pierced are always more easily overcome, though they may have partly closed up again. But although the way was thus to some extent cleared by our vessel, the *Ismaïlia*, the *Embába*, with the boats in tow, found great difficulty in getting through the sedgy masses in our wake.

"Next day, after getting through some smaller masses, we were arrested for several hours by a huge barrier of a felt-like consistency, and nearly the third of a mile in extent. In the course of another hour's steaming through open water we reached the confluence of the Maiyeh bita el Deleb, as I was assured by the pilot; he also informed me that this watercourse is joined by a stream from the south, presumably the Jau, which rises far to the south in Abakáland.

"The Maiyeh is fringed by strips of woodland, and the prospect is also relieved by euphorbias, which occur here somewhat frequently. The papyrus also grew more profusely, and in the shallower parts of the stream along the river-banks this reed was associated with a young growth of *ambach* (*Herminiera elaphroxylon*). The wooded banks of the Maiyeh are occupied by the Nuers, whose huts were visible from the steamer.

"The last great barrier, some 2,000 yards long, was soon followed by another fully as large. We anchored before it for the night.

"The *sudd* at which we were now arrested was of a peculiarly tough consistency, and, being about a mile and a quarter long, it took nearly a whole day of combined efforts to force it. The barrier occupied a bend in the river, leaving only a narrow channel in the centre free of herbage.

"On the 26th February, after passing another sudd nearly 500 yards long, I took soundings, and found the Bahr el Ghazal at this point ranging in depth from 20 to 30 feet. A little higher up the fluvial scenery assumed a different aspect. The river gradually grew wider, while the banks stood out more distinctly, being both higher and better wooded than lower down. Some native dwellings also came into view, and at one point the north side was fringed with a regular forest of *ambach*, a plant which had already been passed some days previously. Here, for the first time, the observer is able to form some idea of the actual size and volume of the river, which in some places was nearly 350 yards wide between its wooded banks.

"At the Ghaba bita 'l Arab, on the north side, the main stream is joined by the Bahr el Arab; owing to the slight incline, the confluent waters here expand into a spacious basin, which appears, from a communication made to me by Schweinfurth, to have had no existence at the time of his explorations (1869-71). Farther on follows another expanse of stagnant waters, beyond which the open channel contracts at first to 50 or 60, and then to a little over 20 yards. Here, also, the woods become thinner, and at last again give place to boundless flooded grassy plains, with patches here and there of tall *ambach*.

"In the narrow channel we were again delayed two hours by a mass of *sudd* about 160 yards deep, above which the stream broadens to 55 yards; but nothing is visible except an endless expanse of grass and *ambach*. At this season the stouter *ambach* stalks grow to the thickness of an arm, or even a leg, and rise from 12 to 18 inches above the water. From the top sprouts the tufty foliage, the stem proper, from 10 to 15 feet long, lying below the surface.

"In the vicinity of the arboreal vegetation shallow water may generally be expected, whereas the *ambach* reed often shoots up from considerable depths. Just now it was beginning to blossom, and the tufts were already in many places covered with a pretty yellow flower. With the extremely light stalks the Shilluk negroes make their primitive river craft. The plant is not an annual, but lasts several years, and when full grown attains a height of 16 feet. In its lower part the stem bulges out to a thickness of 10 or 12 inches; it greatly resembles the Indian *Aeschynomene*, which is used for making summer head-gear, dainty toys, house models, and the like. Hence *ambach* is certainly one of the future resources of Africa, as a material that may come into use for technical purposes. The tangle of felt-like root fibre growing about the foot of the stem is built of little bulbs or tubers, whose purpose is not quite evident, as they neither produce sprouts nor appear to increase the buoyancy of the fibrous radicles.

"Towards sunset of the 27th February we passed the confluence of the River Jur coming from the south-west, and next day brought us to the end of our journey. During the last few hours the Bahr el Ghazal had in many respects again assumed a different aspect. Beyond the mouth of the Jur there was little to suggest a river in the ordinary sense of the term. The 'Kit,' as this section is called, presents the appearance of a boundless sea of grass and sedge, with an open expanse winding away to the head of the steam navigation at Meshra er Rêq. The real navigable channel can be detected only by those familiar with the locality, so sluggish is the current, though the Kit is joined farther south by the Molmul. This relatively flat expanse, spreading out like an inland sea, is to be regarded as a result of the pent-up waters of the Jur, increased by the contributions of the Molmul also from the south-west, and probably by a branch of the Tonj, which permanently flows to the south-eastern part of this labyrinth of water, grass, and sedge." (A plan and sketch of this locality is given by Dr. Junker, Vol. II, p. 49.)

[The shores of the Kit are firm; its waters rise and fall, but have no other motion. It widens at its extremity into a basin of papyrus frequently choked by weed. In this basin are numerous islands, which serve as refuges for boats from hostile attack. The regular landing-place is on the southern shore of the basin. The first boat which entered the Bahr el Ghazal was that of a Khartum merchant surnamed El Habeshi, in 1854. Two years later Consul Petherick followed, and was the first to open mercantile transactions with the tribes.]

"Early on the 28th I was shown the spot, indicated by no particular landmark, to which, and even beyond which, the waters had retired after the heavy rainfall of 1878. The steamer from Khartum had on that occasion to cast anchor at this place, where, the water still continuing to subside, it was soon left high and dry above the stream. At that time people could go all the way by land to Meshra from this station, which stands at the head of the low-water navigation, and which has received the name of Matrak el Vapor, or 'Place of the Steamer.'

"The almost stagnant expanse of the Kit is in many places carpeted with the superb *lotus nymphœa*, and other aquatic plants. Of an evening the peculiar crackling sound is frequently heard, with which the magnificent milk-white calyx of these huge water-lilies bursts into bloom. Here and there the surface is broken by dry spots, which are partly nothing more than flooded termites' nests, a proof that in previous years the Kit had long remained free from the inundations. But some of these dry places are also real islands, on which the tall *Balæniceps Rex* may occasionally be seen mounting guard in his peculiarly motionless attitude.

"At some distance from the left bank I noticed a Negro village, beyond whose conic mud huts the southern horizon was bounded by a semicircular fringe of woodlands, a sure indication that we were at last approaching more elevated dry land. Presently our weary eyes were gladdened by the sight of the straw-thatched huts and the masts of some Nile boats grouped about the landing-stage.

"Four hours after leaving our last anchorage below the Kit we reached the new station of Meshra er Rêq. a little to the south-east of the now abandoned Meshra el Tujár ("Landing-place of the Traders"), which was formerly the starting point for all expeditions to the interior. The *Ismaïlia* cast anchor for the last time off a little island, on which nothing was to be seen except a few Government huts. Beyond it the flooded land still stretched away southwards to the already-mentioned amphitheatre of low-wooded rising grounds.

"We had entered the Bahr el Ghazal on the 21st February, consequently we had taken nearly eight days to ascend the river, owing to delays caused by the numerous floating obstructions. In order to render possible the cartographic survey of the river, I estimated for the *Ismaïlia* six different rates of speed, and in my calculations applied this scheme according to the nature of the obstacles. The course of the stream, as determined by 1,781 angular measurements, I found to be 214 kilometres, or say 130 miles long. It may be incidentally remarked that these results were found to agree in a surprising manner with a chart afterwards prepared by Marno, as well as with the section surveyed by Lupton Bey."

(e) THE BAHR EL ARAB.

The Bahr el Arab rises in Southern Darfur and flows for a distance of about 400 miles before reaching the Bahr el Ghazal. Very little is known of its course; it is

120 yards broad 300 miles above its mouth, and has at that point been crossed in boats (Felkin). Natives state it is navigable from above Taimo (330 miles) down to the Bahr el Ghazal,* but it appears to pass through marshy depressions on its course.

(*f*) SOUTHERN AFFLUENTS OF THE BAHR EL GHAZAL AND BAHR EL ARAB.

The characteristic of all these affluents is that in their upper reaches, coming from the hilly Nile-Congo watershed, they keep to their own beds at all seasons, while on the middle and lower reaches they overflow during the rainy season. On these reaches the rivers during the dry season serpentine in their narrow beds along the bottom of broad, sharply defined, trough-like depressions, which they fill to the banks in times of inundation. These depressions, 1 to 4 miles broad, lie 10 to 20 feet below the level of the surrounding country, and are mostly covered with reeds and grass.

The rainy season begins about July in these parts and lasts for about two months. After a particularly heavy downpour the rivers become impassable, but as the water runs off quickly, the troughs empty in a few days, and the rivers resume their ordinary channels, and may, even during the rains, become fordable in parts.

The chief rivers, supplied by numberless streams and tributaries, are the Rohl, the Jau, the Tonj, and the Sueh; the latter becomes the Jur about the seventh parallel, and flows into the Wau. These all flow into the Bahr el Ghazal.

The chief affluents of the Bahr el Arab are the Dembo and the Bili.

None of these rivers have been traversed in their entirety, and it is probable that none of them are navigable throughout the year. The natives do not appear to use them for transit, and for trade purposes navigation from the Bahr el Ghazal has always stopped at Meshra er Rek, whence goods have been transported by land.

---

* Statement to De la Kéthulle (Belgian) in 1894.

Judging from the accounts of travellers who have crossed these and other rivers in the country at certain points, they are mostly fordable during the dry season, and in flood time are from 6 to 20 feet deep. They seem to be full of fish at all times. Some of the beds are as much as 250 yards broad.

Dr. Junker found that the Rohl, Jau (Ayel), and Tonj were easily fordable in July and August, but that the Jur (or Geddi), having a deeper bed and a less-defined trough than the others, was, in the neighbourhood of Wau, in the middle of August, 10 feet deep, with banks 15 to 20 feet high, and a breadth of 230 yards. A native ferryboat holding 35 men was here available. The Wau River, traversed a few days later, was very similar, but rather deeper. The banks of the Jur and Wau are heavily wooded. The water is greenish-yellow, but good.

[For some other details about the country through which these rivers flow, *v.* Junker's "Travels in Africa," 3 vols.]

CHAPTER III.

COUNTRY ON THE LEFT BANKS OF THE WHITE NILE AND BAHR EL ARAB.

(a) KORDOFAN.
(b) DARFUR.
(c) DAR NUBA, SHILLUK, DAR FERTIT, &C.

(a) KORDOFAN.

General Description.

THE region which extends between the Nile and the eastern frontiers of Darfur consists entirely of vast plains, which rise gradually towards the south, and which form a tableland whose extreme altitude rises little over 2,000 feet above the level of the sea. The surface of this tableland is not interrupted by any chain of mountains. Towards the north are found a number of hills, rarely over 500 feet in height.

Further south are found isolated peaks, rising not over 800 feet above the surrounding plains. It is a country of steppes in which there exist no rivers, no streams of water however small; there are only a few wells at long intervals, furnishing but a scanty supply of water, which has to be drawn from very great depths. In the north-eastern region one can barely see here and there the "khors," or ravines of little depth, through which the rainwater finds its outlet during the season of *kherif* (rainy season). Most of these khors disappear in the sands which finally absorb the waters of the rains. There is good reason to believe that only a very small portion of this water reaches the Nile towards the south-east after the heavy rains. In the region surrounding Debbeh, towards the north-east, the ground is higher on the banks of the Nile than in the interior, and the little rainwater that falls is absorbed by the sandy soil.

In appearance, Kordofan is a monotonous rolling steppe

country formed of undulating plains. In the west, isolated peaks rise from 150 to 600 feet above the plains, such as Jebel Abu Senûn and Jebel Kordofan.

In the north-west, the groups of Kagga (Kaja) and Katûl, and in the south, that of Daïer, are compact mountain masses offering strongholds to brigands.

South of the 13th parallel of latitude, the country changes to flat, fertile, and thickly wooded plains, from which the rugged mountains of Takalla and Dar Nuba rise abruptly. The triassic formation extends over the whole province, of which the new red sandstone alternating with hypogen rocks is the most important feature. Over the sandstone, the ground is firm and gravelly, and contains much oxide of iron. The soil is bad, except when improved by the clay and potash resulting from the detritus of hypogen rocks where they crop up. Near El Obeid, igneous rocks, quartz, gneiss, and granite abound. On the *atmurs* or deserts, the signs of vegetation are very scarce. The steppes of Kordofan are from about 1,350 to 1,850 feet above the level of the sea, the greatest altitude being at El Obeid, and near the mountains in the north and south. They present a dull brown appearance, with here and there thickets of small acacias, a huge adansonia or two, and villages of conical straw huts; broad red patches mark the dokhn fields, which are green during the *kherif*, as are also the plains, which latter, however, by the middle of October, have again assumed their burnt-up appearance; this lasts till late in the following June, and, as Major Prout says, "only a waste of sand can be more forlorn."

Jebel Daïer, a compact group of mountains, which from a distance appear to present on every side a lofty unbroken front, are the highest mountains relative to the surrounding country in Kordofan, rising at least 1,000 feet above the plains. There is reported to be, in the interior of the group, a great basin well watered with ponds and springs. The inhabitants live on the mountain side safe from the Baggara. {J. Daïer.}

Takalla.—Jebel Wadelka is a detached group of the Takalla mountains lying to the north-west of them, and at about 20 miles distance from Jebel Daïer. It consists of bare precipitous granite peaks. The mountain country subject to the King of Takalla is very vaguely defined, but extends some 30 miles south of Jebel Wadelka. The {Takalla.}

height of the latter is about 500 feet, and the slopes have been terraced by the inhabitants in a remarkable manner. Water is supplied by springs which trickle out of the rocks, among which the inhabitants dwell.

Between Wadelka and Daïer is a flat, fertile, densely wooded country traversed by watercourses tributary to Abu Habl. It is, however, uninhabited.

There is also a luxuriant valley, thickly wooded, between Jebel Wadelka and the main range. The trees are mostly acacia, and a low thornless tree called *Libban*. There are also many deleb palms, tamarinds, and baobabs.

Limits. The limits of the province in the old days were ill-defined. The most northerly villages are Katûl, long. 30° E., lat. 14° 15′ N.; Safiyeh, long. 31° 45′ E., and lat. 15° 40′ N., and Shegeg, long. 32° 15′ E., and lat. 14° 30′ N.; but the Kababish, who roam over the steppes between these villages and the Nile used to pay tribute to the Government of Kordofan. On the south, the Baggara tribes and negro tribes of Takalla and Dar Nuba were nominally subject, and used to pay an uncertain tribute. Dar Nuba (or country of black slaves) lies at the southern corner of Kordofan, but its limits cannot be fixed with any precision, *v.* p. 82. On the west, the western limit of the range of the Beni-Hamid Beduins forms the boundary, a very uncertain one, passing near Abu Haraz and Kagga, between long. 30° 30′ and long. 29° 30′.

To the east, the authority of the Governor used to cease at a line running roughly parallel with the course of the Nile, and at from 10 to 20 miles west of its left bank.

Soil The soil of Kordofan is uniform, and is a granite sand mixed with clay; sometimes the clay, but more generally the sand, predominates, and this especially in the north and east, while in the small basins of Bara, Abu Haraz, and Melbeis, and, in general, south of El Obeid, there is a larger admixture of clay; and, as we pass still further south, the bed of the watercourses rising in Dar Nuba and sinking in lat. 13° long. 32° 25′, becomes somewhat plastic. In this neighbourhood also there are wide areas of forest country covered with a rich black mould formed by the decaying vegetation, this being especially the case between El Birket and the mountains of Nuba, and between Jebel Daïer and Takalla.

Some weeks after the termination of the rains the black soil cracks in wide and deep fissures.

South of parallel of 12° 30′ and west of longitude 32°, is the richest soil of Kordofan, composed of clay loam, with a certain admixture of felspar, which, if it could be watered, would produce magnificent crops of sugar-cane, corn, tobacco, and cotton.

The rest of the district is, though inferior to the above, a strong soil, and capable of being made productive; it is largely felspathic, with more or less iron, and considerable mica. It only wants water to make it fertile.

The land is in many places impoverished by the recurrence of the same crop for centuries; this is most common about Bara and Taïara.

Means of Transport.

Kordofan being a country of plains, carriageable roads might be made there with very little labour. Colonel Colston stated in 1875 that "a good teamster could without any difficulty drive a loaded six-mule wagon from Debbeh to El Obeid. The route to Khartum is still more practicable. There is no doubt that a Dutch Boer from the Cape or Port Natal colonies, if living in this country, would promptly supply himself with splendid ox-teams. It seems strange that the natives have never tried to make use of wheeled vehicles, nor even to use their fine oxen for ploughing. The wood found in the country would make tolerably good wheels, for sakiehs are made of it. The deep and shifting sand which prevents the use of vehicles in Lybia and other deserts is not found here. The chief difficulty would be to make wheels able to hold together in spite of the great heat and extreme dryness. I feel sure that wagon trains might be organised for the service of the troops stationed in Kordofan and Darfur, and that they would save expense to the Government. It would be necessary to use camels as draught animals, for which purpose they are well fitted. The trial I made of them in hauling the artillery, with simple ropes, proves that their enormous strength can be utilised with even more advantage for draught than for burden. A wagon, with four camels supplied with suitable harness, would easily transport the loads of 12 to 15 camels—40 to 60 cantars. The wheel tyres should be 10 to 12 inches wide,

Wagons.

Kordofan.

Itineraries.

in order not to sink in the sand, and it would probably be best to have wheels entirely of iron. A train of such wagons, under military organisation, with intelligent officers, would render important services for the transportation of troops, supplies, ammunition, telegraph, materials, &c."

As the region of Kordofan is uniformly of the same character throughout, *i.e.*, a vast hard plain, dotted with low hills, and its surface either cultivated, steppe-like, or covered with patches of scrub and mimosa, it has not been considered necessary to give itineraries of any but the main routes; the descriptions would be all monotonously alike, and, in any case, there is little detail available.*
As regards water, during the *kherif* there is plenty everywhere, but in the dry season the wells are few and far between.

[For a description of the Debbeh El Obeid road, *v.* "Report on the Nile and Country between Dongola, &c." 1898. Part II, Route V.]

Route I.—Khartum (or Omdurman)—Abu Kurat— El Obeid.

Abu Kurat is the usual point from which caravans start inland from the Nile to Kordofan. It is 10 miles west of a point on the Nile about 92 miles south of Omdurman.

Alternative Routes—Khartum (or Omdurman) to Abu Kurat.

 (i) Left bank *via* Tura el Khadra.
 (ii) Right bank *via* Woad Shelai (crossing at this point).
 (iii) By water, leaving the Nile opposite Getaineh.

The usual time occupied by a caravan from Omdurman to El Obeid *via* (i) is 15 days; Mr. Marno, *via* (ii), took 12 days.

(i) *Major Prout* (May, 1875, 6 days).

From Omdurman to Tura el Khadra,† about 96 miles, on the west bank of the White Nile, there is a strip of

---

* Marno's "Reisen im Aegyptischen Kordofan" is the best authority on Kordofan routes, but even this book generally omits all reference to water supply.
† The "Greek Canal."

alluvial soil, which varies in width from 1 to 4 miles, and is evidently overflowed by the river in the season of high water. To the west of that there is a narrow slope of gravel, bounded by rather low hills, generally situated at from 2 to 6 miles from the river.

The above-mentioned strip of alluvial soil widens as one goes south. It seems to be very fertile, but it is not well cultivated.

At the time of Major Prout's journey it was not the harvesting season, but from time to time traces of the cotton plant, and yet more frequently, those of dhura, were noticed. The cotton had a coarse and short fibre.

Here then is a tract of 300 square miles of fertile land, which could be watered by small canals, and which, for the want of organised labour and system, produces hardly enough to feed a sparse and savage population.

Large herds of handsome cattle, as well as flocks of goats, graze on the western hills. A few sheep also are seen, and the people own many donkeys.

Everywhere throughout this country are seen gum-producing acacias in isolated groups, or in small low forests; and from time to time magnificent groves of acacias.

The villages are numerous, especially along the southern half of the route. They are invariably composed of huts built of dhura stalks and grass, in the well-known conical tukl form, or in small and very low parallelograms.

At Tura el Khadra (about 96 miles from Omdurman) the route definitely leaves the Nile, turning to the west-south-west across the plains.

At the distance of about $4\frac{1}{2}$ miles from the Nile there is a permanent lake of about 2,000 yards in length, and 1,000 yards in width, and apparently quite shallow. In all parts of the lake are to be seen trees and small islands covered with vegetation. Water full of organic matter, nasty, and probably unwholesome.

This lake is formed by infiltration of water from the Nile; but it is evident that during the annual overflow of the river the lake receives water directly from it. Here are found many small villages, and the usual cultivation of dhura, as well as a little cotton.

To the west of this lake the face of the country thence to El Obeid is uniform.

(ii) Mr. E. Marno (August, 1875).

Place.	Miles.		Description.
	Inter-mediate.	From Khartum.	
Khartum ..	—	—	Riding a fast camel, Mr. Marno followed the east bank of the Nile across green turf and through sweet-smelling acacias past Jebel Auli to
Kar en Nebbi	35	35	Kar en Nebbi; slept there, and on the next day through thick woods to
Katenah ..	25	60	Getaineh (Katena), v. p. 10, for description. From here to
Sheikiyeh ..	8	68	Sheikiyeh it was good going, but from here onwards the country was flooded knee deep (height of rainy season) as far as
Kurasa ..	16	84	Kurasa. Hence a bad, swampy road to
Woad Shelai	5	89	Woad Shelai. Crossed the river here (took three hours crossing), and struck in a south-westerly direction through woods and over swampy, bad ground to Abu Kurat.

(iii) *Mr. Felkin* (February, 1880).

After leaving the Nile opposite El Getaineh, the track leads S.S.W., gradually leaving the river, over a burning plain, on to the top of an immense sandbank. Following this for several hours, the traveller has a good view of the country. To the east is an expanse of grey mud, covered at high Nile; otherwise the country is flat, and only broken by the towering height of Gebel Arashkol in the south. The inhabitants in this district retire during the *kherif* to pastures far distant from the Nile, but follow the water back again, till in the dry season the river banks are very thickly populated.

Abu Kurat, 10 miles from the Nile. Brush, grass, many scorpions and snakes. From here is a six days' march to Bara. Very good road, huts (surrounded by thorn fences) for travellers, hyenas; much thorn bush.

(iv) ABU KURAT—EL OBEID (*viâ* Khursi or Bara).

N.B.—The wells being as a rule so deep, it would be necessary for an advancing force to be well provided with arrangements for hauling up water at a quicker rate than by the ordinary rope and skin bucket.

Kordofan.

Place.	Miles.		Description.
	Inter-mediate.	From Omdurman.	
Abu Kurat..	—	106¼	Abu Kurat, the usual starting place for Kordofan; rising sandy ground; the old telegraph line passed through here; some tukls and wells, small quantity, pretty bad water. From here onwards all hard, sandy going. Jebel Arashkol to the south. The truck hence bears somewhat south of Jebel Téss, or Teyus, in a W.S.W. direction. The country for the next 65 miles is "akaba," *i.e.*, uncultivated desert, inhabited only by wandering Kababish and Beni Gerar; stony at first, but at the junction of the Tura el Khadra south-easterly track acacia bush begins; red, sandy, undulating soil (Gôs, Gezan = sand hill); much grass (in August) and ant hills. Jebel Terish, west of Jebel Téss, gradually comes in sight, both hills covered with bush at the base, and a small pyramidal hill, Jebel Helba.
Helba	32½	139	Helba; a depression in the ground; some 20 wells, 110 feet deep, sufficient for 500 men and their animals; water slightly brackish and diarrhetic; many mosquitos. From here the ground gets poorer in vegetation.
Atd el Ibekh	25	164	Atd el Ibekh (Id el Nibeg). Numerous deep (100 feet) waterholes, sweet water; a favourite watering-place for nomads. A track leads north-west to Om Naleh soon after starting; over dreary country—many gazelle and bustards—to
Abu Shoka..	25	189	Abu Shoka; two wells 160 feet deep, large quantity excellent water; the village lies 2 miles to the north.

Abu Kurat—El Obeid.

El Uan	11	200	Some straw huts called El Uan. The village of that name lies further to the south, and contains some wells, including a large and deep well, with large quantity good water. The dokhn cultivation begins about here, and the country up to El Obeid is almost entirely a huge plain of dokhn, cut up into fields by thorn hedges (in 1875).
	27?	227?	Past the well (?) of Bir Om Sumemah and the villages of Hellet el Fogara (or Farraged—large quantity of good water) and Kawama—network of paths round the former—to
Tendar	4	231	Helle Tendar, a village situated in a thick osier wood; red ferruginous sand; scrubby, sandy plain to
Rokab	12	243	Rokab, lying amongst dokhn fields. Past Hellet es Serafin and other straw villages, and
Om Ghiba ..	5?	248?	Om Ghiba; abundance of good water—to
Khursi*	12	255	Khursi, the first village since Woad Shelai with rectangular mud houses (tankat); abundance of good water. Thence over dokhn fields, then tree-covered plains with bare sand showing through in places, to
Om Harasah ..	10	265	Om Harasah, a miserable hamlet. From here Jebel Kordofan and Jebel el Ain (Gebelén?) are visible in the distant south. Over fields and through trees, with numerous baobabs (*Adansonia digitata*—locally termed Kankale—in flower in August),
Jebel Kurbag ..	21	286	Between the two halves of Jebel Kurbag, a low hill. El Obeid thickets visible in the south-west, and many other hills visible from the top. Past small rain-ponds, dokhn fields, and baobabs, into
El Obeid	6	292	El Obeid.

* Bara lies 7 miles north-west of Khursi, and caravans sometimes touch here on the way to El Obeid. Pretty town, many gardens and vegetables; much water. Very little water between Khursi and El Obeid on the direct road. On the Bara—El Obeid road water is found at two points, but not in large quantities.

Kordofan.

Water Supply.

North of parallel 14° 30′ Kordofan is hopelessly arid; that portion between 14° 30′ and 12° 45′ is a rolling steppe country, between 1,400 and 1,900 feet above the level of the sea. There is no particular direction of drainage, and although the soil is light, marks of running water are not to be seen. Under the thick stratum of detritus is found, at from 100 to 150 feet below the surface, a stratum of mica schist. At various places on the surface of the ground, isolated peaks of granite crop out, showing the direction of the ancient ranges now abraded down.

The region west of the line connecting Abu Haraz and Jebel Katûl, and that north of 14° 30′, are wastes with wells at rare intervals, and are only visited by the nomad tribes, wandering shepherds, and camel breeders during the rainy season.

In the area chiefly inhabited by the villagers, not including the basins of Abu Haraz, Kagmar, Bara, or Melbeis, Major Prout's expedition estimated the number of wells of drinkable water, contained in upwards of 16,000 square miles, at 900. Except certain groups of shallow water holes found in the khors and at the base of the mountains, these wells are narrow shafts, from 80 to 160 feet in depth, going down into the mica schist. Many of them are brackish, at least a quarter of them dry for half the year, and the majority yield but little water, except during the last weeks of the *kherif*.

The water supply of Kordofan is derived from:—

1st. The wells.
2nd. The rainfall during the *kherif*.
3rd. The three small lakes, El Birket, El Rahad, and Shirkéleh in the south.

Apart from these three sources, there is no water in all Kordofan. Every other lake and pool except the three mentioned is dry a few weeks after the rains cease; and there is no running stream or spring to be found even during the rains.

The watercourses (khors) contain water for a few hours, while rain is falling. In all probability no water finds its way from Kordofan to the Nile.

Kordofan is in consequence an arid unproductive land, with a sparse population, yielding a scanty revenue. To increase the water from the three sources above named is the question on which depends the future value of the province.

Colonel Colston's theory is as follows:—The wells of Kordofan are supplied only by the rainfall on its own area, as there are no mountains sending down their drainage, or any lake or river system filling the reservoirs by infiltration. On the north the rainfall is less, and the general level of the country lower; on the east the Nile is 500 feet lower than any considerable area of Kordofan. On the south the regions of Nuba and Takalla generally drain south and east; on the west Darfur is of a generally lower level, and separated from Kordofan by a waterless tract. *Rainfall.*

The supply of water is thus obtained from the rainfall on the upper porous stratum, which filters through to the impenetrable beds of mica schist, where it flows over the surface, and is collected in any depressions. If a well strikes one of these depressions, there is an unfailing supply of water; if on the other hand it strikes the general surface, the supply is soon exhausted. The mean annual rainfall may be taken at 14 inches.

As might be expected, many wells become entirely dry, and most yield but little water late in the year. After the dokhn is gathered, whole villages migrate to the more permanent wells till the beginning of the rains. In El Obeid, where the supply is exceptionally large, water becomes an article of commerce, and late in the summer usually sells for 12 piastres (Egyptian) the vase of $1\frac{1}{2}$ to 2 gallons.

Outside El Obeid there are no wells within a circle of 20 miles radius which can be relied on later than December, excepting at Melbeis, 10 miles to the south. Water being thus so scarce, little is available for agriculture or stock raising.

Reservoirs have been established at certain places, principally at El Obeid, where the natural drainage can fill them, and where the soil contains sufficient clay for their construction. They might be made on the watercourses which drain to Melbeis, and on those conducting water from near Abu Haraz, Melbeis, and Jebel Kordofan *Reservoirs.*

to Lake El Rahad, but such reservoirs are only useful during the rainy season.

There are two large reservoirs at El Obeid, each of which is sunk about 6 feet 6 inches, and enclosed by a bank about 6 feet in height, and covers about 600 to 1,000 square yards of surface. There are several smaller ones; those 5 or 6 miles down the valley were, during the *kherif* of 1875, filled nearly to the natural level of the ground. The smaller reservoirs dry up within a week after the rains cease, and the larger ones before the end of January.

Supposing the system of economising the water perfect, the amount of rainfall is insufficient to irrigate for agriculture one-fifth of the area of Kordofan. Dokhn requires little water, but much of the crop dies annually from want of it.

In the south of Kordofan, where more rain falls on the mountains, the case is different. The rainy season is said to last six months in Takalla, and, the soil being more tenacious, it enables water from wider areas to drain into the general system. For example, khor Abu Habl rises in Dar Nuba, and flows 190 miles before it sinks; and during the rainy season running water is found for days together. It is even said to have at times found its way to the Nile.

Lakes.

In its course this khor forms three small lakes, El Birket, Birket El Rahad, and Shirkéleh, which cover areas of about 2, 4½, and 6 square miles respectively.

El Birket dries up as the season advances, but water can always be found by digging a few feet. It is surrounded by trees and villages.

El Rahad becomes entirely dry in some seasons, while in others a little water remains until the beginning of the next rains.

Shirkéleh generally becomes dry before the *kherif*; in all these basins water is found at the depth of from 6 to 10 feet. Along the whole course of the khor, up to 32° long., water is found by digging 6, 10, or 13 feet in the bed.

Between the khor and the mountains on the south, water would probably be found at similar depths; but the country, though much richer than Northern Kordofan, is uninhabited because unsafe.

Kagmar, Abu Haraz, Bara, and Melbeis are depressions, where the surface of the ground is so near the impermeable stratum, that water is found in abundance all the year round, at depths of from 3 to 20 feet.

The area of the basin of Bara, as well as that of Melbeis, is not more than 10 to 20 square miles; that of Kagmar and of Abu Haraz not more than 40 square miles, at a liberal estimate.

These basins are important as water stations for passing caravans, and furnish water to the villages for many miles round.

Population and Tribes.

The total population of Kordofan was in 1875 reckoned as high as 280,000, including nomads. In all probability it does not now exceed half that amount.

The population falls naturally under three headings:—

1. The village and town population.
2. The nomad tribes.
3. The hill tribes.

The inhabitants of the province itself principally reside in villages, while various nomad tribes roam about the outskirts. The vilages are most numerous in the central region, especially about El Obeid. They consist of groups of *tukls* and *rabukas*, the former cylindrical with a conical roof, the latter rectangular, and both made of stalks of corn (dokhn) lashed to a framework. The fact of a village being planted at any place is no proof of a constant supply of water, as many of them are only occupied during the rainy season, and in many cases the inhabitants have in summer to make journeys of two or three days for water.

The following table shows the distribution and numbers of the village people as given by the Governor in 1875. Prout considers them probably exaggerated:—

El Obeid	30,000 ?
Department of Khûrsi, 359 villages ..	42,000
,, Taïara, 119 ,, ..	18,000
,, Bara, 171 ,, ..	23,840
,, Abu-Haraz, 80 villages	16,830
District of El Ghodiat, 32 villages ..	6,870
6 villages Sheikh Mohammed.. ..	1,500
16 ,, Fellata	4,000
14 ,, Hamaoni	7,700
12 ,, Abu-Safiyeh..	4,000
25 ,, Jebel Kagga and Katûl ..	5,000
7 ,, Haraza	2,000
12 ,, Dar el ?	3,000
Total population	164,740

Villagers.

1. *Village People.*—The village population is very heterogeneous, especially about El Obeid; the most ancient race is found in various villages north of the 13th latitude under the names of the Ghodiat, Gilledat, and Gowanieh; they form the mass of the agricultural population, and are the original population of El Obeid. Mixed with these are the Kungarra, who, originally coming from Darfur, conquered Kordofan, and were in their turn subdued by Mehemet Ali. The Egyptian conquest introduced Turkish blood, as well as that of all the races of Asia Minor represented in the Bashibazuks. In addition to these, Greeks and Levantines have left their mark, and the slave trade has been the means of introducing a great influx of the negro tribes from the south.

The colour of the generality of the people is dark brown with slightly reddish tinge; they have woolly hair worn long.

The Kungarra and the M'Sabât tribes, who originally came from Darfur, still live apart, and each has its Sultan equivalent to the lesser Sheikhs el Belad of Lower Egypt. These races are black, with woolly hair.

In the mountains of Katû, Kagga (or Kaja), and at Jebel Kohr and Jebel Daïer, colonies of negroes from Dar Nuba are found, and various other colonies from the Nile and elsewhere are scattered through this province.

The villagers are a lazy people; raising the grain crop (Dokhn), and preparing the grain for food and drink, are almost their only occupation.

During the rainy season they plant, cultivate, and gather their one crop. The meal of the dokhn is prepared by crushing the grain between two stones; and beer, *merissa*, is made from the same material. The procuring of water is a serious question for them, as it has to be drawn from deep wells perhaps at 5 or 6 hours distant. Some of the villagers have small herds of cattle, goats, and a very few sheep; and in certain places small plots of beans, pea-nuts, cotton, and sesame are grown.

Special trades are very rare: occasional basketmakers are to be found, and in some villages ironworkers, who forge rude hoes, knives, and hatchets.

The villagers of the interior are poor spirited and unambitious. Extreme sloth is their principal characteristic; neither food nor money will tempt them to work, and only the lash is effective for the purpose. For centuries they have made no improvement in their system of cultivation, which is most primitive; though in constant contact with the Baggara, and other neighbours who use horses, dromedaries, and camels, they have never learnt to breed and train any animal for burden except a miserable race of donkey.

2. *The nomad tribes* comprise cattle-breeders (Baggara) and camel-breeders (Siat Ibil). Although the Baggara have come to be looked on as one large tribe or race, this is not the case: the word simply means "connected with cattle," and under this heading there are many tribes distinct in race. On the whole, however, all the Baggara have much the same characteristics. They cultivate little, and have no trades, living principally on the produce of their herds. Their chief occupations are hunting and war; the latter they wage incessantly upon each other, and upon the mountain tribes. These thousands of turbulent and daring horsemen plunder cattle and slaves, and are a most dangerous element in the population of Kordofan. They speak a tolerably pure Sudan-Arabic, and seem to spread rapidly at the expense of less favoured races. They are far superior mentally and physically to the village population: as a rule, they live in camps, seldom in permanent villages; they wander about with their herds according to the varying conditions of water and pasturage. The favourite camping-grounds of the Baggara are along the watercourse known as

Nomads.

Baggara.

Khor Abu Habl, and about the valleys of the west bank of the White Nile. During the *kherif* they pass into the valleys south and west, but again come north when water becomes scarce and the flies get troublesome.

Major Prout says in 1875:—

"The Baggaras who come to the market of El Obeid are mounted on their bulls, which are fine animals and apparently very docile. A large cushion of plaited straw serves as a saddle. A rope passing through the animal's nose answers perfectly for a bridle. These cattle are also used as beasts of burden. The costume of the Baggaras consists merely of a loose cotton sack with wide sleeves. Although they manufacture excellent broad-brimmed hats of plaited straw, which are an excellent protection against the rays of a burning sun, they are always seen with their heads not only bare but shaved. The Baggaras, like all the Bedouins, always go armed. They carry no shields like the other tribes, but they generally wear a sword and always hold in hand three or four lances, whose heads exhibit a great variety of forms. Most have that of an elongated leaf, but there are some which are barbed with much art and ingenuity. The handsomest lance heads come from Darfur and the south."

The chief tribes which come under the name of Baggara are as follows* :—

Name.	Local Origin.	Fighting men.	Remarks.
Taaisha	In S.W. Darfur	7,500	Khalifa Abdullah is of this tribe.
Habbania	80 miles S.E. of El Obeid and in South Darfur	3,500	Related by blood to the Taaisha.
Rizighat	250 miles S.W. of El Obeid	3,000	Considerably split up.
Beni Halba	Round Dara, in Darfur	1,400	
Messeriya	100 miles S.S.E. of El Obeid	200	
Hawazma	50 miles south of El Obeid	50	
Homr	Round Foga, and 100 miles S.W. of El Obeid	2,500	Very hostile and savage.
Gime	Between El Obeid and the Nile	1,000	

* Slatin Pasha, 1896.

As these tribes are nomad, it follows that the localities given above are subject to alteration.

It must also be remembered that the Khalifa Abdullah summoned the bulk of the Baggara to Omdurman in 1889, since which time they have lost considerably in numbers.

It will be noticed that the Baggara of Darfur are included in this list.

The camel breeders (Siat Ilbil) of Kordofan are much fewer in number than the cattle breeders. They comprise only the Kababish and the Beni Gerrar. Of the former very large tribe, which used to inhabit in great numbers the desert between Dongola, Es Safiya, and Omdurman, barely 1,000 fighting men are now left; of these but few reach as far south as Kordofan. In 1884–85 this tribe assisted us greatly with transport, but on our retirement they were left alone to cope with the Mahdist forces and were almost annihilated by them. *Camel breeders.*

The Beni Gerrar, perhaps 700 fighting men in all, pursue their occupation in the neighbourhood of El Obeid, between that town and the Nile, and in the northern portion of Kordofan.

Of other nomad tribes which breed neither camels nor cattle, the following are the principal ones:— *Other tribes.*

Name.	Local Origin.	Fighting men.	Remarks.
Zayadieh	Round El Fasher (Darfur)	800	
Mahariya	Northern Darfur	350	
Hamr	Darfur-Kordofan frontier	1,000	
Maálieh	North of Shakka	200	

3. *The hill tribes* are confined to the Jebel Daïer and Takalla (Southern) districts. They are negroes, very black in colour, but small in stature. They are hostile to the Baggara, and are well armed and warlike when roused by the raids of the nomad Arabs; but when left alone they are peaceful and pastoral in their habits. They are superior in intelligence to the Shillûk and Dinka tribes. Their neighbours to the south, the Dar Nuba, are similar in character (*v.* p. 83). *Hill tribes.*

Towns and Localities.

El Obeid.   *El Obeid*, the capital of Kordofan, is situated in lat. 13° 10′ N. and long. 30° 7′ E. The height above the sea level is given by different authorities as 1,402, 1,570, 1,899, or 1,919 feet. It is a straggling collection of mud huts, comprising six different villages, each forming a separate quarter, inhabited by a distinct class, and stands in a vast plain. The dwellings are mere huts of straw and mud, with the exception of a few built of clay, and the late Government House, one of the mosques, three barracks, and a hospital built of sun-dried bricks. Like at Berber, there are many pits in the streets from which building mud has been dug. These are used as refuse pits in the dry season, but in the rainy season are full of stagnant water and breed much fever.

The market place presents a scene of much animation during the day; it used to be a great trading centre for gum, ostrich feathers, &c.

Before the Mahdist rising there was a Roman Catholic mission established here, a branch of that at Khartum. The priests stated that they did not find the climate very trying.

The wells are very deep, some as much as 100 feet, and at times the water is very scarce (*v.* p. 48).

The annual export of El Obeid used to be reckoned at 100,000 cwt.

The town, under Muhamed Pasha Said, made a gallant defence against the Mahdi from 3.9.82 to 17.1.83, when it fell owing to starvation.

Other towns.   *Bara* is a pretty town; the wells are 20 feet deep or less, and there used to be splendid gardens. All kinds of fruit and vegetables could be bought. It was at one time intended to remove the seat of government from El Obeid to Bara on account of the superior water supply of the latter; the rebellion prevented the accomplishment of this purpose.

The following notes as to places of some interest may be of use.

Melbeis (or Mulbes), 12 miles south of El Obeid. A tukl village at the foot of a hill of the same name. North-east of it the plain is thickly covered with bush and intersected by small khors. Khor Mulbes has in places banks 7 feet high. The importance of this place lies in its water capacity. The wells are shallow and numerous, and the water is drawn up by shadufs. In the *seff*, or dry season, flocks are brought here to water from El Obeid. There are a few date palms and vegetable gardens here.

Abu Haraz (30 miles south-west of El Obeid). A large and fertile village of tukls and mud huts. Lies on a khor 6 to 10 feet deep and 10 to 20 yards broad, which contains numerous pools in the wet and wells in the dry season. Many ostriches here.

Fula Mshek, 6 miles north-east of Abu Haraz, is a large water-holding depression during the *kherif*, and has numerous wells in the dry season.

Jebel Kordofan, 13 miles south-east of El Obeid, rises to about 500 feet above the plain. Thick forest round the base; difficult to climb to the top, but air very refreshing half-way up. Holds much water in clefts except during dry season. Between here and Jebel Tunkultu (a few miles to the north), thick wood, lion, parrots, and much small game.

Taiara, 35 miles east of El Obeid. Large village and important market for dokhn and gum.

Jebel Katul, 110 miles north-west of El Obeid, a rocky group of hills, reaches to about 600 feet above the plain. Numerous villages. Inhabitants great thieves. Between here and Jebel Kaga (35 miles further to the north-west) is a large plain without bush or tree; grey clay soil holding considerable water, chiefly at Aîd Sodari. Many large antelope. The two ranges are inhabited by Bederiyeh, originally from Dar Nuba.

Produce.

The following is an approximate estimate furnished to the Governor of Kordofan by the merchants in 1871:—

Consumed yearly in the Provinces—

Dhura and Dokhn	400,000	ardebs
Sesame	5,000	,,
Fuli Kordofani (peanuts)	500	,,
White beans	2,000	,,
Wheat	300	,,
Dried bamieh (okra)	200	,,
Salt	3,000	,,

Onions	1,700 ardebs
Tobacco	300 cwts.
Cotton (with seed)	500 ,,
Iron	1,000 ,,

Exported—

Gum	from 35,000 to 70,000 cwts.

Feathers (Ostrich)—

Owam (first quality, white)	40	,,
Black	200	,,
Rubda (mixed short female)	350	,,
Abu Hariba (from short young birds)	2	,,
Raw hides	7,000	,,

These quantities include all the commerce in feathers in Cairo, of which much the larger part used to come from El Obeid.

The value in Cairo of the exports from Kordofan was, in 1877, approximately :—

Gum	£55,000
Raw hides	2,500
Ostrich feathers	75,000
	£132,500

The ivory trade was never great, and is now dead.

Imports approximately :—

Cotton fabrics	£40,000
Other imports	10,000
	£50,000

Among the latter are included cutlery, metal work, liquors, tobacco, sugar, rice, coffee, glass, beads, &c.

Large quantities of cotton fabrics pass through El Obeid to Darfur.

Corn.

Corn.—Dokhn is the sole food of nine-tenths of the people, and they build their huts of its stalks.

It grows during the *kherif* on sandy ridges, and requires little water. It takes four months from planting to harvesting.

On a journey the grain is eaten raw, or simply boiled; in the house it is crushed between stones, mixed with water, and baked in thin wafers, *kissera*, or boiled into a thick soup, *asida*, with bits of meat or leaves. It is also made into a crude sweetish beer, *merissa*, which is drunk in enormous quantities.

The dokhn is also produced north of the 13th parallel, and in the neigbourhood of lakes El Birket and El Rahad.

A succession of unfavourable years for dokhn caused a famine about 1874, and many people died of starvation.

The quantity of dhura produced is small as compared with that of dokhn, and comes chiefly from the mountain districts.

Cultivation is performed in a most primitive manner, with hoes and instruments for making holes in which to place the dokhn. When ripe, the ears are broken off, dried, and beaten with sticks to separate the corn, which is finally winnowed by small fans.

Sesame, wheat, bamieh (*okra*), onions, cotton, and tobacco are cultivated in the districts where water is most abundant, but owing to the scarcity of moisture the crops are insignificant.

Salt.—Salt is produced by evaporation from three groups of wells in lat. 14° 20' long. 30° 45'; it is dark coloured and bitter. Salt.

Iron.—There are two ore beds, one almost 60 miles to the north-east of El Obeid, and the other about 50 miles to the north-west. The ore is brown hematite, and is found in small fragments at a little depth in the sand. It may exist in large quantities. This iron can never be worked economically, as there is no material for building furnaces, or fuel; nor could it be shipped with profit without a railroad. Iron.

Gum.—The best comes from the gray-barked acacias (*hashab*) which abound in East Kordofan, between latitudes 12° 30' and 13° 30'. Taïara is the chief point for collection. It is more or less abundant in all parts of the province. Considerable quantities come from Magenis, in the north-west. Gum.

There are immense forests of red-barked acacia (*latch*) in the south; the gum is of a certain value, though inferior to that of the gray bark. Other gum-producing acacias are scattered over the province in large numbers.

It appears that the gum forests of Kordofan are not worked to anything like their capacity; the labour of gathering it is tedious and unremunerative.

Baobabs. *Baobab trees* (Adansonia digitata), native name *hamre*, or *kankale*. These trees play an important part in the life of the inhabitants. Their northern limit is a few miles north of El Obeid. The tree is 70 or 80 feet high, and the trunk from 30 to 40 feet in circumference; the leaves resembles the sycamore leaf. In addition to its fruit, it is very valuable as a storage for water, many trees being capable of holding 20,000 gallons; these are not filled by nature, as is often imagined, but by the people during the rains.

Ostrich feathers mostly come from Darfur and Dar Hamar, El Obeid being merely the collecting station. Ostriches are seldom seen in Kordofan, but are numerous west of the mountains of Kagga. With care, however, ostrich farming in Kordofan ought to be most successful.

Animals.

Cattle. *Cattle.*—The raw hides come from the Baggara, and the slaughter-houses at El Obeid.

The herds of the Baggara are large, and the cattle of excellent quality, though they do not seem to be very prolific, and yield but little milk. They are of the humped variety seen throughout the Sûdan, are docile, and the bulls are trained to the saddle and to carry burdens. These cattle seem to have a capacity for living with little water. They are said to require drink only every second or third day. Hence large areas round the wells become available for grazing. Prout estimated in 1875 the extent of grazing ground of the Baggara at about 4,000 square miles, and the stock on it at about 100,000 head of cattle.

It must be remembered, however, that the vegetation is not renewed by constant rains, and the cattle have to subsist on the herbage which grows during the *kherif*.

In northern Kordofan the cattle are few in number, and cannot be counted on as one of the resources of the country.

Camels.—Those of the Kababish are to be counted by thousands, and camels are also plentiful among the Hamid Arabs and the Hamr of the north-west and west. They are very scarce among the village people of Kordofan, and cannot be bred successfully south of latitude 13° or 13° 30′. South of this they are degenerate animals, without speed or endurance; there are none among the Baggara, where, on the other hand, a few thousand horses are to be found.

In the villages of Kordofan are goats, donkeys, and sheep.

Camels.

Horses.

Other animals.

Climate.

The year in Kordofan is divided into three seasons of varying durations and uncertain limits, viz. :—

> The *kherif*, or rainy season.
> The *shitta*, or winter.
> The *seff*, or summer.

The *kherif* begins early in June. Some hot afternoon, dense clouds, appearing in the south, will bring a heavy shower of some hours' duration. After this, days may pass without rain, and the wind will probably not settle in the south and south-west before July. From this, till late in September, showers may be expected any afternoon, but probably only every third or fourth day. They cease at the end of September or the first week in October.

During these four months the temperature is remarkably uniform, the thermometer indicating :—

	Centigrade.		Fahrenheit.	
	Wet.	Dry.	Wet.	Dry.
At 7 A.M.	23°	25° =	73·4°	77°
,, 1 P.M.	24	28 =	75·2	82·4
,, 9 ,,	24	32 =	75·2	89·6
,, 3 ,,	24	33 =	75·2	91·4

The wind is almost constantly from the south and south-west, and large masses of cumulus clouds overhang the sky.

Notwithstanding the moderate temperature, the weather is very oppressive; even the strongest are sure to be attacked sooner or later by fever. This is intermittent,

Disease. and generally of a low typhoid character. In general, only the native escapes; even Arabs and Turks, who have been in the country for years, succumb towards the end of the rainy season.

The mortality is very great; Major Prout lost 6 per cent. of the men under his command in four months, though they were well sheltered and attended to.

Major Prout says he does not consider the climate of Kordofan, during the rainy season, positively dangerous to persons who can take care of themselves; but, as Dr. Livingstone has written, "men may escape death in an unhealthy place, but the system is enfeebled, and life reduced to its lowest ebb."

Ophthalmia. Ophthalmia, so common in Egypt, is rare in the Sudan, but is more severe in its form.

Frenhit. A malady to which new comers are specially liable is the so-called *frenhit, fertit*, or *farantit*. It shows itself by a swelling generally in the foot, which has to be cut open. A worm then comes out, said to be sometimes a yard in length; the Guinea worm is the ordinary name. There are many theories as to its origin, but it is generally found in the legs; it probably enters while the person is wading, and is not induced by drinking the water.

In extracting the worm, great care must be taken not to break it off short. It should be drawn out as far as possible, then made fast to a twig, and the process repeated in a few days. Great cleanliness is said to be a preventive. Single worms, though causing much pain, are not fatal, but when 20 or 30 are present, the prognosis is very bad. Travellers should be most careful in drying themselves after being in water, and avoid resting their arms and legs on the bare ground. The natives, as a remedy for this complaint, use a strong solution of a plant called *goák*, both internally and externally.

Winter.—The wind is changeable towards the end of September, and often blows from the north, while high light clouds take the place of the cumulus masses; by the middle of October, the wind is settled in the north, and continues to blow steadily from that quarter during the winter.

The thermometer falls gradually. The means of a number of observations in November show:—

	Centigrade.		Fahrenheit.	
	Wet.	Dry.	Wet.	Dry.
7 A.M.	16°	24° = 60·8°		75·2°
12 N.	20	30 = 68·0		86·0
9 P.M.	16	32 = 69·8		89·6

The means for December—

7 A.M.	15°	18° = 59·0°		64·4°
12 N.	21	31 = 69·8		87·8
3 P.M.	24	34 = 75·2		93·2

The means for January and February—

7 A.M.	12°	15° = 53·6°		59·0°
1 P.M.	19	27 = 66·2		80·6
2 P.M.	20	31 = 68·0		87·8

The dry air, north wind, and fresh nights soon terminates the fevers of the *kherif;* the winter is delightful.

Summer.—In March, the summer begins, and with it come drought, sultry nights, and terribly hot days. In May, the afternoon temperature is 41° Centigrade, = 105·8° Fahrenheit.

Altitudes above sea level compiled by Major Prout.

Helba	1381·7	
Bara	1622·6	Wells 20 ft. deep.
El Obeid	1919·5	,, 80 ft. to 130 ft.
Faki Dow	1743·0	,, 120 ft.
Hamaoni	1734·0	,, 110 ft.
Meguénis	1820·0	,, 80 ft.
Om Doban	1704·0	,, 15 ft.
Gumburra	1853·0	
Tibri	2072·0	
Om Rahali	1994·0	
Shitangul	1998·0	
Abior Tiné	1789·0	
Abu Senûn (Hella)	1928·0	

(b) Darfur.

General Description.

Darfur proper, or the country of the Fors, is, according to the assertions of the inhabitants, the territory comprised in the central group of mountains of Jebel Marra and its offshoots.

Although the boundaries of Darfur have never been ascertained with precision, the country may be considered as lying within and nearly filling the area bounded by the parallels 9° and 16° N. lat., and the degrees 22° and 28° E. long. In shape it is a more or less regular parallelogram, measuring about 500 miles from north to south, and 400 miles from east to west. In the centre stands Jebel Marra, a range of mountains a 100 miles (4 days' march) from north to south, and 60 miles ($2\frac{1}{2}$ days' march) from east to west, and varying in height from 1,000 to 1,500 feet above the general level of the surrounding country.

The main characteristics of the country are the large and numerous khors which traverse it on the west, south-west, and south. These are, it is true, only channels for rain-water, and hold it only during the rainy season; but at the same time they are of great value, for in all of them water is to be found, held up by the clayey strata, at a few feet below the surface.

Broadly it may be said that the Darfur country to the north and east of the Marra range resembles that of Kordofan in its character and usual dearth of water, whilst to the west, south-west, and south it is very much more fertile.

The greater proportion and the largest of these khors, such as the Sonot, the Bargo, Baray, the Gheldâma, and, above all, the Adsom, with its many affluents, flow towards the west and south-west. The smallest of these are from 200 to 300 yards across; in the rainy season they are perfect torrents, and, although their beds are dry soon after the cessation of the rains, water is always to be found in abundance at a depth of 5 or 6 feet. Two considerable streams, the Ghendi and the Bulbul, flow towards the south, and, uniting about a hundred miles from the mountains, are said, in seasons of excessive rainfall, to reach the Bahr el Arab. Like all the other streams in Darfur, these are dry in the dry season. On the eastern side of the mountains rise the Wady el Kho and the Wady Amur, the fall of the ground eastward towards the Nile being only very gradual, their course is almost due south. Neither of them reach the Bahr el Arab, but are finally lost in the sand about 200 miles to the south of El Fasher.

In the eastern part of Darfur the wells are of a considerable depth and at great distances from each other. The people are dependent to a great extent, in cultivated parts, on the baobab reservoirs and on melons (*batikh*).

This part of the country is described by Gordon as "most miserable—a sandy, bush-covered desert—quite useless for any food purpose, with no water for distances of 40 or 50 miles." The deepest wells are at Karnak, where water is only reached at 250 feet. At Brûsh, on the El Obeid road, and on the road to Towaïsha the wells average 100 to 130 feet. In El Fasher the wells are of no great depth, and before the beginning of the rainy season water is reached at 35 feet. Here the Wadi system begins; valleys into which the drainage from the north and north-west flows to lose itself in the wide plains to the south. At Towaïsha, as well as throughout the portion of Darfur under consideration, the wells pass through layers of marl and chalk which renders the taste of the water unpleasant.

The nearer one approaches the central group of mountains the depth at which water is found diminishes; at 3,200 feet above the sea it is found by excavating in the sand, but at 4,000 feet there is running water which becomes more abundant still further to the west of Jebel Marra.

The drainage from Jebel Marra flows to all points of the compass. On the north and north-east it is taken by the Wadi em Milkh (or Malik), which debouches at Debbeh on the Nile; on the east, by the Wadi el Kob, which further on is lost in the plains to the south; on the west, there are the two great Wadis of Barreh (or Turah) and Azûm, which are both branches of the Wadi Kadja. The natives assert that the water in these three last is so plentiful during the rains that crocodiles and hippopotami are common, and fish are in abundance.

A great valley, the Wady Gendy, has its origin on the southern slopes of Jebel Marra, and probably runs into the Bahr el Arab; whilst those already mentioned on the west are likely to be affluents of Lake Tchad.

To the south of Dara the watercourses are insignificant. Wells are usually found in the small depressions where rain water collects, but this becomes scarce in the dry season.

During the *kherif* the southern portion of Darfur becomes a huge lake and impassable.

The geological formation is very varied; in the west, the mountains show a volcanic origin; in the north and south, granite and sandstone are the prevailing rocks; in the east, the soil is sandy and contains a quantity of iron which is worked to a small extent.

In the east and north-east, granite predominates, with the exception of a strip between Foga and El Fasher, where red and white sandstone crop up.

In the north, Wadi Millît and the hills in its neighbourhood are of gneiss. To the north-east of this granite again predominates at Saya, whilst still further north Jebel Tagabo is of sandstone.

Jebel Midubh contains both sandstone and granite; this group has been much distorted by volcanic agency, and beds of lava are to be seen in all directions. To its south-west lies Bir em Malha, an extinct crater which, to outward appearance, is an insignificant hill, but has a depth of about 150 feet. Here is a small lake strongly impregnated with alkaline matter, while sweet water springs issue from the sandstone and granite declivities.

The greatest elevation of Jebel Midubh does not exceed 3,500 feet, and the plateau between it and Jebel Tagabo is about 1,200 feet.

The Jebel Marra group is also of volcanic origin; lava and granite are to be found everywhere; but there is no sandstone; small peaks of pink granite crop up here and there between the mountains and El Fasher.

About Jebel Turah, one of the offshoots of the main group, the height of the plateau is about 4,400 feet, whilst the peak itself is about 5,500 feet.

Stretching from the main group in a westerly direction for a distance of 30 or 40 miles, is a huge dyke of white quartz with a plateau of sandstone raised some 300 feet above the plain, which is itself about 3,200 feet above the sea level. To the south-west of Jebel Marra, the plain is about 4,000 feet above the sea, and the main peaks of the group rise to an altitude of about 6,000 feet.

The inhabitants report a large lake of brackish water from which salt can be obtained on the north-eastern part of the mountain; while at a day's journey to the west, salt is also found at Karunga, and the Wadi Burka is strongly impregnated with soda.

In all the depressions sand rich in iron is met with.

In a southerly direction from Jebel Marra, there stretches a broad alluvial plain which is dotted all over with peaks of granite, giving the impression of a range of mountains, buried all but its highest points. This plain falls rapidly towards the north-west and south-east, and the whole country has a constant fall towards the east and south-east.

On the road from Dara to Shakka, not far from the latter place, there is an isolated tract of sand about 40 miles long and broad; here water melons are the chief production.

The road from Shakka to El Fasher for three days passes through a dense wood where the soil is of sand and clay mixed; it then debouches on a sandy steppe country which stretches up to El Fasher.

Inhabitants (v. also pp. 54, 55).

The total number of inhabitants may be roughly estimated at 1,500,000, of which half are Fors, 500,000 Arabs, and the rest Tukruri and Fellatah.

The sandy wastes to the east of Darfur are chiefly occupied by the Tukruri and Berti tribes, mixed races of warlike tendencies, to which belong the Leopard tribe, that gave Gordon a certain amount of trouble.

To the north of these are found Homr Arabs, who occupy themselves in camel-breeding; while to the south are the Tukruri and Arab races, chiefly Baggara (v. p. 54).

North of El Fasher, Tukruri and Zayadieh Arabs appear; south are the Fellatah, and further south the Baggara.

The Marra Mountains are exclusively inhabited by the Fors, and further west we again find Arabs occupying the northern districts, the negro race of the Masalit the central, and the Baggara the southern.

The Arab population have, as a rule, kept themselves unmixed from the For, the Tukruri, and the other races. The Homr tribe originally came, it is said, from Marocco.

There is, in addition to the above, a nomad tribe called the Zoghawa, but these are of negro extraction, and have only assumed the nomad life.

The Arabs are, for the most part, great hunters; they go out after ostriches to the desert, for five or six days at a time, in small bands with about 10 camels. They are also warlike, constant feuds taking place either between the Arab tribes themselves or with the village-dwelling people, the *casus belli* being usually cattle stealing or some such provocation.

Truth is little known among them, and immorality universal, in consequence of which there is much disease.

The Fors are clean and industrious. They will be found assembled under trees, spinning, weaving cotton, or plaiting mats; the children being employed in herding the cattle. On the women falls the heavier occupation of grinding corn and carrying wood and water.

The Fors are not particular in the matter of food; corn is the main article of consumption, and they drink quantities of *merissa*. On festivals they make a compound of meal, water, and a gravy made from meat, and flavoured with pepper. They occasionally add roasted grasshoppers or caterpillars.

They are religious and even fanatical. In every village there are several fiki, who teach the children and perform the office of scribes for the older part of the population.

The Fors live in tukls or conical huts, five or six of which, arranged in a circle, form a habitation.

Very few foreign wares are found among the Fors, but they have home manufactures of their own, which suffice for the wants of the mass of the population, the chiefs alone using imported stuffs.

The men wear a large mantle and trousers, but have their heads and feet bare. The women use a piece of cotton stuff, which they throw over their shoulders and make fast about their hips.

When under the rule of its own Sultan, Darfur was divided into four provinces, which answered to the four quarters of the compass.

Dar er Rih (north), Dar es Soba (east), Dar es Saïd (south), and Dar el Gharb (west). Each province was governed by a *Magdum*, who had three or four *Chotias* to assist him; and each village had its own *Melik*, or headman. These villages were united in groups, the names of which correspond to those of the Chotias.

There was no regular system of taxation; but each Magdum carried it out as best he could.

In each province there was a kind of head collector, *Abu el Gabân*, who had underlings in every village to gather the taxes.

In case of difficulty, they got assistance from the *Abid es Sultan* (Sultan's slaves), who were scattered through the land. These were in reality soldiers, who, to avoid expense, were quartered in the various villages.

In order to give some idea of the distance of Darfur from the civilised world, it may be mentioned that the expedition under Colonel Mason in 1874–75 took 147 days to reach El Fasher from Cairo. They had, however, a large caravan, and were delayed for some time at Dongola. The return journey *viâ* Khartum was done in 96 days.

Produce.

The country may be divided into three sections with reference to the vegetation, *i.e.*, the eastern zone of sand, the central mountains, and the western zone.

In the eastern zone, the cultivation of corn, in the shape of dokhn and a little dhura, is the chief industry. A small quantity of sesame, cucumbers, pumpkins, and water melons are also grown. In certain depressions of the ground, where the presence of clay gives a stronger soil, cotton is produced, but in no great quantity. *Corn.*

The northern part of the country is almost uncultivated; and in the west, agriculture is pretty much the same as described for the eastern portion, except that, owing to the greater quantity of water, more vegetables are grown.

The central mountainous district is the richest, and accordingly the most thickly populated. Small terraces are formed all over the slopes of the hills, upon which gardens are laid out. Here wheat, dokhn, dhura, sesame, pumpkins, and melons are grown. In the small watercourses in the valley, onions are planted during the dry season, and here also honey of very good quality is collected.

Cotton. The cotton grown is excellent. Arabs manufacture from wool a coarse stuff, but the Fors are ignorant of the process of turning this raw material to account.

Salt. The production of salt is also carried on.

Camels. Camel breeding is the principal pursuit of the Arabs in the north and east of Darfur. North of 14° latitude the camels are very numerous; those at M'Badr, the head-quarters of the Homr Arabs, have been estimated at 30,000 head; those at Millît belonging to the Zayadieh tribe, at upwards of 10,000; and a similar number at Saya. Further west, those of a tribe called Mahamid are countless.

The Arabs who breed camels occupy themselves with no other industry, and have even to buy the corn used in their households, which, with camel's milk, satisfies all their wants.

Cattle. In the south, among the stationary inhabitants, cattle and sheep are to be found.

The cattle are of two kinds; the humped species and the so-called African species, with long horns. The former are compact, well-made animals, and become very fat: the others are not worth much.

Sheep. The sheep have but little wool, but their flesh is good; among the Zoghawa there is a species with long curly hair.

Goats. Goats abound everywhere.

The Baggara Arabs confine themselves to breeding cattle.

Horses. Horse breeding is only carried on by the Mahamid tribe, while the Homr Arabs obtain theirs from Kordofan. They are small in size but very strong, and are said to be able on an emergency to travel for 60 hours without water.

There is very little import trade, but ostrich feathers, ivory from the south, and damûr cloth are yearly sent into Kordofan.

The ironwork of the Fors is good, and tanning is carried on to a small extent.

Currency. In Darfur the currency is curious. Forty small pieces of damûr cloth about a foot long and 4 inches broad = one white cloth, two of which = one dollar, or 3s. 9d. to 4s. 2d.; a small blue cloth is used to represent half a dollar.

The standard white cloth is called a Tob, the blue cloth Farakhieh, and the smallest pieces of cloth Rubieh.
The following were the approximate prices in 1876:— Prices.

An ox costs	12s. to 24s.
A sheep costs	3s.
A goat costs	2s.
A good riding camel costs	£10 to £14
A pack „ „	5 „ 6
A horse costs	10 „ 12
But sometimes a good horse fetches	60 „ 85

The slave trade was, before Gessi's campaign, one of the chief occupations of the inhabitants. Large expeditions used to proceed across the Bahr el Arab, returning with slaves and ivory.

Towns.

El Fasher is the chief town. Colonel Gordon in 1877 El Fasher. described it as a most miserable place, though once a populous and thriving town under the Sultans.

El Fasher or Tendelty stands on the western bank of the Wadi Tendelty, in an angle formed by the junction of the latter with the Wadi el Kho.

The Tendelty has no current of its own, but is filled during the rains by the overflow from the Kho, and a dam, constructed near the junction, retains the water for some time. The wells supplying the town are all sunk in its bed.

The town consists almost entirely of tukls and box-shaped straw sheds. On the east of the Tendelty stand the palace of the late Sultan, a group of mud huts, and a few tukls surrounded by a mud wall about 20 feet high.

On the town side opposite the palace, the Egyptians constructed a square fort with ditch and parapet.

The population of the town was, in 1875, about 2,650. Of these—

      1,700 were natives.
       300 Zayadiyeh Arabs.
       250 Sâbah Arabs.
       400 Melhah Arabs.

Dara is the second town in Darfur. Mr. Wilson says Dara. (in 1880):—" It is well fortified by a stone wall, which has a tower at each corner; the walls are massive and there is a deep trench outside the wall. The fortification forms a square, each side of which is a quarter of a mile long. Inside are the Government magazines and barracks. The townspeople live in straggling lanes of huts, irregularly built, to the south and east of the citadel. In 1880, the houses were being gradually rebuilt in a more substantial manner of brick. There is a daily market, where meat, milk, merissa, vegetables, beads, and odds and ends are sold, and which is attended by all the tribes in the district."

Dara is situated about a mile from the left bank of the Wadi Amur, which drains south-east into the Bahr el Arab. Sandy surroundings, town of tukls with Government buildings. The old Mudirieh on a sandy hill.

N. lat. 12° 10′ 35″; E. long. 25° 21′ 6″ (Mason Bey). Height above sea-level 1,622 feet.

Towaisha.   *Towaisha* is a collection of large villages, and lies at the mouth of a valley running north.

Shakka.   *Shakka.* Gordon describes Shakka as quite a town, and a much larger place than El Obeid. It was at one time the headquarters of slave dealing, and was an important Dervish post up to 1896. The water supply is poor.

Om Shanga.   *Om Shanga* was in 1880 a considerable town, with houses and stores well built of bricks; some really fine buildings. The wells are half a mile from the town and are 120 feet deep—excellent water. Large market, starting-point for caravans for long distances, many camels.

A sort of bread (*abri* or *kisreh*) for long journeys is prepared here, made of sun-dried dokhn dough flavoured with herbs.

ROUTE II.—EL OBEID TO EL FASHER.

There are two routes from El Obeid to El Fasher.

The main caravan route leads by a northerly bend *viâ* Jebel Katul, Magenis, and Guradi to Foga, and thence to El Fasher; this is fairly supplied with water.

The more direct route leads straight to Foga and joins the caravan route at this point; but from El Obeid to Foga there is no water at all, except what has been placed in the baobab trees along the track; there is not sufficient for camels. The old telegraph line followed this latter route, which was only used for quite small parties and post-couriers.

(i) El Obeid—Katul—Guradi—Foga—El Fasher.
(Major Prout, March and April, 1875, 35 days.)

Place.	Miles.		Description.
	Intermediate.	From El Obeid.	
Nezeha ..	20	20	For the first 62 miles, as far as Magenis, the route lies through cultivated country; here the traveller will seldom be out of sight of villages, and can always find grain and meat, guides, and fair pasturage. The country is perfectly open and slightly rolling; the soil is light, but the sand not deep. The following account refers to the dry season.
Esh Shei ..	27	47	At Nezeha, near Om Shemma, are some scattered groups of wells, known as Om Shemma and Om Leha. Sufficient for villagers, but could not be depended on for a large force.
Magenis ..	15	62	Wells of Esh Shei, Kurra, and Om Shewai, 130 to 140 feet deep; plenty of water for a large party.
			Group of many wells, 45 to 60 feet deep: some salt, but many sweet. One of the most important water stations, yet in March, 1875, it was impossible, owing to their slowness in filling, to take in one day three days' water supply for 75 men and a few animals.
			At Shehahete, 10 miles to north-east, is an abundant supply of good water. From Magenis to Gurradi there are three routes: the first direct across uninhabited steppes, south of Gebel Om Hashas; no water in dry season; 72 miles. The second, *viâ* Tinneh (26 miles), and Bir Soderi (35 miles; abundant water throughout the year) to Gurradi (25 miles)

Place.	Miles.		Description.
	Intermediate.	From El Obeid.	
			—total, 86 miles. The third, taken by Major Prout, *viâ* Tinneh, and thence direct to Gurradi. All these routes pass through a rolling steppe country, inhabited only at the base of the hills by negro tribes from the south. Easy going, little wood, much grass, fine pasture in the *kherif*.
Tinneh ..	26	88	Always a little water in the wells, and an abundant supply for three or four months after the rains. No water from here onwards to
Gurradi ..	52	140	Gurradi. White clay plain almost destitute of herbage or vegetation. Ten or twelve wells, 30 feet deep, an abundance of excellent water. Bacali and Asserar El Buger villages near. Camel pasturage scanty; kept fed down by caravan animals, which must rest here before starting across the *atmur* to Foga. From here to Foga, 81 miles, is a steppe, quite uninhabited, and absolutely without water, except in the rainy season. Hamr Arabs pass with their flocks during the *kherif*, but otherwise hardly a soul is seen. Throughout, the steppe is rolling; for the first 30 miles so much so as to add greatly to the labour of the loaded camels. The last third of the journey is quite flat, and the soil, which was hitherto light red sand, becomes intermixed with clay. Thickets throughout of acacia, becoming dense low thick thorny forests, disagreeable to traverse and easy to get lost in. Country well grassed everywhere.

Fogs	..	81	221	At Fogs is a basin covering about a square mile, which receives the drainage of a large area, and is a lake during the rainy season. Abundant water at all times 4 to 6 feet below surface of ground. Resort of Hamr Arabs with many flocks and herds. In 1874 this was made the capital of the district, *vice* Omshanga. Around Fogs are dense low forests of acacia. From here the old route used to pass *viâ* Omshanga, but it is longer than the direct route to Karnak; the latter route is waterless, so provision of water must be made at Fogs.
J. Surug	..	13	234	On leaving Fogs, the first 13 miles are through thick forest, across a level and somewhat clayey bottom, to the hills of Surug, where there are several villages of negroes; these obtain their water from clefts in the rock.
J. Megsan	..	14	248	From here on to Karnak the track lies across rolling country, with light sandy soil, well grassed and thickly wooded. The forests are of acacia, heglik, and godén, and baobabs are numerous. The Debba road joins the track somewhere between J. Megsan (27) and Jebel Adashir (32 miles from Fogs).
Karnak	..	37	285	At Karnak is one immense well, 250 feet deep and 12 feet across, cut in the sandstone. Abundant and perpetual supply of excellent water. Bucket and rope work tedious. Village of tukls. Zeyadieh Arabs. Little cultivation. Lies at eastern foot of extensive plateau running north and west. Skirting the southern base of some picturesque sandstone cliffs and hills, the track reaches
Buti	..	10	295	Buti. Village. Slight cultivation. Three wells, 140 feet deep, cut through the rock. Good and abundant water.
Jebel Hella	..	5	300	Village. Two wells, 200 feet deep. Ditto, ditto. Good camel pasturage. The region is hilly, well peopled and cultivated.

76   *Darfur.*

Place.	Miles.		Description.
	Intermediate.	From El Obeid.	
Brúsh ..	17	317	Brúsh; large village; three wells, 92 feet deep; ostriches, cattle, sheep, and donkeys. Lies a little north of the track. Country open and hilly. Sandstone. Much cultivated.
Om Zeriba ..	13	330	One well, 115 feet deep. Plenty of water.
Om Kedada	7	337	One large well, 100 feet. Abundance of good water. Frequent villages to the north.
Abiat ..	22	359	20 or 30 wells, about 45 feet deep; little water in each, and not very good.
Derra ..	30	389	The track now bends south-west. From Abiat to Ergûd (44 miles) no water for a caravan in the *seff*. Ground rolling, well grassed, many thickets. No villages up to Derra or Derrat el Hamra. Water for a few people here most months. Between here and Ergûd are many villages.
Ergûd ..	14	403	Three groups of wells; water in abundance 10 to 20 feet below ground. Large basin, full of trees. Numerous villages around. Dokhn cultivation.
J. Sarganat..	20	423	From Ergûd the track leads first over dunes of light sand, then across rolling, grassy steppes to the Sarganat hills. Leaving these, a gravelly basin 3 miles wide is traversed, and so to the sandy ridges of El Fasher. There is no water at all between Ergûd and El Fasher. A few villages in the hills may get their water from cisterns in the rocks or water-holes in the khors.
El Fasher ..	23	446	El Fasher (*v.* p. 71 for description).

(ii) El Obeid—Foga (Telegraph Route).
(Major Prout, December, 1876, and January, 1877.)

Fula Menderaba ..	16	16	On leaving El Obeid in a direction a little south of W. the track passes through much cultivation and thickets, with scattered villages, to Fula Menderaba, a depression which only holds water in the four months of the rainy season.
Tianneh ..	11	27	Village; water only during rainy season; at other times it is fetched from Abu Haraz, lying 12 miles to the south. Rising ground now on the left, and valley full of thickets.
Beriab (or Om Gamarra)	18	45	Beriab. Baobabs, with water brought from Abu Haraz, the sole supply of villages near; 7 miles further on, the track passes through dense forests, and curves to the W.N.W.
Dudieh ..	19	64	Dudieh, a village with cultivation and many baobabs. Country wooded, but not densely so.
Ildai ..	16	80	Village with considerable corn and very many water baobabs. Through country now rolling and wooded, but uninhabited, to
Shallota ..	18	98	Shallota. Considerable cultivation, and a little water in baobabs. Village strongly fenced against lions (Felkin). Over undulating land, wooded, no villages.
J. Misón ..	21	119	Past the southern foot of Jebel Misón, through forests of acacias, leaving
(Three hills ?)	26	145	Three hills to the south, through more dense forests to
Frokit ..	3	148	Frokit. Three reservoirs; water only in rainy season. Four miles further on, the track turns due west, through thickets and small corn-fields to
Kabra ..	22	170	Kabra. A large village, and a little water in wells. From here the track bears a little east of north for 4 miles, and then swings N.N.W. through forest country to
Foga ..	16	186	Foga.

Darfur.

Southern Darfur, between Dara and Hofrat en Nahas.

Everywhere, south of Dara, there is plenty of water, except in El Goz, the plain extending for 20 miles south of Om S'ghir. In the dry season water can be found 12 to 30 feet below the surface in the wadis.

Always water in the lake at Taimo, and in the Bahr el Arab.

In the El Halla country are forests of gum trees, ebony, and tamarinds, and many fruit-bearing trees, e.g., the "*abu behessa,*" which bears a sweet orange-like fruit.

Bread is made from dokhn, dhura, koreb, sammn, and other plants.

The Habanieh are the chief inhabitants of all this district; formerly at war with the Massalit. They cultivate the ground and possess great herds of cattle. Few sheep, but many goats and donkeys. Camels cannot stand the climate. Poisonous fly (tsetse?) very bad in parts.

Much wild animal life: elephant, giraffe, hippo (in the *kherif*), rhino, buffalo (now extinct?), wild ox[*] (grey, with white head), wild sheep, *katamburo*,[†] *tetel* and other antelopes—no true gazelle—baboon, wild boar, ostrich, heron, partridge, &c., &c., and much fish and crocodiles in the rivers.

---

[*] *Abu orf* and *om boga.*
[†] Ox-like animal.

ROUTE III.—DARA TO HOFRAT EN NAHAS.
(*Colonel Purdy, February, 1876.*)

Place.	Miles.		Description.
	Intermediate.	From Dara.	
El Obeid ..	10	10	From Dara the route passes south-west across a plain covered with bush; here and there a tamarind or baobab. Wells numerous; water 20 feet down. Zoghawa from North Darfur, Borgawi, Beni Helba. Cultivation. Lime near here. Many villages.
Kirkiri ..	11	21	On the Wadi Kirkiri, a branch of the Wadi Amur. Zoghawa and Bisharin. Cotton trees and fields.
Wadi Om S'ghir ..	8	29	Six villages. Seventeen wells, 50 to 60 feet deep. Mixed inhabitants. Hence for a day and a half, over El Goz, an undulating sandy plain covered by a forest, most of the trees killed by white ants. Road trends now S.S.E.
Allari ..	23	52	Bir Allari el Fellata, or El Tosiel. Massalit country begins. Rich soil, little cultivated.
Moella ..	10	62	Residence of (former) Sultan Abd el Rahman of Massalit.
Tigla ..	2	64	Two or three houses.
Sul el Benaza ..	1	65	Seventy wells, 10 feet deep. Boundary of Darfur and Bahr el Ghazal Mudiriehs. Entry into Dar Kalaka. The route now leads through forests of acacia, past a well called
Tawila ..	16	81	Tawila (village of Habanieh Aruba), and El Hamir wells (?) (large gemaiza tree, with dom palm growing from it), across open sandy country to

	Miles.		Description.
Place.	Inter-mediate.	From Dara.	
Kobesh ..	14	95	Kobesh. Several villages. Many merchants. Rich soil; dokhn, maize, tomatoes, &c. From here to Shakka is a three days' camel ride, with water and numerous villages every few hours. From Kobesh one turns south-west, across dhura fields and small gum forests, to
Gemamizo (?) ..	7	102	Gaemahrieh (?). Wells and villages. On leaving this, one traverses a very rich and well-wooded country, with grasses 5 to 10 feet high, inundated during rainy season in lower parts.
El Akhdar ..	16	118	El Akhdar. Wells. From here to Hofrat en Nahas the country is a vast succession of forests, broken by a few uninhabited spaces. Forests chiefly gum acacias. Country called El Halla ("wilderness"). Much wild game—elephant, ostrich, giraffe, &c.
Lake Kundi ..	17	135	Lake Kundi, the enlargement of the Bahr er Rigl. Much water and fish all the year round.
Taimo ..	6	141	Taimo, at the south-west corner of the lake, on the R. bank of the Rigl, is a group of three or four Habanieh villages. Deserted during the *kherif*, when it is submerged. It is the headquarters, during the dry season, of hunters of giraffe, rhino, &c. Tamarisk forests. Road very bad hence, 10-feet grass and many holes, to the
Bahr el Arab ..	16	157	Bahr el Arab. Much water in February, but no current. Many crocodiles and fish.

Dara—Hofrat en Nahas

Birket Yiff	13	170	On the L. bank of the Bahr el Arab. Eight miles to the south-west the Bahr el Fertit joins the Bahr el Arab at Birket esh Shoka. ("Birket" here means a deep part of a river.)
Jobel Dango	23	193	From Birket Yiff the road leads due west, through great forests, to Jebel Dango. A small granite hill. Dokhn, dhura, and cotton. Four villages, two wells. From here onwards the woods are not so thick, and the going is easier.
Hofrat en Nahas	36	229	Hofrat en Nahas is situated on a plain half a mile from the R. bank of the Bahr el Fertit. N. lat. 9° 48′ 23″. E. long. 24° 5′ 38″. Small village; no supplies. Three inches of water in the Bahr el Fertit in February; running water, deep and full of fish, a mile below. The famous copper mines lie 1,000 yards south-west of the village, 100 feet above the river. The vein runs north-west and south-east, and sticks 2 feet out of the ground. In 1876, 500′ × 50′ × 9′ had been dug out. Well 10 yards to the west, through white clayey matter. This ground is very rich in almost pure carbonate and bicarbonate of copper; only the richest parts worked. Smelted on the spot in clay furnaces. Numerous other old workings. Poisonous camel-killing fly ("Omo Bogano") in neighbourhood (killed nearly all Colonel Purdy's camels).

From Hofrat en Nahas back to Dara.

	From Hofrat en Nahas.		
Jebel Hadid	46	46	Back *via* Jebel Dango; hence northwards by Jobel Hadid; iron mines; thick bamboo forests on granitic soil (not flooded during *kherif*) to
Ras el Fil	20	66	Ras el Fil village. Enter Dar Kalaka, cultivated country.
Millem	20	86	Millem village. Ground becomes sandy, with small acacia trees. Dokhn, dhura, and cotton cultivated in parts.

Dar Nuba.

Description.

Dar Nuba may be best considered from Jebel Dilling, where four granite peaks rise to 400 or 500 feet above the plains, on which other similar peaks crop up here and there. At a distance of from 8 to 12 miles, the view is shut in to the north-west, west, south, and south-east, by high rugged mountains. To the north, broad plains slope down to El Birket, and the watercourse draining the northern and eastern faces of the mountains runs in the same direction. These plains are uninhabited, and densely wooded. The trees have no value as timber, and consist principally of acacia.

The people live in caves and on the terraces of the mountains in comparative security from the predatory horsemen of the plains.

Whilst Kordofan is merely an extensive plain with little change of scenery, Dar Nuba presents an entirely different aspect. Here chains of picturesque hills, running in various directions, rise out of the plain, interspersed with numerous watercourses. Jebel Delen, on which the late Catholic Mission station was situated, is one of the smallest of the hills. The other principal groups are Naïma, Kurun, Dobab, Dair, Kedaro, Tagalla, Gedir, and Tira, in which gold is found, besides a number of smaller hills. It is estimated that in all there are upwards of 100 inhabited mountains.

The intervening plains and valleys are rich in vegetation of every description; trees of colossal dimensions are found, more especially in the khors (the beds of perennial streams), and the thick luxuriant growth is so dense that the rays of the sun cannot penetrate. The soil is exceptionally fertile and rain abundant, consequently for six months in the year the density of the undergrowth makes it almost impossible to traverse these rich valleys; but when the rains are over and the grass becomes dry, it is generally fired, and thus the plains and valleys become passable again. A quantity of the rain from these hills flows into Lake Birket, some passes also into the Khor Abu Habl, which becomes lost in the sand

Population. 83

before it reaches the White Nile. The rain from the southern Nuba Hills finds its way into the Bahr el Arab. The plains abound with quantities of deer, giraffe, antelope, and wild boar, whilst the woods contain myriads of birds of lovely plumage, and apes and monkeys of every description. During the winter season elephants are frequently to be seen in the neighbourhood of Delen, which also abounds with snakes, amongst which the python is not uncommon.

Population.[1]

The population of Dar Nuba, which at one time was considerable, does not now exceed 50,000; the scattered sub-tribes of Baggara, who roam the plains with the Bederieh and Ghodiat Arabs, have decimated the Nubas, and forced those that are left to fly to their mountain recesses, where they eke out a wretched existence, their protection being the inaccessible nature of their retreats.

Father Ohrwalder found the Nubas a pleasant and well-disposed people; indeed, they have the reputation in the Sudan of being the best of all the negroid races; they cultivate only sufficient quantities of corn, sesame, and beans to serve for their livelihood, whilst the wild fruits and vegetables of their country are so plentiful as to furnish almost sufficient food for their maintenance should they be unable to cultivate. They possess numbers of goats and cattle which supply them with milk and butter; they are much addicted to drinking merissa (a kind of beer made from dhura), and great quantities of this beverage are consumed at their feasts, principally at the feast known as Zubehr. On this occasion men and women drink and dance together; but notwithstanding this unusual familiarity nothing is done which might be considered an outrage to society. With the exception of the Khojur and the head sheikh monogamy is practised.

The Nubas are governed entirely by their own traditional laws and customs, the Khojur only intervening in case of necessity. The Khojur is in reality a sort of religious chief, whose power over the people depends entirely on his skilfulness and sagacity.

(d) Shillûk District.

Description.

The Shillûk tribe of negroes inhabits the entire bank of the White Nile for 200 miles northwards of the mouth of the Bahr el Ghazal. Their territory, however, is not more than 10 miles wide. Formerly, they extended much further north than at present, and had settlements on all the islands of the Nile; now they only exceptionally penetrate to lat. 12° 30' N.

The Baggara Arabs hem them in on the west, and are constantly extending their encroachments along the river bank, and have, moreover, with their flocks ventured far to the east of the stream into the land of the Dinka. During the dry season the Baggara hold all the left bank, but return to the steppes of the interior during the rains. Wherever they settle they drive out the Shillûks.

The Shillûks had an ancient dynasty of kings, and a form of government which was destroyed by Mehemet Ali. They are said to have numbered 2,000,000 before the Egyptians occupied their country.

Since 1884 the Shillûks have often been at war with the Dervishes; in 1894 a protracted rising led to heavy reprisals on the part of the latter, who annihilated a large portion of the tribe and killed their Queen. Notwithstanding this, the Jehadieh comprise a number of Shillûks, many of whom fought on the Dervish side during the recent campaigns.

Population.

In the year 1871 their subjection to the Egyptian Government was completed. At this time a census was taken of the villages, by which their number was estimated at 3,000. Taking the number of huts in a village as varying from 45 to 200, and the inhabitants of each hut at four or five, the number of inhabitants in the country must have exceeded 1,000,000. No known part of Africa has a density of population so great. Everything here is favourable to support a teeming population—agriculture, fishing, pasturage, and the chase.

The soil is very fertile, for in addition to the rains,

it is watered by the rising of the river and artificial irrigation.

A certain amount of emigration goes on in a south-westerly direction, where considerable numbers of the Shillûks, as well as of the Dembo and the Jûr, have settled on the borderland between the Bongo and Dinka. There are also settlements of Shillûks about the mouth of the Sobât River.

The entire west bank of the Nile, as far as the district of the Shillûks reaches, has the appearance of a continuous village, the sections of which are separated by intervals varying from 300 to 1,000 paces. These clusters of huts are built with great regularity, and closely crowded together. Every village has its overseer, whilst there is a superintendent over 50, 70, or 100 villages, who has the control over a district. There are about 100 districts, each distinguished by its particular name. *Villages.*

In the centre of each village is a circular space, where the inhabitants congregate.

They are of medium height and unpleasing in appearance. The men wear no clothes, but cover their bodies with red and grey ashes. The women wear a leather apron. *Inhabitants.*

The hair of the men is worn clotted together in all sorts of fantastic shapes with clay, gum, or dung.

They carry clubs similar to the knobkerries of South Africa, but their only other arms are long flat-headed spears.

The Shillûks breed oxen, sheep, and goats; they also keep poultry and dogs. *Produce.*

The dogs are shaped like greyhounds, but are smaller; they are exceedingly active, and are used in chasing antelope.

The Shillûk canoe, in which they navigate the Nile, is formed of long pieces of the *ambach* wood, which is lighter than cork. These canoes or rafts generally carry two persons, and are especially adapted for the navigation of the marshy parts of the river, as they can be carried on the head without difficulty, when it is necessary to cross an island or morass.

Cotton grows wild, but the people are ignorant of the art of its manufacture.

Large quantities of dhura and some maize are grown.

Tobacco is also found.

The country consisting simply of rich alluvial soil, there is no iron, which is accordingly much prized by the natives.

The rains begin in May and are regular during four months, so that cotton might be cultivated without the expense of artificial irrigation.

The acacia forests produce gum in unlimited quantities, but there is no trade in it from here.

The northern limits of this country are rich in forest of the Acacia Arabica (*sunt*)—a wood that is invaluable as fuel for steamers, and is the only really durable wood for ship-building in the Sudan.

CHAPTER IV.

COUNTRY TO THE EAST OF THE WHITE NILE.

(i) COUNTRY BETWEEN THE WHITE AND BLUE NILES.

(a) SENNÂR.

This province lies principally in the angle formed by the White Nile above Khartum and the Blue Nile or Bahr el Azrek, and between lat. 12° and 15° 45′ N.

In lat. 15° 37′ N. is situated the junction of the two great branches of the Nile, the tract between which, increasing towards the south to 50 to 60 miles in width, is called by the Arabs the "Island of Sennâr." The indigenous population call it "Hui."

The towns lie chiefly along the banks of the Blue Nile, and are numerous, from the 13th parallel for 200 miles.

The province is bordered on the north by the country known as Dar el Halfaya, and on the south by Dar Fazokl.

To the east of the Blue Nile, the province extends as far as the forests which surround Abyssinia. The actual boundary is but vaguely defined.

The west side of the "Island of Sennâr" is more or less a wilderness, Hellet el Ais, a poor hamlet at the ferry on the road to Kordofan, and, lower down, Manjera (Mangara), a former station for hewing timber and building boats, being the principal places.

History.

The popular traditions of Sennâr represent that country as the original seat of the Macrobii, whom Herodotus mentions as the most remote of the Ethiopians, and a people whose gold provoked the cupidity of Cambyses. The same historian also speaks of the Automeli (emigrants) or Egyptian soldiers, who, deserting Psammeticus, marched south and settled in Ethiopia above Meroe. These were the Sebridæ or Sembritæ of later writers, and prove that the Island of Sennâr was occupied by Egyptians.

Tradition also says that, after the time of Cambyses, 12 Queens and 10 Kings reigned in Sennâr. Then the tribe of the Fungi came from Western Sudan, forded the White Nile, and established themselves in a part of the country.

In Sennâr, at the beginning of the present century, several rival factions disputed for sovereign authority. Two usurpers, Adlan and Rêgeb, had made themselves masters of the State to the prejudice of Bâdy, the rightful heir, when Ismail Pasha entered the country in 1820 at the head of a Turkish army. Adlan was assassinated by Rêgeb, who had to fly the country, and Bâdy surrendered his rights to Ismail.

This ancient Egyptian settlement of Sennâr seems to have risen superior to Meroe, and to its influence may be ascribed the imitations of Egyptian art found scattered over the plains in the latter district.

As Christianity spread up the Nile, it was soon accepted by the descendants of the Egyptians, and in the 10th century the most flourishing State of "Ethiopia" was the Christian Kingdom of Alwa on the Blue River, with Soba for its capital. The ruins of Soba may now be seen about 15 miles above Khartum.

Topography.

The territory of Sennâr is, in general terms, a great level plain, from which masses of rocks protrude at wide intervals, and to no great elevation. West of the town of Sennâr, however, about 10 or 12 hours' distant, are the mountains Moia, Mandera, and Segadi, apparently extending as a chain from south to north, but in reality disconnected. Granite is the prevailing rock, associated with micaceous schist and greenstone. The red granite of Segadi is of the finest quality, and superior to that of Syene (*v.* p. 95).

Jebel Moia, the largest of these hills, has a length of some miles, and rises to a height of about 1,200 feet above the plain.

Baboons are the only inhabitants of the bare rocks; apes, parrots, and Guinea fowl inhabit the woods at their feet.

The ebony tree grows round Jebel Moia; the sycamore round Segadi.

The plain of Sennâr, for some distance above Khartum, exhibits only a sandy soil, mixed with river deposits. But, from Mesalamieh up, its character changes entirely, and the level flat, now higher above the river level, becomes a deep bed of argillaceous marl, containing calcareous concretions in great quantity. Over its surface are scattered boulders of granite, and fragments of greenstone in great numbers; of the latter are made the mills of the country, of which every household has one.

The plain is covered with a black mould, the result of decomposition.

The argillaceous soil is retentive of water, and when refreshed by rain (for these rich plains are nowhere reached by the waters of the Nile), becomes exceedingly fertile. But in the dry season it has an aspect of the most dismal sterility; no tree, little herbage, and the naked ground cracked and gaping in all directions with the burning heat.

The belts of thick wood which extend along the banks of the Nile below the junction of its two great arms, continue along the Blue River above the junction.

The foliage of all trees in this region, with the exception of the *Acacia senegalensis,* is scanty, and gives little shade. With the species just named are also associated the *Acacia seyal* and *Acacia nilotica,* or *Sunt,* producing gum arabic, *Balamites Egypticus, Rhamus spina Christi,* and *Sodada decidua;* the last leafless, and presenting only a bunch of slender boughs.

The fruit of the tamarind, called Ardeb in Nubia, is in great request for its medicinal qualities.

Above Khartum the palms increase in number; the dôm and date palm are seen towards Sennâr; but more

90   Sennâr.

Banks of Blue Nile. characteristic of the climate are the Deleb palm and the Baobab, which latter and the tamarind make their first appearance at Kamlin, increasing in numbers southward, till two days' journey above Sennâr they shade the lounging place of every village.

The plain around Sennâr town is destitute of trees, and though naturally prolific, rarely exhibits any luxuriant vegetation.

Harvests. For six or seven months of the year Sennâr offers the aspect of a sterile waste. But as soon as rain falls, the arid and dreary waste becomes a sea of mire, and on this, without any preparation, is sown the dhura (*Sorghum vulgare*), the characteristic produce of Sennâr.

In three months and a half, or towards the end of October, the whole place is covered with ripe grain, and the harvest is gathered.

Below Messalamieh, where the river here and there rises above the bank, and irrigation is carried on, the crops are somewhat earlier.

Near Khartum, the extensive inundated tracts on the White Nile are sown, on the retirement of the floods, with kidney beans, and afterwards with dhura.

The inhabitants only cultivate a very small portion of the soil, and yet a good harvest is sufficient to provide for the wants of two or three years.

The principal crops are dhura, beans, lentils, tobacco. On the plains about the Dinder, cotton and sesame are grown without trouble. In gardens, watered every day, the pomegranate, lemon, fig, &c., are found, covered with fruit or flowers at all seasons. The vine, banana, onion, water-melon, and other vegetables are also cultivated.

In Sennâr, dhura used to be sold for 20 to 25 piastres the ardeb, or about 3*s.* to 5*s.* per 100 lbs.

The Kalaba, or small merchants, collect and transport it on donkeys for distances of seven or eight days' journey from their localities.

Inhabitants.

The population is very mixed, and no traveller has succeeded in determining distinctly the aboriginal race. According to Cailliaud six classes may be readily distinguished :—

(1) Asfari (yellow) of manifestly Arab origin.
(2) Hamar (red) mulattoes, one remove from the preceding.
(3) Azrek (blue), darker than the Hamar, and including the people called Fungi.
(4) Akhdar (green).
(5) Elkat Fatelolu (very dark), and little removed from No. 6.
(6) The Sudan blacks or negro slaves.

The existence of a once dominant white race, distinct from the Arab, cannot be doubted.

The pastoral tribes of the island are the Aelt and Haraza.

On the right bank of the Nile are the Jaalin, the Kawalah (between the Rahad and Dinder), the Rufaa, and Dobena.

The pastoral tribes of Sennâr move north with their herds in May, and return in September.

The northern portion of the fork of the Niles is inhabited by the Degheim and Kenana Arabs, horse-breeding tribes. Khalifa Ali Wad Helu is head of them. They are fanatical Mahdists.

· The bodily vigour of the men is soon undermined by climate, &c., and they grow rapidly decrepid in declining years. The women, on whom all the drudgery of domestic life devolves, soon become repulsively ugly.

The dress is the *ferda* or toga, which is folded in a variety of ways.

The elaborately dressed hair and ornamental sandals exactly represent the fashion of ancient Egypt as painted on the tombs.

Slavery was one of the chief conditions of social life; when Sennâr was an independent State, every man was an abject slave, either of a private master or of a despotic King.

The inhabitants have scarcely any other occupation than that of cultivating the ground, which they do very imperfectly; it could be made to produce three times what it does at present, but they themselves say that the old Egyptian rule totally suppressed all habits of industry.

The land is thinly peopled and little cultivated, and there are no proprietors of the soil. Anyone can take a piece of open ground and cultivate it, but cannot claim the produce as a right until he has taken in all the crops.

The work of the fields is all done by slaves.

The upper classes spend a life of indolence and dissipation. All classes love intoxication, and drink either merissa or brandy distilled from it.

They are not particular in their food, and, though Mohammedans, do not refuse pork, or the entrails of camels, sheep, or cattle.

Their favourite dish is liver, which they devour raw.

They live, however, as a rule, on nothing but dhura cooked with water; and frequently fast for several days without complaining.

Belilah is a decoction of dhura and water.

Merissa, a kind of beer, is made from dhúra or dokhn by boiling it for a whole night and then letting it ferment. That subjected only to a slight fermentation is reserved for the priests and devout Mussulmans.

Bilbel is merissa more carefully made from the best grain.

Logma, the chief article of food of the poor, corresponds to the *polta* of the Italian peasantry. It is a sort of paste made out of ground dhura and water and milk.

Ebreh is the same paste made into thin wafers.

Kesra, or bread, is also made of thin paste, baked for a few minutes on a hot iron or stone.

Meat is roasted or hung up and smoked. When dried for keeping it is called *El-kadid*.

Salt is scarce and not pure.

Some of the natives chew a preparation of tobacco or stramonium, which frequently produces fits of insanity.

They possess some surgical art, can amputate and perform other difficult operations; they also practise inoculation for smallpox.

They are skilful as weavers, goldsmiths, curriers, potters, &c., and in the Sudan are celebrated for superior workmanship.

The people, though professing the faith of the Koran, observe hardly any of its precepts; they never wash nor pray, and most of their villages are without mosques.

The houses of Sennâr of the present day are built of sun-dried bricks, and roofed with *halfa* (a grass), dhura straw, or reeds. Formerly there were many houses of two storeys in Sennâr, but few of them now remain. The architecture, however, is still far superior to that of surrounding districts.

Scattered among the rectangular brick houses are the far more numerous huts of the black population. These are made of clay and straw, and of the various shapes peculiar to the different races.

Animals and Climate.

The horse, the ass, and camel all suffer severely from the rainy season in Sennâr. The cattle are small and ill-conditioned, the sheep tall and without wool. *Animals.*

The dog appears to be a degenerate greyhound, and is very subject to hydrophobia.

The wild animals are not numerous.

The elephant, rhinoceros, giraffe, zebra, and antelope keep to the wooded districts of the Abyssinian frontier, or to the forests to the south, and rarely approach the inhabited banks of the river.

The hippopotamus and crocodile are very numerous. The maraffin (hyena) enters the villages at night in search of dead bodies.

Apes, parrots, baboons, and wolves, leopards, &c., are plentiful in the woods.

The *suretah*, or fly, that attacks cattle, does not come within two days' journey of Sennâr, though other travellers assert that it is most destructive to camels during the rains.

Mosquitoes are very troublesome. Various kinds of scorpions and other reptiles abound; the bite of the snake known as the *assal* causes instant death.

Though the limit of tropical rains is marked in maps in lat. 17° 40′ N., yet, about the Nile, these rains can hardly be said to reach far beyond the 15th parallel. At Khartum, in lat. 15° 37′ N., rain falls irregularly, and droughts of long continuation are not unfrequent. Even higher up, where rain never wholly fails, it is still but scanty. But on the marshy plain of Sennâr three or four tropical showers are enough for the dhura. *Rains.*

The rains seem to be occasioned by east winds, though winds from the south prevail during the wet season, which generally begins in July and continues for two months.

Generally speaking, the *kherif* (rainy season) may be said to commence early in May, and continue off and on up to the end of October.

In November and December the crops are gathered.

The Nile swells fitfully in May, begins to rise steadily in June, and attains its greatest height early in September. Immediately before, and at times during, the rains, the heat is insupportable, and the air oppressively humid. Then come fever and dysentery, which are most fatal on the argillaceous plain.

Disease.

Sandy spots near the river, and places on the verge of the rains, are said to be most exempt from disease.

The *Farantit* or Guinea worm, another plague, which comes with the rains, and is here attributed to the use of rainwater, is more frequent south of Sennâr (*v.* p. 62).

In winter the thermometer falls to 60°, and the air becomes very dry.

The climate, tolerably cool, is yet unhealthy, though less so in the direction of Khartum.

The Blue Nile.

The Blue and White Niles do not receive, north of latitude 12°, any notable streams from the intervening watershed. But, as the whole country visibly slopes west, it is probable that some intermittent rivulets flow into the White Nile.

The Blue Nile is joined within the limits of Sennâr by the Dinder, and lower down by the Rahad (lightning) or Shimfa, as it is called by the Abyssinians, in whose territories both these streams rise (*v.* p. 101).

They are both great rivers in the rainy season, and when this is over, the Rahad stands in pools.

The villages and settled population of Sennâr are nearly all planted on this river, the ordinary width of which varies from 500 to 1,000 yards.

Route IV.—Sennâr Town to Kawa.

(*Pruyssenaere, May,* 1863.*)

A road leads between the White and Blue Niles from Sennâr town to Kawa. It takes 5½ days' journey; country near the Blue Nile covered with bush; wells and water-holes at several places on the road; used to be much used

---

* In Petermann's "Mittheilungen," 1877, Supplements 50 and 51.

by large caravans (slaves, &c.) from Darfur to Kordofan. Country bare and sandy for the western two-thirds of the journey. Level throughout.

Water supply on road from Sennâr westwards:—

		Miles from Sennâr.
1. Jebel el Mâ, Moia, or Moyé—large well		23
2. Jebel Sakati or Segadi—many water holes		38
3. Waliya village—wells		65
4. Kubosa ,, ,,		83
5. Gamusa ,, ,,		89
White Nile—river..		100

Besides wells in the numerous villages between the Blue Nile and Jebel el Mâ.

(b) Dar el Fungi.

Description.

The Dar el Fungi (or Funki) comprises the country between the White and Blue Niles lying to the south of the Dar Sennâr. It is a vast steppe-like expanse, dotted with isolated hills here and there, of which many hold water during the dry season. Fertile in parts in the rainy season, during the rest of the year the steppe is dried up and bare, except for occasional woods of mimosa, &c. There seems to be a fair amount of small game, and lion and hyena spoor are met with on occasion.

The inhabitants are mostly of the Hameg negroid tribe, whose religion is a thin Mohamedanism overlying a groundwork of fetish-worship. There are also settlements of Burûn and Jaalin.

Few Europeans have traversed this country. Pruyssenaere made a fine journey in 1863 from Karkoj southwards, almost to the Sobat, but has left little record of value.

The land takes its name from the Fung, a Darfur tribe which long ago overran the country and took possession of it. They are a fine race, but are now closely intermingled with the Hameg and the Burûn.

About N. lat. 10° 15', the fertile grass and woodlands of the Dinka form the southern boundary of the Dar el Fungi, a boundary often overrun by the inhabitants of the steppes in search of slaves and plunder.

To the east and south-east of the Dar el Fungi, the country is raided by the Inkasana, a robber people, from the direction of Beni Shangul and the hills of Dar Bertat.

(c) BENI SHANGUL.

Description.

From Famaka on the Blue Nile, the Dar Bertat, or Dar Fazokl, district stretches due south for 150 miles. It is a mountainous country, well supplied with streams, chief of which are the Tomat and Yabus, full of game, and with beautiful scenery. Its chief attraction, however, lies in the fact that it is rich in gold, which metal is chiefly to be found in the Beni Shangul hills.

The Beni Shangul occupy the mountainous zone formed by the westernmost edge of the Abyssinian tableland, and limited on the east and the north by the Blue Nile, on the south by the River Yabus, an affluent on the left bank of the Blue Nile, and by the country occupied by the Komas. The country of the Beni Shangul is intersected by the 35th meridian, and is very auriferous. They trade in gold with Abyssinia and the Sudan, and their money is formed principally of pieces of that metal.

The Beni Shangul are a people of mixed Arab and Sudanese blood, nearly connected with the Dervishes in the language which they speak, which is Arabic, and by religion, habits, customs, and government. They are not nomads and but little agricultural, but possess large quantities of cattle. Their villages are constructed, for reasons of defence, on isolated peaks. Hitherto they were independent of both Abyssinians and Dervishes, but they paid to the latter a tribute in gold; to the former they were always hostile.

The leaders of the Beni Shangul are two Emirs. One resides at Agoldi and is called Kogeli, the other resides at Beni Shangul, and is called Ali Abdul Rahman, and also Tor (or Wad Tur) el Guri. Each of them disposes of, it is said, 10,000 rifles, obtained from the Dervishes or bought from the Abyssinians at Tille.

Besides the two towns mentioned where the Emirs reside, there is the centre one of Gomosha.

The village of Beni Shangul lies on the south-east

slopes of Jebel Singe in the midst of the gold-bearing district, and 75 miles south by west of Famaka. It is very healthy, cool, and prettily situated. Here a battle was fought by Ismail Pasha, son of Mehemet Ali, in February, 1822, and the country was annexed to the Egyptian dominions. The gold is washed out of the streams during, or immediately after, the rainy season. Convicts were at first sent there from Egypt to work the gold, but the proceeding was so unremunerative that Said Pasha gave it up. A certain amount is, however, still obtained.

The possession of the country is still in dispute. Wad Tur el Guri, a recalcitrant Dervish Emir, fled here about 1887, and pacified the Khalifa by sending him an annual tribute of gold dust. On the other hand, the country, or at all events a large part of it, the southern half included, is claimed by the Emperor Menelik of Abyssinia. There is no doubt that the chief portion of the gold is sent to Abyssinia, and of this a considerable quantity finds its way through Harrar to India.

The inhabitants are negroid, warlike and generally restless.

The Inkasana, in the north of the district, are robbers, and unsubdued. They use as weapons, besides spears and occasional rifles, throwing-sticks like boomerangs (*trumbash*), and throwing-knives (sickle-shaped, *kulbeda*). Further south, the inhabitants approximate more to the Gallas.

An Abyssinian expedition, under Ras Makunnen, is reported to have gone in this direction, to repress a rising, in 1897, and to have inflicted a severe defeat on Wad Tur el Guri in the spring of 1898.

(ii) COUNTRY EAST OF THE BLUE NILE.

General Description.

East of the Blue Nile, between Khartum and Abu Haraz, the country towards the Atbara is little known, and offers but few inducements to further explorations. It appears to be a steppe-like country, growing more stony as one proceeds eastwards.* Running water there

---

* See "Report on Nile and Country between Dongola, &c.," Part III, Route VIII.

is none, and wells are few and far between. Mimosa forests cover the ground in places, and low hills are occasionally seen. The chief inhabitants are the wandering Shukriyeh tribe, akin to the Hadendoa, but of a lower type. In the early days of Mahdism the Shukriyeh were loyal to Egypt.

South of a line drawn eastwards from Abu Haraz to Tomat, the country changes in character. The ground becomes more hilly and cut up as one proceeds south, and numerous large rivers, full in the rainy season but at other times dry or nearly so, water the region. Of these, the chief ones are the Rahad and Dinder, flowing north-west into the Blue Nile, and the upper reaches of the Atbara, which is joined at Tomat by the Setit. All these rivers have their origin in the highlands of Abyssinia.

The triangle between the Rahad, the Atbara, and the line east and west from Abu Haraz to Tomat comprises two regions: the northern one is known as Gedáref,* and the southern as Gallabat.† These have been strongholds of the Dervishes for many years, and from these points hostile incursions have been made against Kassala and Eritrea.

(d) GEDÁREF.

Description.

Gedáref is an undulating plain, barren, brush-covered, and generally waterless except during the rains. Here and there low ranges and isolated hills are visible, and in places, especially round Suk Abu Sin, the ground is fertile and capable of much cultivation. Wells are few and far between. The inhabitants are mostly Shukriyeh. There is little pasture, except some scanty herbage for camels and sheep. Horse forage has to be carried.

The road from Kassala *viâ* Suk Abu Sin to Abu Haraz has been frequently traversed by Europeans, but outside the immediate neighbourhood of this road there is little information available.

[V. "Report on Nile from Dongola," &c., Part III, Route VIII (iii).]

Suk Abu Sin (Gedáref market) is situated on the border of immense prairies, which in the rainy season—

---

* Chief town Suk Abu Sin.   † Chief town Matamma.

June to September—are covered with long grass, but in the dry season form an arid and waterless desert.

Captain De Cosson says:—"The desert between Suk Abu Sin and Abu Haraz is not sand, but mud, and nothing meets the eye as far as it can reach but the dead skeleton grass of last rain season, which rises dry and white in the burning sunshine, making the plain look at a distance like a gigantic field of over-ripe corn. The track is worn bare by the feet of camels, and strewn with their bones. An unwholesome smell of dead vegetable matter rises from the cracks in the black mud, now all parched and baked, and reflecting back the almost vertical rays of the sun, like heated fire-brick. It is easy to understand how fever lurks on these plains, both when the tropical rains are melting all the decayed vegetable matter of which the mud is composed, and when the sun is boiling the blood in one's veins, and the very air one is breathing is at the temperature of a baker's oven" (May, 1873).

At Jebel Araing (Galaat Aranj), a range 40 miles north-west of Suk Abu Sin, there is often water, but with this exception there is none until Hellet esh Sherif is reached (105 miles from Suk Abu Sin).

The country between Gedáref and Gallabat is level, and thickly covered with mimosa trees. Doka is a large village about half-way. Little water in this district. The ground begins to rise south of Doka, towards the group of hills, Ras el Fil, which is termed the Gallabat country. Here the scenery is excessively pretty and mountainous, with several streams. Many leopards, lion also numerous.

(e) GALLABAT.

Description.

The district of Gallabat comprises (1863) about 20,000 souls, distributed among 24 villages. Of these, after Matamma, the chief ones are Rumeli, Abd er Rasul, Hellet ed Dervish, and Doka. No running water north of Hellet ed Dervish. Very fertile country, but little cultivated.

Gallabat lies at the foot of the Ethiopian highlands, and in former days, up to 1862, belonged to Abyssinia. It was taken by the Egyptians in that year.

Inhabitants. The inhabitants are a very mixed race, the wild Takruri* tribe predominating. These are negroes originally from Darfur. They ride oxen, and use the *trumbash* (boomerang) and long barbed spears.

Matamma. The town of Gallabat, or Matamma, is a considerable market town, composed principally of round houses thatched with conical grass roofs. It used to have a market on Tuesdays and Wednesdays, and much exchange goes on here between the products from the Nile and those from Abyssinia.

The chief articles of barter are cotton, coffee, wax, mules, and slaves. The town was formerly a celebrated centre for the latter form of merchandise.

The Dervish garrison of Gallabat was reported in the spring of 1898 to be 4,500 men, under Ahmed Fedil.

The Upper Atbara is in the vicinity of Matamma. In August, 1862, it carried a large head of water. In April it is 60 yards broad and hardly knee-deep.

(*j*) Country between the Blue Nile and Gallabat.

Between the Blue Nile (from Karkoj to Famaka) and Gallabat the country is one vast alluvial plain, divided by the sinuous Rahad and Dinder rivers into three long strips. The two western strips are undulating ground, and the banks of the river are covered with thick mimosa bush. Away from the rivers the interior is much more sparsely wooded. Country very fertile, but little labour or cultivation.

The third (eastern) strip, comprising Gedáref and Gallabat, has been described. The Rahad and Dinder are practically dry from November to May. The flood comes down in June, and during July and August they are at their height. During August and September nuggers can ascend them assisted by the north wind.

Between Karkoj and the Dinder a small river, the Mebera, or Abdogul (?), flows into the latter. It is a pretty river, running with clear water when the others are muddy.

---

* A name formerly given to negro bands who had made the Mecca pilgrimage.

The Dinder River.

The usual limit of navigation on the Dinder is Deberki, which is a collecting place for grain and native produce.

The Dinder, about the 14th parallel, is, in May, 110 yards broad; banks 50 feet, thick jungle, much game, deep pools, quantities of crocodiles and hippopotamus. Fertile banks.

The river, which in February has ceased to flow, rises about the 26th May, and much dirty brown water (as opposed to the red water of the Blue Nile) comes down. On the 13th parallel, at its highest flood, it is 180 yards broad, with an average depth of 14 feet. Left bank steep, right bank sloping; flood rises 2 feet over right bank. Current $4\frac{1}{2}$ miles an hour.

The Rahad River.

The Rahad at a point due west of Matamma is 80 yards broad (April), not much water. Banks 45 feet high. Flows through rich alluvial soil, gentle current. All along its banks country very fertile in supplies. When full the river would average 40 feet deep; course free from shoals or rocks; admirably adapted for small steamers. Dry in parts (April). (Sir S. Baker.)

From the point above-mentioned on the Rahad to Rumeli (37 miles eastwards) there is no water.

The Rahad flood is similar to that of the Dinder, and comes down about the same time. In lat. 13° 19' it is, in flood time, 250 yards broad, with an average depth of nearly 10 feet. Current 5 miles an hour.

(iii) COUNTRY TO THE EAST OF THE BAHR EL JEBEL.

General Description.

The Sobât district formerly belonged to the Mudirieh of Fashoda, but in 1882 was included in the Lado Mudirieh (v. p. 110) and transferred to Emin Bey's Government.

The western boundary of the latter may be taken as having been the River Rohl as far as it goes, but all the Makaraka country on the south was afterwards included, and stations also organised in the Monbuttu land.

The eastern boundary is in no way defined; the province here embraced all territory where it was found advisable to establish stations garrisoned by Egyptian troops; its most easterly districts were in the Lattuka country between lat. 3° 30′ N. and 4° 30′ N., and in the neighbourhood of long. 33° E.

The southern boundary was marked by the northern shores of Lake Albert Nyanza, the Somerset River, or Victoria Nile, as far as the station Mruli, and the territory of the King of Uganda, which lies to the north-west of Victoria Nyanza.

Sir Samuel Baker had, before he left Egypt, constructed three military stations, Gondokoro, Fatiko, and Foweira. He had been unsuccessful in establishing a station at Massindi, in Unyoro.

On the east, the mountain spurs and ridges, which touch upon the river between Lado and Dufile, are bordered on the south by wide-spreading prairies and marsh-lands, intersected by numerous watercourses (khors) and dotted over with isolated hills.

Former Stations and Communications.

The district just described used to be held for the Egyptian Government by military stations, each with a garrison of 10 or 20 men, and at one and a half to three days' journey apart; the principal ones being as follows: — Gondokoro, Okkela, Loronio, Tarrangole, Agaru, Fadibek, Obbo, Laboreh (on the Bahr el Jebel).

To the south of the hilly country, there were the stations Fadyellu, Fatiko, Fabbo, Faloro, Dufile, Wadelai (the last two are on the river), Foweira, Magunga.

Description.

From Gondokoro eastwards towards the station Loronio, the country, for the first few miles, is a sandy flat, and then further to the east is succeeded by low hills of iron clay mixed with quartz, which gradually rise into the mountain spur known as the Lokoya. This group is composed chiefly of grey granite, and has many prominent peaks. Numerous watercourses run northwards; a great number of these are dry except during the rainy season, whilst others contain a certain amount of water all the year round, which is left standing in pools and depressions in the lower ground. This water is, however, frequently turbid and discoloured by the loamy deposits from the hills, and is not always drinkable.

In the valleys, the soil consists of a dark brown iron-holding clay, overlying granite detritus; the slopes of the hills are well wooded with acacias, and numerous other kinds of trees, including large quantities of bamboo.

The country for about 30 or 40 miles east of Gondokoro is inhabited by various small clans of the Bari tribe, the principal among whom are the Liria.

From Jebel Oppone, at the eastern extremity of this group of hills, the land subsides into wide stretching flats, through which the several watercourses flow northward. The country at first is sparsely covered with groups of acacia trees, but towards Okkela becomes more wooded and park-like in appearance.

Most of the khors hold no running water except during the rains, but there are many pools, stagnant lakes, and tracts of marshy ground. A few hours' rain, however, is sufficient to render the khors impassable. The water found in the standing pools is, as a rule, muddy, and much fouled by troops of wild animals.

At Okkela, the khor Ginetti holds running water all the year round, and during the rains is 5 or 6 feet deep; its waters are turbid and unpleasant to the taste.

Vast swampy flats stretch away to the north of Okkela, extending to the Bahr el Zeraf and White Nile. Immediately to the north of the Lattuka and Bari countries, these flats are inhabited by the Berri tribe.

Okkela is the first station reached in the Lattuka land. It lies in a fertile richly wooded country.

From here a road runs to Bohr direct, but it is only available during the dry season. It passes at first through wide, grass-covered, treeless plains, but, on approaching the Bohr territory, runs into a bush country.

The western boundary of the Lattuka country is marked by the khor Loddo, which separates it from the Liria district.

Running in a north-west and south-east direction from Loronio is a valley about 50 miles in length, and 8 to 10 in breadth. It is bounded on the east by a mountain spur known under various names, Larfît being the principal one. On the west, the boundary is the Langia spur. This valley is the principal habitation of the families of the Lattuka tribe.

It is traversed throughout by the khor Kohs, essentially a rainwater stream, empty at the dry season, and, during the rains, fed by numerous rainwater channels from the adjacent mountain slopes. Many small hills crop up here and there through the valley; these are frequently flat-topped, and crowned by the huts of the inhabitants.

The soil of the valley is in part composed of iron-clay, but there are also tracts of sand, marsh, and yellow loam.

The vegetation is luxuriant, and large varieties of trees clothe the slopes.

To the north-west and north of Lattuka land, lies the district of the Berri tribe; to the east, at about three days' journey distant, the mountains of the Irenga tribe. In this direction is the broad valley of the khor Tu, a stream of large dimensions during the rains, but of little importance, though constantly running, during the dry season. The country further to the east has not been explored, but there is reported to be another river of much greater importance with a large and constant stream in that direction.

Towards the southern extremity of the valley the country is covered with large masses of rock, and the soil is a deep red.

The end of the valley is closed in by ranges coming from the south-west and east; and, passing from the khor Kohs, in a westerly direction, the country of the Shuli tribe is entered.

Agaru is situated in this neighbourhood, and here there are several permanent streams flowing southward; these unite in the khor Okorro, which, it is said, loses itself in a marsh still further to the south.

The mountain country is composed of granite and is broken into deep ravines; in the villages there is a deep red clay formation, and in places this is mixed with loam and sand. The hills are thickly wooded.

Agaru is situated at a height of about 3,700 feet above the sea, and forms a species of sanatorium for the inhabitants, for which it seems well qualified.

From here to Fadibek there are a succession of ridges, valleys, and marshes, with one or two permanent streams running southward. There is much bush, high grass, reeds, and bamboo.

Fadibek is the chief village of Shuli land; the whole country to the south-east is known generally as Lango land.

Fadibek is at the southern limit of the group of mountains; at this point they cease, but from the peaks lying eastward towards Agaru numerous spurs are thrown out in a north-west direction. Various isolated groups and peaks of considerable height crop up between this and the Bari country to the north, the most notable being Jebel Okkiri, which has a height of about 5,000 feet above the sea level.

The gentler slopes of the spurs lying to the south-west of the Lattuka country are rich pasture grounds, and present a park-like appearance.

The country between Fadibek and Obbo is diversified in character; undulating prairies, swampy bottoms, woods, and park-like tracts succeed each other; numerous khors run towards the Bahr el Jebel, but their water is generally thick and turbid.

Between Obbo, which is the most northern station in the Shuli country, and Laboreh the land is low, and in places swampy, but it rises again to the range of hills which borders the Bahr el Jebel between Dufile and Laboreh.

To the south of Fadibek, the high ground is succeeded by a vast undulating prairie. Solitary hills start up here and there, while the ridges bordering the Bahr el Jebel throw out a spur in the direction of Faloro.

The prairie lands are in parts covered with bush, but are generally flat and open, with few trees. Numerous khors, some holding permanent water, intersect the lower grounds, while in other places there are interminable swamps. These districts are mostly uninhabited, and more or less impassable in the wet season.

Inhabitants.

The chief tribes of the district east of Bahr el Jebel and between latitudes 5° and 2° N. are:—

Commencing from the north, the Berri, the Bari, the Lattuka, the Shuli, the Madi; to the north-east of the Shuli, the Irenga; the Lango, to the south of the Shuli. This latter comprises the country of Umiro, which has its northern boundary four days' march south-south-west and south-east from Fadyellu. It is made up of numerous clans with separate dialects, and called Kidi by Speke. In the south-east, the inhabitants of Lango lands are nomads.

To the E.S.E. of Fadyellu lie the Dyahle districts, and beyond that the mountainous country of the Lobbohr, who speak the Shuli dialect.

To the north of Lobbohr is the Lorehm country, also called by the inhabitants Adieh land. It is very populous.

To the east of the last-named follows the Koliang country, and to the E.N.E. of this the Bognia district.

Beyond Lobbohr is the Termajok, and to the north of Koliang the Rohm country. None of these latter countries have been explored.

Mr. Felkin, in "Uganda and the Egyptian Sudan," describes the Bari tribe as inhabiting villages the picture of neatness; the huts built of tiger grass, with large eaves and very low doors.

Their cattle constitute their chief wealth, and they value them above their wives and children.

They are a fine muscular race, the men better looking than the women.

Small-pox is very prevalent among them, but it is believed it will be stamped out by inoculation.

Small shells, strung on string, are used as money.

They appear to have no religion, belief in a Supreme Being, or a future state.

That portion of the Bari tribe proper which inhabit the eastern bank of the Bahr el Jebel are an industrious people. They employ themselves in the cultivation of sorghum and cattle breeding. Their herds are very numerous.

The Liria are a branch of the Bari living to the east, up to the borders of the Lattuka country. They are a fine race, but of thieving propensities; they carry their raids into the Berri country to the north, and that of the Kiri to the south.

They have also gained a reputation for being "rainmakers," a calling much in request among the native tribes.

They are industrious in the cultivation of corn

(sorghum), but pay little attention to that of tobacco, the best of which comes from the Lattuka district.

Hunting is a very profitable employment, as antelopes and elephants abound, though beasts of prey are not very numerous. In the dry season hunting excursions are made into the low-lying country to the north, where countless herds of elephants are to be found.

The Lattuka appear to be a totally distinct race from their neighbours both in appearance and language. They are a slight, well-built people as regards the men, whilst the women are of a strong and thick-set build.

Lattuka.

The women far outnumber the other sex, and perform all the heavy portion of the manual labour, such as carrying water or material for constructing huts, and tilling the ground.

The huts are built of grass, straw, palm leaves, &c., have doors about 2 feet 6 inches high, and are generally packed closely together and surrounded by filth, but are clean inside. In the hilly country they are grouped on tops of hills, and surrounded by thick hedges and palisades to keep out the wild animals. Each village has its watch-tower.

The nation is divided into small tribes or classes under different local chiefs, who generally obtain their influence by a reputed power for rain-making.

The inhabitants wear little or no clothing. The men carry numerous ornaments of iron, copper, and brass, and a helmet made of hair, covered with ornaments, and topped by a plume of ostrich feathers. Every man has several wives; the price paid for each is, where cattle are plentiful, 22 cows, elsewhere 20 goats or sheep, or, as an equivalent, 40 spear-heads or 40 spade-heads.

Taxes to the chiefs are paid in corn, sesame, honey, leopard-skins, cows, and ivory.

The arms carried are three spears and a shield; bows and arrows are unknown.

Produce.

Hunting, cattle breeding, and agriculture are the chief occupations; but the two latter are sacrificed to a large extent for the first, which is followed with great zeal.

Basket-making and the manufacture of tobacco are also among their industries.

Agriculture is neglected for hunting, although the ground is most fertile. The soldiers at the various stations cultivate sorghum, maize, earth nuts, water melons, &c.

The chief agricultural products are sorghum (dokhn in the south), sweet potatoes, bananas, ground nuts, &c. The bark of the acacia tree is used for tanning.

Tobacco is much cultivated, and the best produced in the countries of the White Nile is considered to come from the Lattuka. It is known under the name of *Kaniett*, and the finest is grown on Jebel Molong.

Cattle, sheep, and goats are found in great quantities.

Elephants, buffaloes, giraffes, zebras, lions, leopards, baboons, hyenas, and antelopes are the principal, and are all plentiful. The leopards are the most dangerous to men and cattle.

Snakes are also numerous.

Formerly there were great numbers of ostriches, but these have generally disappeared.

Crocodiles are found in the ponds and lakes, where fish is also abundant.

In the lowlands about Okkela, cattle, donkeys, mules, &c., do not thrive, probably from the absence of salt, and the impurities of the water.

Tarrangole, the principal village, was occupied by Nubian merchants for 25 years; it was a central depôt for ivory, but, owing to the warlike character of the natives, the slave trade never gained a footing.

Agaru, as mentioned before, is a species of sanatorium, being placed high up among the hills.

Okkela is situated in the low country on the borders of the marsh land, and is thickly populated.

This tribe are also good hunters, but not to be compared to the Lattuka. They only carry two spears. Corn growing is one of the chief occupations.

They carry on a certain amount of traffic with the Lango people in ivory and ostrich feathers. There are great quantities of ostriches to be found on the wide savannahs of Lango land.

As in Lattuka, the women greatly outnumber the men.

The Shuli cultivate red dhura as well as the sorghum corn.

Lado, the capital, was a well-built town; the divan, offices, mosque, and Government buildings being made of burnt bricks, and roofed with corrugated iron. The streets were wide and straight, and there was a broad promenade surrounding the station, a clear space of 30 yards being kept between the houses and the fortifiation. There were large gardens outside the fortifications, where Arab and European vegetables were grown.

On the arrival of Chaltin's force in 1897, Lado was found to be in utter ruin and uninhabited.

Gondokoro, a station built in 1871 by Sir Samuel Baker, has long been abandoned. It is more unhealthy than Lado, and cannot easily be reached by water at all times of the year.

<small>Gondokoro.</small>

The transport in the Equatorial provinces has still to be carried on by porters; ox wagons might in places be employed, but elephant transport would be the most suitable.

The porters used to form squads of 10 to 20 each, with a soldier in charge.

The natives refuse to march at night partly from fear of wild animals, and partly from their belief in the evil influence of the moon.

They likewise object to start early in the morning on account of heavy dews.

CHAPTER V.

BAHR EL GHAZAL COUNTRY.

The Southern Provinces.

The Southern Provinces in former days, up to 1878, included four mudiriehs, as follows:—

1. *Bahr el Ghazal.*—This mudirieh was vaguely defined, but may be described as enclosing the entire district watered by the southern tributaries of the Bahr el Arab and the Bahr el Ghazal Rivers. Its eastern boundary was the River Rohl.

2. *Lado.* — Comprising all Egyptian stations in the country, from Bor* southwards, bordering the Bahr el Jebel, and extending to the most southern and southeastern parts of the Sudan then under Egyptian control: *i.e.*, the southern boundary was the Somerset Nile to Mruli and the northern shores of the Albert Nyanza; the eastern boundary was about 33° E. long. The chief portion of the mudirieh therefore lay on the east bank (*v.* p. 101). The northern boundary was subsequently (1882) extended to the Sobât district* (inclusive) and the White Nile between the mouths of the Bahr el Ghazal and the Sobât.

3. *Rohl.*—The country between the left bank of the Bahr el Jebel and the Rohl River, bounded on the north by the Bahr el Ghazal, and on the south by—

4. *Mâkaraká.*—Which comprised the country between the latitude of Lado, the Nile, Congo watershed, and the Bahr el Jebel, from Lado to the Albert Nyanza.

Mâkaraká was in 1878 merged into Rohl, and Rohl was in 1881 merged into Lado, the "Equatorial Province" thus formed being placed under Emin Bey's jurisdiction.

---

* Formerly belonging to the Mudirieh Fashoda.

The whole of these four former mudiriehs west of the White Nile are now generally termed the "Bahr el Ghazal Country."

(a) BAHR EL GHAZAL (Mudirieh).

Some of the earliest settlements of the slave and ivory trade were in Darfertit, the most western part of the province. These settlements were made by small resident traders known as Kalabas, who paid taxes to the native chieftains of the Krej (or Kreish) tribe.

History.

About the year 1854, trading companies from Khartum began to arrive, and, accompanied by armed bands of Nubians, established stations all over the country, which became the hotbed of the slave trade.

The country of the Bongo (or Dohr) became their headquarters. This is one of the largest tribes, agricultural and industrious in their habits, and, being easily subdued, it was soon bound down into vassalage and slavery by the slave dealers. The position of the Bongo country likewise favoured these settlements, as it was no great distance from Meshra er Rek, the highest navigable point on the Bahr el Ghazal.

The smaller neighbouring tribes of the Jur, Dembo, and Golo, were soon reduced to vassalage in like manner, and the traders then established their out-stations at a greater distance towards the south-east in the Mittu country, &c. But to the north-east they could make no impression on the Dinka, protected by their impenetrable marshes, and were more unsuccessful still against the numerous, powerful, and warlike nation of the Niam-Niam (Azande) lying to the south-west.

About the year 1870, the Egyptian Government undertook the administration of the province, with the avowed object of putting down the slave trade. The administrators, however, and the officers of the troops sent for the purpose, instead of carrying out this object, became themselves not only the open abettors, but also the most energetic traders.

It was not till 1878–79 that the country was opened up, and the nefarious traffic put an end to by Gessi.

In the meantime, what had once been a thriving population, living in a fertile country, and possessed of flocks and herds, was reduced to starvation and misery. By the wholesale exportation of the women and children, and by the emigration of others to avoid the cruelties of the traders, the populations were so reduced that many districts became totally uninhabited.

The Zeribas, Jur Ghattas, Dem Idris (or Ganda), and Dem Zubehr (Dem Suliman) were among the principal stations of the traders, and were named after them.

Wau, on the River Wau, is well situate for becoming the chief station of the Bahr el Ghazal Province. Large flat-bottomed craft could convey goods throughout the year to Meshra er Rek and bring back stores and supplies from Khartum.

Topography.

Dinka country.
That portion of the province to the north-east inhabited by the Dinka tribe, and included in the angle between the Bahr el Arab and Rohl Rivers, is a vast alluvial flat, rising but slightly above the Bahr el Ghazal River, of which it is the basin. The soil of this region is an unfathomable clay, in places covered by wastes of sand about 10 feet thick. Great areas of forest are met with, and innumerable marshes, lagoons, and sluggish channels of water left by the annual inundations of the river. From July to the end of the rainy season, a great part of this country is under water. In March the water is at its lowest level.

The inhabitants devote themselves exclusively to cattle breeding.

Bordering this alluvial plain is the foot of a steppe country which gradually rises towards the mountainous regions to the south. The line of demarcation between the alluvial and the steppe country runs close by Jur Ghattas in a north-west and south-east direction.

Here the borders of the huge tableland of ferruginous soil are reached, which, unbroken except by gentle undulations or isolated mounds of gneiss, gradually ascends to the Equator. This plain appears to cover the greater part of the centre of the continent.

Bongo country.
The steppes are, in the Jur and Bongo country, composed of a ferruginous soil known as swamp ore. This extends in broad plains and plateaus, and produces the ore which is, or rather was, worked to a considerable extent by the tribes.

Description. 113

The character of the country is very varied. In former days large stretches of cultivation alternated with bush, forest, park-like meadow land, swamps, bamboo, jungle, &c., but the slave trade ruined much of the agricultural prosperity. Occasionally, low hills to the north-east of Bongo Land vary the scenery.

To the north-west of Bongo Land rocky country is met with, swampy depressions and forests of Termalia, also many open plains and plateaus.

In passing westward from the north-west of Bongo Land, through the Golo country towards Dem Zubehr (Dem Suliman), a notable change takes place in the character of the country. Immediately after passing the Pango River, the soft, absorbent soil of the lower steppes, where water is only found in the streams during the *kherif*, is succeeded by a country rich in springs, and very similar to the Niam-Niam hills.

In the Jur and Bongo lands, which are on the edge of Jur country. the red swamp ore, there are no springs, but only such water as is left by the rains in the various khors and depressions.

The country gradually rises up to the station Zubehr, which is 2,282 feet above the sea, and 737 feet higher than Jur Ghattas.

Dem Zubehr, on the Bili River, was visited in December, Dem Zubehr. 1894, by a Belgian, M. Colmant. He found it to consist of 50 or 60 fine, yellow-grey brick buildings, of considerable height, covering about 1,000 yards square. It was, of course, in a ruinous state and uninhabited, but it produced on him the effect of "une grande ville européenne, mais de singulier aspect." Lemon trees, cactus, streams, and much vegetation in the neighbourhood.

When this country was handed over by the Belgians to the French in 1895, and the Marchand expedition was formed, M. Liotard proceeded to Dem Zubehr as advanced party, and was there the greater part of 1896 and 1897. During this time he devoted his energies partly to cultivating the surrounding district.

The place lies 12 days' march from Jur Ghattas (Meshra es Rek lies five days beyond Jur Ghattas). Much game in district. Roads lead hence to Liffi, Shakka, and Kordofan.

From Dem Zubehr westwards towards Dem Gudyu,

(386) I

the altitude increases, the latter station being 2,275 feet above the level of the sea. The country is broken and intersected by numerous streams. Blocks of hornblende and schist are met with, as also masses of red granite, flats of gneiss, and swamp ore.

In passing south-east towards Dem Bekr the hills continue; alternate flats of gneiss and swamp are passed, also marshy depressions and woods, while meadow land and the characteristics of the steppe country are absent; there are no springs, only the dry beds of various watercourses.

<small>Dem Bekr.</small> Dem Bekr lies on the little River Duro; broad, grassy depression; flat country; much bush.

On proceeding towards the south, ridges of hills appear in all directions of the character universal in Central Africa, consisting of ranges with isolated peaks, or plateaus of grey gneiss rising up from the beds of iron ore. They are probably the remnants of earlier chains of mountains.

The elevated land—*i.e.*, the Nile-Congo watershed—now runs to the south-east, while towards Bongo Land are a series of steppes, extensive marshes, ranges of low, flat-topped hills, stretches of forest, and khors—dry, except during the rains.

To the south-east of the Mudirieh, in the Bongo and Mittu countries, are hills of considerable height, an off-shoot from the more southern highlands, which serves as a watershed between the Tonj and Jur Rivers.

<small>Population.</small> The following are the principal tribes included in the Bahr el Ghazal district:—The Dinka, Jur, Bongo, Dembo, Golo, Krej, Sehre, Bellanda, Babukur.

Bongo.

<small>History.</small> Bongo Land was the most important and most representative district of the Mudirieh.

This country lies between 6° and 8° N. lat. on the south-western boundary of the depressions of the Bahr el Ghazal basin, and on the lowest terraces of ferruginous crust bordering the alluvial land.

Its area is about the same as that of Belgium, but it is a deserted wilderness. In 1870, it averaged only 11 or 12 inhabitants to the square mile.

It extends from the River Roah to the Pango, and embraces the middle course of nearly all the affluents of the Bahr el Ghazal.

It is 175 miles long by 50 broad. On the north, it is separated by the Jur country from the Dinka, but joins the latter along the north-east frontier.

The south-east boundary is the Mittu territory on the Roah, on the west the Golo and the Sehre countries, and on the south the Niam-Niam. Between the latter and the Bongo, the small settlements of the Bellanda and Babukur are wedged.

When the Khartûmers first arrived, they found the whole country divided into a number of small independent districts, each with its own chief, and not combined in a commonwealth like the Dinka.

The people were thus an easy prey to the traders, who reduced them into slaves and vassals, establishing a sort of feudal system, and forcing them to live round the zeribas. The Bongo were docile and yielding, and, being agricultural, supported these zeribas to a great degree.

The Jur, Golo, Mittu, and other smaller tribes shared the same fate as the Bongos, and in 10 years there were more than 80 zeribas between the Rohl and the River Biri. Some of the population took refuge with the Dinka and the Niam-Niam, but the greater portion were reduced to slavery.

The slavers treated the country in a pitiless and overbearing manner, destroying the population and seizing their corn and cattle. But after some years, when they had exterminated about two-thirds of the people, they discovered the value of their services for the cultivation of corn and the transport of merchandise.

In Central Africa, every nation has different names for its neighbours.

Jur and Niam-Niam are Dinka names for these two tribes; the Bongo they call Dohr.

The colour of the Bongos is a red-brown. It would *Inhabitants.* seem that the soil they inhabit has a marked bearing on the colour of the races. Here the red iron rock prevails, while, in the low-lying dark alluvial flats, we find the Dinka and Nuer of a deep black tint.

The Bongos have short woolly hair, are of medium stature, and, as regards their occupation, are essentially an agricultural people, devoting, however, occasional periods to fishing and hunting.

Agriculture. The labour bestowed on the culture of the dhura corn is very great, and it is through their indifference to cattle breeding that they owed their comparatively peaceful relations with the slave-dealing communities.

When the Khartumers first came to the country, the Bongo, unlike other tribes, inhabited extensive villages, enclosed by palisades; now these are no longer found, except in the neighbourhood of the Government stations.

They bestow great pains on the construction of their huts, which are conical in shape, and made of stems of trees, faggots, bamboo, clay from the ant-hills, and grass. In diameter they are about 20 feet, and in height the same.

Besides agriculture, much of their time is devoted to the working of iron, which is found in great abundance in Bongo Land. They manufacture arms and tools of excellent quality.

Industries. Their smelting furnaces are made of clay, and the iron is afterwards worked on anvils of gneiss or granite by hammers of stone or iron, rude bellows being used for the purpose.

Their dexterity in wood-carving is also very great, shown in the various utensils, spoons, &c., which they make.

They are also very fond of music, and have instruments, both stringed and wind.

Compared with the other tribes, the Bongo devote great attention to basket work, with which they line their huts, make beehives, and other articles for household use.

The manufacture of pottery is carried on by the women, who make different kinds of vessels and pipes.

The preparation of skins also forms an important branch of industry.

Their covering is scanty, being usually restricted to an apron or strip of stuff or skin; but they disfigure the body in various ways, and their partiality for ornaments is very strong.

Arms. Their weapons consist mainly of spears and bows and arrows, shields being rarely used. Their spears are of great size, and they poison their arrows with the milk of a species of euphorbia.

A man may have only three wives; he buys them for so many plates of iron from their fathers. The people have no religion or any name for a deity except *Loma*, which denotes luck or ill-luck. But they have an extraordinary fear of witches, devils, and spirits.

They have rude methods of surgery; deformed persons and cripples are seldom seen, and previous to the settlement of the Khartumers there was no syphilis, which now makes considerable ravages.

The dialect spoken throughout the country is generally the same. It is very simple in its grammatical structure, and has a great variety of terms for concrete subjects.

Bongo Land is traversed from south to north by five important tributaries of the Bahr el Ghazal, with numerous smaller rivulets, not permanent streams, though the pools which remain during the dry season furnish a sufficient supply for the vegetation of the country. *Water.*

Water for drinking never fails, although from November to end of March a fall of rain is exceptional. In case of necessity, water can always be obtained from the pools above mentioned.

The crops are far more frequently injured by a superabundance of water than by drought, and the continuance of wide inundations has been followed by famine. *Crops.*

Towards the end of August, the sorghum harvest commences by the pulling of the light crop sown at the end of April. The ingathering of the heavier kind of corn does not take place till the beginning of December, after the rains.

In this district, sorghum takes eight months to come to maturity, though only five or six in Sennâr and Taka. Both the early and late sorts attain a height of nearly 15 feet.

Schweinfurth says:—"In all descriptions of sorghum as given by travellers there seems to be a considerable confusion with respect to the distinctive names of this ordinary cereal. It is called promiscuously 'Kaffir corn,' 'negro cane,' 'bushel maize,' 'Moorish mille,' or sometimes 'durra.' Durra is an Arabic definition which can be traced in literature as far as the 10th century. . . . . In Egypt this sorghum is called 'durra beladi' (durra of the country) to distinguish it from maize, which is known as 'durra Shahmi' or Syrian durra. In Syria itself, where the sorghum is little known because rarely cultivated, it is simply called 'durra.' Throughout the Sudan it has exclusively the appellation of '*aish*,' i.e., 'bread.'"

There are three other kinds of corn. Next to the sorghum comes the *penicillaria*, or Arabian dokhn, which is cultivated here more freely than in Northern Sudan. It is sown later than the sorghum.

The second is a meagre grain, called by the Arabs *telabûn* and by the Abyssinians *toccusso*. It is only grown on the poorest soils when the ground is too wet for any other crop. It yields a miserable grain. The Niam-Niam, who are its principal growers, and the Abyssinians, make beer of it.

The third kind is the maize of the country. It is only grown in moderate quantities, and as a garden vegetable. The Madi tribe of the Mittu are the only people who grow it to any great extent.

The flour produced will not make bread such as we are accustomed to. Arab bread is a fermented dough, tough and leathery, or, if risen, it becomes a crumbling mass.

All corn in the tropics has some constituent which produces these effects.

The process of cultivation is very simple, and consists in merely placing the seed in holes. There is no stuff for manuring the land, so that if the crops were increased to any extent with the view of ameliorating the condition of the people, the soil would be exhausted in a year or two.

Wheat does not thrive.

Rice has not been tried, but would probably be well adapted to the soil. In the whole district south of the Bahr el Ghazal the wild rice of Senegal grows freely, and is of good quality.

There are numerous vegetables cultivated by the Bongo, such as the mungo bean, which they call *bokwa*; the earth nut; sesame, to which the Bongo give importance second only to sorghum. Various kinds of yams are also seen; gourds of two principal kinds, the white and the yellow. The onion is unknown below the southern limits of Kordofan and Darfur.

Compared with Africa in general, this district is deficient in spices.

Tobacco culture receives a good deal of attention.

There are two kinds, the Virginian and the common, and the natives are much addicted to smoking.

A great abundance of fruit is afforded by the common trees of the country.

There is a great want of common salt throughout the district of the Bahr el Ghazal: alkali is used as a substitute, obtained by soaking ashes of burnt wood. *Salt.*

The domestic animals of the Bongo are poultry, dogs, and goats; sheep and cattle are rare. *Animals.*

The wild animals are buffalo, antelopes, ichneumons, civets, genets, wild cats.

Elephants appear to have become scarce. Lions, leopards, baboons, hyenas, &c., exist in the forest.

In Bongo Land, the *kherif* or rainy season opens as early as March with occasional showers; up to August the showers increase in number, but are never continuous, and at the most only take place every third or fourth day; up to June they are accompanied by tempests and thunderstorms, but after that their violence abates. After July there is a change of temperature, which only occasionally reaches the extreme point again, and does not exceed about 35° Cent. = 95° Fahrenheit. *Climate.*

The climate is exceedingly uniform, attributable to the absence of mountain ranges. The trade winds exert their influence without hindrance over the whole country.

The *loggoh kullutty* is the circulating coin. It is a flat iron coin 10 to 12 inches in diameter, with a handle on one edge, and serves, equally with spear-heads and spades, for cash and exchanges.

Dinka.

The Dinka (or Jangeh) country in the Bahr el Ghazal includes nearly the whole of the low ground extending from the Jur and Bongo countries as far as the Bahr el Ghazal and Bahr el Arab. It is a vast plain of dark alluvial clay, unbroken by a single hill or mass of rock, and the tracts of forest are limited in extent. This district has already been described under the general topography of the Bahr el Ghazal province. *Country.*

The clayey swamps become in the dry season as hard as stone, the brooks and streams all dry up, and their beds are scarcely perceptible, being covered up by the rapidly growing herbage.

Inhabitants. The inhabitants are essentially a race of cattle breeders, and despise the more agricultural tribes.

Although some branches of the Dinka race are pre-eminent for size and stature, the majority of this western branch rarely exceed the middle height. They are of lank and sinewy form, and are among the darkest coloured of races. The women alone wear clothing, which consists of aprons of skin, and carry numerous ornaments, especially iron rings.

Huts. The Dinka dwellings consist of small groups of huts clustered in farmsteads over the cultivated plains. There are no villages in the proper sense of the word. The cattle of separate districts are collected in a large park called *Murah* by the Khartumers.

The huts are spacious and durable, and frequently 40 feet in diameter. They are built on a foundation of clay and straw, of branches of acacia and other hard woods, the roof being of cut straw.

Habits. They are a cleanly people, and far in advance of the Nubians in their preparation of food. The women, on account of their proficiency in housekeeping, are greatly valued in the slave trade, but give more trouble to their masters than slaves of any other race. The male slaves used to be converted into soldiers, and were conspicuous for their stature and bravery.

They have a species of religion based on an institution called Cogyûr, a society of necromancers and jugglers.

They have the character of being pitiless and unrelenting in war, but their domestic ties are very strong. They are a pastoral people, but always prepared for war.

Arms. Bows and arrows are unknown, but spears, clubs, and sticks are the favourite weapons, and they carry a shield of buffalo hide.

Animals. The domestic animals are oxen, sheep, goats, and dogs; poultry are never seen.

The cattle are in enormous numbers, and belong to the Zebu race. They are smaller than those of the Baggara and Hassanieh. They have a hump, and are generally white in colour.

The sheep are of a breed peculiar to the Dinka, Nuer, and Shillûks, and are remarkable for the shaggy covering on their shoulders. The continual moisture of the pasture produces internal worms, from which they suffer to a great extent.

The goat is of the Ethiopian species, but somewhat larger.

The great object of the Dinka is to acquire and maintain cattle, to which they pay a kind of reverence. A cow is never slaughtered.

The only domestic animal killed for food is the goat, which scarcely represents the thirtieth part of the value of a cow.

The breed of cattle is, however, degenerating. They are incapable of carrying burdens or of travelling.

The yield of milk is miserable.

Neither camels, asses, mules, nor horses are available in Central Africa, and the only animal by which these countries can be opened up—*i.e.*, the elephant—is being quickly exterminated by the demand for ivory.

Agriculture is carried on to a great extent. *Agriculture.*

The corn cultivated is the largest variety of the cereal; it takes nine months to ripen, and the stems become hard and woody.

There are also cultivated three kinds of beans, earth nuts (*arachis*), earth peas (*Voandzeia subterranea*), sesame, yams, and Virginian tobacco.

The character of the vegetation resembles that of Kordofan. The most common trees are the Seyel acacia, hegelig, tamarind, Christ's thorn, cappara, &c.

In the dry season water is obtained from wells, the *Water.* residue of the great pools formed in the rainy season. These are teeming with filth and animal life, and cause the intestine worms among the sheep and cattle.

Among the swamps the miasma is a sure source of fever.

There are numerous snakes in the Dinka country, but these are never met with in Bongo Land.

Nuer.

The Nuer are a warlike tribe somewhat formidable to *Country.* the Dinka; they occupy a territory on the banks of the lower Sobat, and in the country between this river and the Bahr el Ghazal, on both banks of the Bahr el Jebel (Upper White Nile) Rivers. They are somewhat hemmed in between the Dinka and the Shillûks.

In habits they resemble both these races, but differ in dialect.

Pasture is their chief pursuit.

Their huts resemble those of the Dinka, always clean and free from vermin. The men go naked, but the women are clothed about their loins.

In appearance the Dinka, Shillûks, and Nuer, all inhabitants of low marshy flats, strongly resemble each other.

Jûr.

Country

The Jûr inhabit the territory between the north-east frontier of Bongo land and the Dinka country.

Jûr is a name given by the Dinka, and means wild men, or men of the woods, and is used as a term of contempt.

The district is the lower terrace of the ferruginous formation from which the natives extract a large amount of iron; they are all smiths by profession.

They call themselves Lwoh, and claim to be descended from the Shillûks, whose dialect they use.

The area of their territory is small, and their numbers cannot exceed 20,000.

On the north they are bounded by the numerous tribe of the Dembo, and by smaller clans.

They adhere to the Shillûk mode of decorating themselves, though for years they have been in partial dependence on the Dinka.

Industries

Iron manufacture is their principal occupation, and they produce a metal excellent in its homogeneousness and malleability.

Iron smelting is carried on in March, just before the sowing season, when they move away from their huts partly for this purpose, and also to drag the rivers for fish. The men also spend their time in hunting, while the labour in the fields is done by women, who likewise occupy themselves in making wicker-work and pottery.

This is much the same as among the Bongos already described.

Every tribe has its peculiar description of hut, and that of the Jûr is a simple structure of wicker-work, of wood, or bamboo, cemented with clay, and roofed with straw.

The Jûr have large families, and were it not for the depredations of the Nubians would be a dense population.

The Khartumers appropriated their corn, reduced them to slavery, and employed them as porters and builders.

Goats, a few poultry, and dogs are the only domestic animals possessed by the Jûr.

Mittu.

The Mittu country lies to the south-east of Bongo Land, between it and the River Rohl. In its southern part it is broken and hilly, but possesses many very fertile tracts. *Country*

The nation really consists of groups of tribes, the northern of which call themselves Mittu, while the others are designated as:—Madi, Madi Kaya, Abbakah, and Luba.

Their collective country lies between the Rohl and the Roah Rivers, and for the most part is situated between 5° and 6° N. lat.

To the north it touches on the Dinka tribes of the Rohl and Agar. On the south it is bounded by the eastern extremity of the Niam-Niam and the Makaraka. The Mittu call their own land Moro.

The Mittu tribes can all converse with one another, though there are slight differences in their dialects. *Inhabitants.*

In manners, customs, and dress they most nearly resemble the Bongo.

The Khartumers had stations in the country, but never entirely subjugated the more southern tribes.

Physically the Mittu are inferior to the Bongo, and are not capable of sustaining much fatigue.

In the adornment or disfigurement of their bodies the Mittu have distinctive characteristics of their own. A peculiar custom is the distortion of their lips with plates of ivory, &c.

The land is very productive, and they cultivate a variety of cereals, roots, and fruit. It requires little labour, and is specially fertile between lats. 5° and 5° 30′ N. in the districts on the Upper Roah and Wokko, and in the district of Mbomo, between the Lehssy and the Roah, where the growth of maize is extensive. *Agriculture.*

They breed the same domestic animals as the Bongo, viz., goats, dogs, and poultry; they possess no cattle, and, it is said, show a preference for dog's flesh. *Animals.*

Their huts are smaller and far inferior to those of the Bongo.

They are great lovers of music, and have many different kinds both of wind and stringed instruments.

Their dexterous use of the bow and arrow gives them a certain superiority over their neighbours. The arrows are 3 feet long; they despise shields, but keep a liberal supply of spears.

Babukur.

The Babukur tribe inhabits a small tract of about 350 square miles on the south-west portion of Bongo Land to the west of the Tonj River. They came originally from the south, probably impelled northwards by the Niam-Niam. They have been restricted to their present territory by the raids of the Niam from the south, and those of the Khartumers from the north.

They are a warlike, resolute race of very dark colour, short in stature, and of repulsive expression.

They are expert at all work, but have such a love of freedom that they were difficult to enslave. Another section of this tribe lies to the south-east on the southern frontier of Mittu Land.

Bellanda.

The Bellanda tribe inhabits a territory to the west of the Babukur on the south-west frontier of Bongo Land. They use the Shillûk dialect.

They are partly under the King of Niam-Niam, and partly under the Egyptian Government.

Sehre.

The Sehre resemble the Niam-Niam, to whom they were originally subject. Their district lies to the north-west of Bellanda, and the scenery is here very diversified, dense woods being relieved by cultivation and the homesteads of the natives.

In appearance they resemble the Niam-Niam, but are not tattooed, and are of a dark chocolate colour.

They are a well-built, robust race, and in this respect more resemble the Golo and Bongo.

Their huts are carefully built and kept, and are far superior to those of the Golo or Krej.

They appear to have neither goats nor dogs, and their live stock consists in a few cocks and hens.

Their spears resemble those of the Bongo, but their bows and arrows are smaller.

The women's attire consists in bunches of grass and leaves fastened by a girdle. They disfigure their lips like the Mittu.

Hunting is their principal occupation, which is productive, as the district abounds in such wild animals as buffalo, antelopes, lions, &c.

The country is all but destitute of water, for the Pango separates a country teeming with springs from one that is dry. With the exception of a few streams, pools and marshes, scattered at wide intervals, afford the only supply. *Water.*

Sweet potatoes, cassava, horse-beans, &c., are among the products.

The people are most light-hearted, and bear hardships with great cheerfulness.

Golo.

The Golo resemble the Bongo in manners and personal appearance, though their dialects have very little in common.

Their huts are more like those of the Niam-Niam, the roofs projecting far beyond the clay walls, and supported on posts.

Dokhn corn and sweet potatoes are extensively cultivated.

Brooks and springs are plentiful among the gneiss and granite rocks.

Krej and Dar Fertit.

To the west and north-west of Dem Zubehr lies the Krej (or Kreish) country, sometimes reckoned as coming within the Dar Fertit district, Dar Fertit being a name applied by the Baggara Arabs and the inhabitants of Darfur to distinguish tribes south of the Bahr el Arab from the Niam-Niam. In a wider sense the term is applied to all nations south of Darfur.

Whatever its limits may be, Dar Fertit is no doubt one of the oldest domains of the slave trade, and it was in 1870 described by Schweinfurth as a "sold-out land."

The territory of the Krej lies to the west of the Bongo *Country.*

and Golo lands. It is bounded on the north by the Baggara Arabs, on the west by the Mango and Benda tribes, who have their districts on the Upper Bahr el Arab; on the south the territory approaches the Niam-Niam country.

The population is a conglomeration of the representatives of different races, the remnants of a systematic destruction.

The following tribes predominate: viz., the Nduggo, situated about Dem Zubehr; the Bia around Dem Gudyu; and the Yongbongo between the two former.

Inhabitants. In form they are below the average height, thick and unwieldy in figure, and of a coppery colour.

Copper. The caravan roads from Dem Nduggo to Darfur run in a N.N.W. direction; they pass through the Mango country, and, crossing the Bahr el Arab, traverse the region of Hofrat el Nahas, where the renowned copper mines exist (*v.* p. 81).

These mines are about six days' journey north of Mango land.

The copper is brought into market in the shape of rings or cakes, but no systematic mining is carried on by the natives.

In the Krej country are numerous running streams, khor beds, and stretches of fine forest.

Fishing, agriculture, basket making, &c., are among the chief occupations of the people.

The huts are very defective in construction and resemble those of the Kaffirs.

Descriptions of the Monbuttu and Niam-Niam countries, which are on the frontiers of the Mudirieh Bahr el Ghazal, and on the Congo side of the Nile-Congo watershed, are to be found in "The Heart of Africa," by Dr. Schweinfurth, and in "Dr. Junker's Travels" (Vol. 2, pp. 101–220).

(*b*) LADO (Mudirieh).

On the west of the Bahr el Jebel, about 70 miles above Lado, a flat and park-like country is succeeded by a line of hills, which, running from the north-west, abut on the river at this point, and run parallel to it as far as Dufile;

here they bend away to the south-west, leaving between the upper course of the river and the mountains some miles of open country.

. The remainder of the country comprised in this Mudirieh has already been described in Chapter I, pp. 16–20 (Upper Nile), and Chapter IV, p. 101 (country east of the Bahr el Jebel).

(c) ROHL (Mudirieh).

The Mudirieh Rohl used to have several outlying stations in the Monbuttu country, where ivory is collected from the countries still further south. The route along the River Rohl has always been the favourite one for the ivory caravans, and the only one safe from the hostile Niam-Niam.

From the Zeriba Dufalla, where the road from Rabat Shambeh on the Bahr el Jebel debouches, up the course of the Rohl, to the Makaraka country, there used to be a number of small stations, which are on an average two days' journey from one another.

A small colony of comparatively friendly natives is settled in the neighbourhood of each, but the rest of the inhabitants have taken refuge at a distance from the river so as to avoid raids.

Topography.

The Zeriba Gosa is the first station north of the Makaraka country; the land in this district is marshy, but becomes firmer towards Sayadin, where it is covered with thick, high grass. North of the latter station the river is called the Rohl, while to the south it is known as the Aire.

To the east, treeless low-lying lands are visible, bounded by a range of cone-shaped hills which run in the direction of Sayadin. These hills are of granite and metamorphic rock, but chiefly grey granite: their highest points are about 3,000 feet above the sea.

The hills are well wooded, and many bamboos (*Bambusa Abyssinica*) grow in the neighhourhood. The soil is bare, except in the ravines and valleys among the hills, which are clothed with bush.

In the country lying west of the river, a short light-green grass succeeds to the high vegetation of the swamp lands, and covers a large proportion of the province to the north. There is also a great quantity of red ironstone cropping up, the detritus of which makes excellent roadways.

About Sayadin the Rohl has the local name of Yalso, so called after one of its tributaries.

Towards the north the country is principally low, and in some places wooded. Felspathic rock crops out occasionally, but there are no hills except at a considerable distance from the river. About the station of Lori some of the Lori-Moru negroes are settled, but the districts between the stations are uninhabited.

Between Lori and Moffo the character of the country changes, and becomes much more varied by spreading woods and fantastically-shaped rocks, at the foot of which there is a rich vegetation.

Thus on the slopes of Tyack a rank growth is found in all the hollows, while at its foot magnificent palms tower above the lower shrubs.

Elsewhere there are stretches of meadows and trees, reminding one of English parks.

The vegetation differs greatly from that in the Makaraka country. In the latter the trees are large, and have strong leathery leaves, without thorns, while here it is quite the reverse. The western banks of this part of the Rohl present low-lying treeless flats covered with grass and rushes, and it maintains its monotonous character up to Dufalla; all distant view is shut in by woods.

On the eastern side there is a low range of hills inhabited by numerous clans, offshoots of the Dinka tribe.

Towns. Dufalla and Rumbek are the most important stations of the province; they are distinguished by their palisaded dwellings, which are so often found among people of the Dinka race.

Dufalla used to be surrounded by a strong stockade and deep moat, with a few rusty cannon mounted on its ramparts. The houses are built on raised platforms and surrounded by high fences of reeds. The streets are so narrow that two people can hardly pass each other, and the town is very crowded.

Round the zeriba there are large villages with a native population of about 1,500.

In the town the disorder, filth, and stench are beyond description.

The river here is about 50 yards wide and 15 feet deep, with a current of one knot per hour.

The main road branches off from Dufalla towards the Bahr el Jebel, and passes at first through the country of the Agar. Here there are neither woods nor meadows, but an open cultivated district with cornfields. It is most thickly populated, though the inhabitants do not live collected in hamlets, but in detached palisaded huts about the fields.

Rumbek used to be the seat of the Mudir of the province; to the west the country is, as usual, inhabited by numerous small tribes or clans, and in many parts is covered with wood and tall grass; elsewhere it is monotonous and flat, with a few isolated hills.

Rumbek is a very large place, with an Arab population of some 3,000, and about 30,000 natives in the surrounding villages. The streets are narrow and tortuous: the town was once fortified, but the earthworks are now in ruins.

It was described by Junker (1877) as a dirty, crowded town of houses built on posts. Founded by Alfonse de Malzac (a notorious merchant or slave-trader) in 1858.

There used to be large gardens round the zeriba, and quantities of vegetables and fruit could be obtained.

At the Zeriba Dyoht the mudirieh of Bahr el Ghazal used to commence.

(d) MÂKARAKÁ (Mudirieh).

The Mâkaraká people inhabit but a small part of the former mudirieh of the same name, but custom gave the name to the whole, from the fact that the Government found the Mâkaraká much the most trustworthy of the tribes, and employed them, accordingly, as porters and in other employment.

There are a number of other tribes who have been for much longer residents in the country, and are indigenous to the soil, distinguishable in manners and language, and apparently the remnants of more powerful negro tribes, who are now to a great extent amalgamated and scattered in groups over the land. Such are the Liggi, Fadyellu,

Inhabitants.

wooded, and in all directions fantastic masses of rock present themselves.

Here a magnificent view opens to the west and south-west, over undulating plains, diversified by occasional hills and groups of Niambara villages.

While the Miré mountains present a uniform range, out of which rise single peaks, the Rego mountains are a connected series of prominent cones, united by saddleback depressions, traversed by several passes. The peaks of this range attain the height of about 2,100 feet above the surrounding country; the most prominent are named Luli, Kuyuh, and Kero.

From Jebel Kiddi, the most northern elevation, a low spur runs towards the north, on the eastern side of which, in the neighbourhood of Rillek, there are a number of hot springs, the temperature of whose waters is about 58° Cent. The surrounding ground is of a reddish-brown colour, which points to the presence of iron, while ironstone crops up throughout the district enclosed by the two ranges of mountains above described. The water of the springs is clear and tasteless.

The road over the Rego range is a rugged track among a confused mass of rocks and gorges, the pass through which is about 16 miles in length.

The western sides of this group of mountains appear to slope gradually down to the plains, while the eastern are precipitous.

A winding path running down through thick woods soon leads to the western boundary of the Niambara. Their northern neighbours are the Mandari; while on their southern frontiers lie the Kakuak and Fadyellu.

Leaving the Niambara country, whose eastern boundary is about 8 miles east of the River Bibja, the lands of the Moru and Liggi tribes are next entered on the west. All this territory up to the River Yei is a monotonous expanse of rolling uplands covered with bush.

In comparison with the Niambara district it is well watered, even in the dry season, by the numerous watercourses which find their way through the depressions of the country, partly to the Bibé, and partly to the Yei River.

Some of these streams are called *silek*, from a species of tree which grows in their neighbourhood. This tree has a tall slender stem, and foliage totally distinct from the large leathery leaves of the bush vegetation. The stem of the silek resembles somewhat that of our fir, and is used by the natives for the roofs of their huts (tukl).

The country between the Yei and Kabayéndi, the most western station, is watered by the River Torré; in character it resembles that described, and is covered with low bush and occasionally taller trees. There are numerous small watercourses and depressions, which, during the rainy season, are full of water.

The character of the country changes in the vicinity of the old Zeriba Fadl Allah, where to the north and west mountains are to be seen.

On the left bank of the Khor Baballa (a watercourse which is never dry), the country of the Mundu begins, and thence stretches away far to the west.

It is covered with bush, advantageously mixed with forest trees; while in some places during the dry season the stiff stems of the grass, higher than a man's head, are a serious inconvenience to travellers.

Beyond the plains surrounding Fadl Allah, the hilly country begins to the north and west. The ridge Ingiterra to the north-east is about 1,600 feet high, and consists of five combined elevations. In its neighbourhood, as also about the hills of Kura and Langho, and to the west, the Abukaya Oisila are settled.

On the road to Mount Lobogo, the hill of Ambe rises to a height of about 200 feet, and large forest trees cover the district about it.

Many of the hills are named after the resident chieftains, such as Lofoke, Koh, &c. Whilst to the south and east the country is a vast plain, with isolated peaks cropping up here and there, to the north and west there are ranges of mountains, varying in height from 1,000 to 1,500 feet above the surrounding country, some of the more prominent peaks being called Abba, Agallo, Agilbi, Adyuh, Assana, Issi, &c.

To the west of Lofoke there is much bush, and bamboos are found in the low-lying lands in the neighbourhood of Koh.

From Azigo to Kudurma the country is at first hilly, but afterwards falls into a wide plain, which is crossed by various low ridges, running north-west and south-east.

As far as the hills of Labigo and Gangara travelling is difficult, as there is a great growth of bamboo, wood, and bush; and having passed these, there are still many difficulties to contend with in the shape of watercourses and swamps.

The Mundi territory commences south-west of the Moku hill. Near Kudurma, the topographical features consist in low hills and bush, alternating with papyrus-growing marshes.

From Kudurma to Amusei, marsh land predominates; here is the extremity of the plateau which culminates in the hills above referred to; to the south and south-west of the plateau lies an extensive plain, watered by the River Mense, and inhabited by the Bombeh tribe.

To the west and north-west is the land of the Abaka, a country characterised by ranges of high hills, intersected by valleys and tracts of low-lying ground. To the east of this district, the station of the Chief Tomaga is of great importance from a hydrographical point of view, and will be referred to hereafter.

Between Hassan and Kudurma the country is very broken, and intersected by numerous streams, which are running all the year. The hills rise to a height of about 540 to 660 feet, and the banks of the streams are covered with a luxuriant growth, including trees of great size.

Between Kudurma and Konfo, this country is very similar in character to the above; the passage of the Aire or Hire (the source of the Rohl) is difficult, and a rich vegetation is everywhere met with.

At Konfo the hills disappear, and to the north, north-west, and south-west a bush-covered country is found.

The district from Konfo to Gosa is flat alluvial land, bordering the River Aire; and as far as the eye can reach no mountains are visible. Great acacia trees tower over the bush, with which the plains are covered, and travelling out of the trodden path is almost impossible, owing to the tangled mass of reed-like grasses and vines.

To the west of Konfo, the country, though not flat, has no hills of any great size, except towards the wooded district to the south of the Kudurma, where the rocks consist of gneiss and red granite. In the low land to the south-west of this, where some small tributaries of the Aire have their origin, there are large districts of bamboo.

The western portion of the territory of the Abaka tribe is hilly, and intersected by many streams.

West of Ansea there is a plateau, which forms the watershed separating the Aire and Roah (Meriddi) systems, the latter river rising in a prominent hill to the south, named Embe.

To the west of Baudura, the hills are thinly wooded with bush but covered with high grass, and in this direction lies the watershed between the Meriddi and Issu Rivers.

From the hill of Ngirna, near Bellédi, there is an uninterrupted view over the country to the west, which slopes down to the Issu, and at a distance of about 25 miles are seen the hills of Damvolo (Damvo), Baginsa, and Bonduppo.

The country south of Ansea is a uniform undulating plain, with a few isolated hills appearing here and there, such as Embe, Guduku, and Bageda. There are numerous streams flowing southward, of which the Akka and the Garamba are the most important. The marshy nature of the smaller ones, however, makes even their passage difficult. The most prominent landmark seen from this part of the country is Mount Andgu, lying away to the south; but, with the exception of an occasional peak, the entire country in this direction seems a vast plain.

The Zeribas Wandi and Ahmet Agha lie in a hollow, watered by the Torré River. From the south, numerous streams run into the Torré, and around these are to be found most of the habitations of the Makaraka proper. This tribe call themselves Idio, a name given to them by the Niam-Niam. In their district there are two hills of gneiss, Gurmani and Lipako, which constitute prominent landmarks from the south-east, in which direction the country gradually but continually rises, so that not only the range south of Ndirfi can be seen, but also the distant hills to the south-east, as Muga, &c., in the Kakuak and Fadyellu country, as well as those to the east and north-east, Jebel Gumbiri, and the peaks of the Rego range. From Ndirfi itself, one can only see in a northerly direction as far as Degîs, a line of gneiss hills.

To sum up the topography of the Mudirieh Mâkaraká, to the north and west the country is hilly, to the south and east rolling plains.

The country south of the Mâkaraká land had for many years been traversed by Arab traders, in search for ivory, slaves, and cattle. The splitting up of the negro race into small groups was necessary for the safety of their expeditions, which they carried on with the assistance of the more powerful chieftains, who extorted ivory from the weaker tribes, and in return were rewarded by a share of the plundered cattle.

In a southerly direction from the station Rimo lies the country of the Fadyellu. In character it is a flat, and, in places, a marshy district; on the higher spots a certain amount of bush is to be seen, and ironstone occasionally crops up. Slabs and masses of gneiss are strewn over the surface.

The miserable huts of the inhabitants offer a marked contrast to those of their northern neighbours, and the white species of dhura is no longer met with.

Between the River Kabba and the Yei there are numerous watercourses running north-east, to join the latter river. Some of these are dry, some marshy; while others form a series of pools.

About Dumunsu, beyond the fields of sesame, red dhura, &c., there can be seen in a semicircle the hills of Korbe, Muga, and Ottogo; while to the west the high ground south of Ndirfi is visible.

The Yei runs through a broad undulating plain, traversed by many streams and deep watercourses. The land here gradually but constantly rises towards the south, which gives an extensive view towards the north-east and north.

The Muga range of hills which runs from north to south is from 1,500 to 2,000 feet high, and sends forth many streams from its western flanks.

South of the Muga the country falls towards the south into a wide plain, bounded still further south by groups of hills, of which Uado is the principal. On its northern slopes the huts of the Kakuak are to be seen.

To the south-west is a hilly country, in which the River Yessi rises; and to the east an undulating valley, shut in by a distant range of lofty hills.

Between Uado and Uani the country is very broken; hills, some of which reach 1,500 feet in height, alternating with valleys.

The natives of Wani and Ganda live for the most part on the banks of the Kinde, in a fertile and luxuriant valley. Date palms, bananas, and lofty green acacia trees abound.

South of Ganda many tributaries of the Bibé River are crossed, and the boundary between the Kakuak and Kalika tribes is reached. Here also, in latitude 3° 5' N., we come upon the watershed between the Nile and Congo systems.

At Khor Haro, a short distance to the north of this district, a remarkable type of vegetation is met with in the elephant-ear tree (Schweinfurth's *Platycerium elephantotis*).

The district separating the Kakuak and Kalika is a bare rocky mass of broken hills, with a sparse vegetation, but the home of a beautiful species of euphorbia. From the milk-like juice of its leaves the natives procure the chief ingredient for the poison which they, more than any of other negro tribes, use for their arrows.

From the high plateau the country to the south is seen to be an undulating expanse, bordered to the south-west by high hills. At first the dhura fields of the Kalika cover the southern slopes of the plateau, which are succeeded by steppes intersected by numerous watercourses running south-west.

Trees, bush, and high grass, which were general in the Kakuak Land, disappear, and the country is quite open; on the banks of the river alone is there much vegetation.

Grass and wood, the chief material for their huts, failing, we find the habitations of the Kalika made of straw.

The entire district, especially in the south, bears evidence of the industrious habits of this tribe. Dhura fields are to be seen in all directions, and cattle breeding is extensively carried on. The roads are also far superior to those in the other countries.

In the south of this part the hill of Abanga is a notable landmark; there is a certain amount of bush in the neighbourhood of Lemihn, and of forest trees in the valley of the Kibbi: otherwise the country is open and covered with short grass. The ground falls gradually to the west and south, and is more or less undulating, with various hills appearing in the distance.

It appears to be a rich, fertile country. Dhura, beans, pumpkins, and sweet potatoes are seen growing on all sides, and streams and rivulets with their accompanying luxuriance of vegetation water the land in every direction.

To sum up the topographical features of the country from Mâkaraká Land to Lemin, it may be said that the northern and western portions consist of rolling plains with occasional series of low hills, the eastern of a hilly and a mountainous district, while to the west, in the southern part, we again find rolling steppe country bordered on the east by high lands.

PART II.—HISTORICAL.*

CHAPTER I.

HISTORY UP TO 1882.

On the Nile above Assuan the Nubian desert limited for centuries the extension of so-called civilisation towards the heart of Africa. This progress was further impeded by the obstacles presented in the second and third cataracts of the Nile, which render the river almost impassable for over 200 miles. Colonel Gordon wrote:—" From Wadi Halfa southwards to Hannek, a distance of 180 miles, an utter desert extends, spreading also for miles eastwards and westwards on both sides of the Nile. For the same length the river is also encumbered with ridges of rock. . . . . It was, therefore, this boundary of the desert that kept the warlike and independent tribes of the Sudan quite apart from the inhabitants of Egypt proper, and has made the Soudanese and the Egyptians two distinct peoples, that have not the least sympathy one with the other." South of the Nubian Desert lie the lowlands of Ancient Ethiopia,† or Island of Meroe, flanked on the south-east by the Abyssinian hills. Ethiopia was originally, in the days of the Pharaohs, a colony of Egypt, and its

---

* Authorities:—

 A.D. 770 to 1837.—Col. Stewart, "Report on the Sudan, 1883."
 „ 1837 to 1882.—From "Report on the Egyptian Provinces of the Sudan." I.D., 1884.
 „ 1882 to date.—Compiled from various authorities, mainly Col. Wingate's works, Intelligence Reports and Publications, &c.

† Ethiopia is nowadays considered to mean Abyssinia, and is the word employed by the ruler of that country to denominate his dominions.

capital, Meroe, a city of some importance. In later times it became independent, but was reconquered by the Ptolemies. The Romans, however, during their occupation of Egypt, fixed the Nubian Desert as their southern limit.

A.D. 700.

It is said that between the first and second century after the Mohamedan era the Arabs of the tribe of Beni Omr, being hard pressed by the Beni Abbas tribe, began to emigrate from Arabia in small numbers to the opposite shores of the Red Sea, and to settle in the districts about Sennâr, on the Blue Nile. Whether the Beni Omr led the van of the great Arab invasion it is impossible to say, nor is it known whether all the tribes chose the Red Sea road. Some authorities appear to think that several came into the Sudan from Egypt and Marocco.

Be this as it may, the fact remains that the Beni Omr settled gradually in the districts round Sennâr, the inhabitants of which were negroes belonging to the tribes of Fung, Hameg, &c. (*v.* p. 95).

The Beni Omr, becoming gradually stronger, by degrees succeeded in becoming the masters of the whole of the Sennâr districts, and converted the negroes to Islamism.

1493.

By degrees the distinction between Arab and negro diminished, and in 1493 the name of Beni Omr is no longer heard of, and the old tribal names of Fung, Hameg, and others reappear.

In that year Amara Dunkas, the Sheikh of a sub-section of the Fung, either through the fortune of war or his superior capacity, succeeded in getting himself declared king of all the Fung tribes. He then allied himself with Abdulla Gemân el Kerinani, the powerful chief of the Keri district (east of the Blue Nile), and conquered all the country on both sides of the river between Fazokl and Khartum.

These districts were inhabited by negroes belonging to the Nuba tribes, some of whom, after the conquest, remained in the country, while others emigrated into the mountains of Fazokl and Kordofan. Those who remained embraced Islamism, intermarried with their conquerors, and, losing their language and nationality, were soon lost in the tribes known collectively under the name of Fung.

Of these tribes some settled in towns, while others

Early History of Sennâr.

retained their nomad habits, such as the (1) Khamir, (2) Rebia, (3) Kakhtan, (4) Kenana, (5) Kawaklah, (6) Geheena, (7) Beni Shekr, (8) Beni Ziban, (9) Beni Abbas. From this last have descended the (1) Kababish, (2) Ferara, (3) Beni Selim, (4) Ahamdeb. The latter two tribes are Baggara, or owners of cattle and horses.

All these tribes are now to be found along both banks of the White Nile.

In 1523 Amara Dunkas was succeeded by his son Abdul Kader. 1523.

In 1539 Abdul Kader was succeeded by his son Nule. 1539.

In 1545 Nule was succeeded by his son Amara. 1545.

Amara was surnamed Abu Sakakin; during his reign Sheikh Abdulla Gemáa died, leaving the Province of Keri to his son.

In 1553 Amara died. Between that date and 1596 four Kings, all of the family of Dunkas, succeeded each other. 1553.

In 1596, in the reign of Adlan, Sheikh Aghib, a descendant of Gemaá and Governor of Keri, rebelled. Adlan defeated him near Alati. His children fled to Dongola, where Adlan sent Sheikh Idris to offer them a free pardon and invite them to Sennâr. They came, and Adlan invested the eldest with the Government of Keri. 1596.

This emissary of Adlan's, Sheikh Idris, was celebrated for his ability. He is also said to have lived to the great age of 147. During this reign many learned men came from Cairo and Bagdad.

In 1603 Adlan was succeeded by his son Baadi. 1603.

In 1606 Baadi was succeeded by his son Rubat. 1606.

In 1635 Rubat was succeeded by his son Badi Abu Daku (Father of the Beard). 1635.

This King attacked the Shillûk negroes and took a large number of slaves. The Shillûk inhabited the country on both sides of the White Nile south of Kawa. Thence he invaded the mountain of Takalla and destroyed Kordofan, where he again took a large number of slaves. On his return to Sennâr he built a number of villages in that district for his prisoners.

The prisoners named these villages after those they had left, hence the number of villages now near Sennâr with names similar to those in the Jebel Nuba, Takalla, and other districts about Kordofan.

In time these slaves supplied the Kings of Fung with recruits for their armies.

Besides his warlike enterprise, Baadi built the mosque now at Sennâr, and furnished it with copper window-bars.

1671. In 1671 he died, and was succeeded by his son Ansu. During this reign there was a great famine and an outbreak of smallpox.

1683. In 1683 Ansu was succeeded by his son Baadi el Akhmar. In this reign a number of the Fung tribes and the people of Keri, under their prince, rebelled, but they were defeated with great slaughter, and the Prince of Keri was killed. Sheikh Hamid Welid el Terabi, a celebrated Sheikh, lived during this reign. His tomb is now at Sennâr.

1710. In 1710 Baadi was succeeded by his son Ansu II. This monarch caused such great dissatisfaction by his extravagance and debauchery that the Southern Fungs revolted, deposed the King, and placed a noble called Nur on the throne. This happened in 1714.

1719. In 1719 Nur was succeeded by his son Baadi Abu Shillûk. In this reign the Abyssinian King Kedem Yasu invaded the Sennâr with a large army. He was, however, defeated with great slaughter by Sheikh Emin, near the village of Tekiyah, on the Dinder River. It is said that the reason for this invasion was that some presents sent by the King of France to Abyssinia had been seized by King Baadi.

After this great victory the renown of Sennâr spread in all directions, and eventually even reached to Constantinople. Crowds of learned and celebrated men flocked into the country from Arabia, Egypt, and India. Notwithstanding this, in 1758 Baadi, owing to his bad administration, was deposed and exiled. He was succeeded by his son Nasser.

1758. 1758.—Under this reign the Hameg tribe became very powerful, and the Fung lost a great deal of their influence and prestige. In 1765 Nasser was killed by a rebellious vassal, and was succeeded by his son Ismail.

1774. In 1774 Ismail was deposed, exiled to Suakin, and succeeded by his son Adlan. During this reign many intertribal wars went on both in Sennâr and Kordofan, and the power and influence of the Hameg grew so great that they eventually became the masters of the King.

In 1786 Adlan was deposed by the Hameg, and the kingdom of the Fung totally disappears, anarchy prevails throughout the country, and the kings succeed each other in such rapid succession that in the year 1788 four kings successively reigned. During the succeeding 33 years of anarchy the Hameg continued supreme, and under Sheikh Nasser they devastated the northern and eastern part of the Sudan with fire and sword.

In 1819 Mehemet Ali, hearing of the anarchy prevailing in the Sudan, and wishing to introduce the benefits of a regular government of civilisation, and at the same time to occupy his troops, ordered his son Ismail, with a numerous army of regulars and irregulars, with many learned men and artisans, to invade the country.

Ismail reached Khartum without meeting with any resistance, and thence marched on to Sennâr. There he was joined by his brother, Ibrahim Pasha, and they together advanced to Fazokl. Shortly after, Ibrahim returned to Egypt, and the report spread that Ibrahim had been killed in the Fazokl Mountains. The Arab nomads immediately rose, but Ismail returned, defeated the rebels, and appointed new Sheikhs. He then went on to Shendi, on the Nile. The Meg (ruler) Nemr (tiger) of that place, wishing to be revenged of all the cruelties and barbarities Ismail had been guilty of, invited him and his followers to a great banquet at Shendi. During the banquet, and while the guests were all more or less intoxicated, forage was piled round the house and set on fire, and Ismail and all his followers perished (1822).

When the news of this catastrophe reached Kordofan, Ahmed Bey, the Defterdar, who had wrested that province from the Darfur Sultan, put himself at the head of a large army and marched on Shendi. When he reached Metemma, opposite Shendi, the inhabitants sent to ask for pardon. This was granted. One of the people, however, happening to throw a lance at the Defterdar, the pardon was at once rescinded, and a general massacre took place. The Meg el Nemr, however, escaped, having fled towards Abyssinia.

After this the Defterdar marched to Tuti Island, opposite Khartum, where he again defeated the rebels with great slaughter. He then marched to Wod Medani, near Messalamia, and then returned to Kordofan.

It is said that when Kordofan was conquered it was

found that the Governor of the province had the title of Magdum, which is a title only given to Palace eunuchs. It would appear that it was the custom of the Darfur Sultans to send eunuchs to govern provinces and districts.

1822. In 1822 Osman Bey was named Governor of the Sudan, and the Defterdar, Ahmed Bey, returned to Egypt. This was a year of rebellions and famines.

1824. In 1824 Mokhu Bey was appointed Governor.

1826. In 1826 Khurshid Pasha became Governor. He is renowned for his rectitude and honesty. He led some expeditions up the White Nile against the Dinka negro tribe, opposite Fashoda, and also into the mountains of Tagalle.

1834. In 1834 he went to Egypt for a few months. Towards the end of that year he went to the Abyssinian frontier to repel the attack of the Abyssinians, who were coming to the assistance of the Sennâr rebels. The Abyssinians were defeated, and Adlan, their leader, was taken and impaled. During this year cholera and other diseases ravaged the country. In 1836 the Abyssinians, after attacking the Gallabat provinces, retreated into their mountains.

Khurshid Pasha was the first Governor who taught the people of Khartum to build with bricks, and to give up their huts made of skins and reeds. In 1837 he was recalled to Egypt, and was succeeded by Achmet Pasha Abu Udan (Father of Large Ears).*

1837.

The annexation of the Sudan provinces thus took place more than three-quarters of a century ago. Mehemet Ali, having dispersed the Mamelukes, and made himself master of Nubia, turned his attention towards the districts bordering the White and the Blue branches of the Nile. Gold was doubtless his main object, for he had heard rumours of mines of vast wealth; but we must also give him credit for an honest intention to introduce commerce and civilisation into the midst of the negro tribes.

Expedition by Mehemet Ali, 1838. In the autumn of 1838, Mehemet Ali himself started to visit Fazokl, and in 1840 and following years three large expeditions were organised. Although gold was not found in any important quantities, the provinces were reduced under Egyptian sway, the navigation of the White Nile was declared free, military stations were

---

* For subsequent Governor-Generals, v. Col. Stewart's Report, p. 5.

Organisation Introduced. 145

established on both rivers, and many slaves were brought back to swell the ranks of Mehemet's army. Whatever may have been his dreams of civilisation, the result of Mehemet's expedition and consequent government was to establish at Khartum, not only the capital of the Sudan provinces, but also a central mart for a huge slave trade.

The provinces thus annexed were Kordofan, Sennâr, and Tâka (Kassala).

Abbas Pasha, grandson of Mehemet, who ruled Egypt from 1849 to 1854, kept up his authority in the Sudan provinces by means of a large force, which was necessary for the purpose of collecting taxes from a discontented population. In 1853 the most southern Egyptian settlement was about 120 miles south of Khartum, but in that year the first trading voyage to the Upper Nile was started by Mr. Petherick, the English Consul for the Sudan. He was soon followed by other traders, who established posts far up country, and organised armed bands under the command of Arabs. It was soon found that slave hunting paid even better than ivory, and raids were made on the surrounding tribes. *Abbas Pasha, 1849—1854.*

Said Pasha, the successor of Abbas, found the country in a deplorable condition; exorbitant taxes, a depressed agriculture, a disordered administration openly encouraging an open slave trade.

With the resolution of organising a better state of things, Said, in the year 1857, made a rapid tour through the provinces in question. At Berber he proclaimed the abolition of slavery, and at Khartum he organised a new government for the five provinces then comprised in the Sudan, *i.e.*, Kordofan, Sennâr, Tâka, Berber, Dongola. He ordered that the excessive taxes on the lands and waterwheels (sakiyehs) of the people should be discontinued, and postal services on fast camels organised across the desert. About the year 1860 the European traders sold their stations to their Arab agents, who paid rental to the Egyptian Government, and the misery and ruin were increased tenfold. *Said Pasha reorganises Government at Khartum, 1857.*

To Said Pasha is also due the first idea for making a railway to unite the Sudan with Lower Egypt; Mongel Bey was ordered to report on the subject, but the probable expense caused the project to be abandoned.

146   *Expeditions.*

Source of the Nile discovered.

The sources of the Nile had long been the object of much speculation, but comparatively little had been done to solve the question. Towards the latter end of the 18th century, Bruce had tracked the Blue Nile to its origin in the Abyssinian mountains, but the White Nile remained unexplored till Speke and Grant, carrying out, in 1860–62, an expedition organised by the English Government, proved that the Victoria Nyanza, discovered by Speke*

1858.

in July, 1858, was the source of the Nile.

Sir S. Baker's expedition in 1861.

In 1861 Sir Samuel Baker started on an expedition from Cairo *viâ* Khartum, with hopes of meeting the travellers in question, and of making independent investigations on his own account. He was successful in both ways, and his explorations resulted in the discovery, in

State of the Sudan in 1864.

1864, of Albert Nyanza Lake. His description of the Sudan at this period, under the governorship of a certain Mûsa Pasha, gives a melancholy picture of the results of Egyptian rule. He describes the provinces as utterly ruined and only governed by military force, the revenue unequal to the expenditure, and the country paralysed by excessive taxation; shut in by deserts, all communication with the outer world was most difficult; and the existing conditions rendered these countries so worthless to the State, that their annexation could only be accounted for by the fruits of the slave trade.

Ismail Pasha, 1863.

On Ismail Pasha coming to the throne in 1863, orders for the suppression of the slave trade were issued, and on Baker's return journey in 1865, he found an Egyptian camp of 1,000 men established at Fashoda in the Shillûk country for the purpose.

Scheme for railway again brought forward, 1865–66.

In 1865–6 the Khedive again brought forward the scheme for a Sudan railway, and a study of the country from Assuan to Khartum was made by Mr. Walker and Mr. Bray, but nothing came of it. About the same time Mr. Hawkshaw recommended the canalisation of the 1st Cataract, but this was strongly opposed by Mr. Fowler, who proposed, as an alternative, to construct a ship incline over land, using the mechanical force supplied by the descending water.

Ismail Pasha not only determined to extend his territories, but seemed in earnest to put down the slave trade.

J   * On a journey from the East Coast.

The Slave Trade.

The traders were chiefly Arab subjects of the Khedive, and the traffic was being carried on under the cloak of legitimate commerce. Khartum was the headquarters for the trading companies, who leased from the Governor-General of the Sudan certain districts, nominally for carrying on the ivory trade, for which they bought the monopoly. In these transactions the Government did not hesitate to lease territories over which they had not a vestige of right; in fact, any portion of Central Africa south of Khartum was considered open to them for selling the monopoly. The result was that certain traders established themselves in, and claimed a sort of proprietary right to, large districts, especially in that part of Central Africa which lies to the south of Darfur and Kordofan, and borders the course of the White Nile. Traffic in slaves was the real business carried on, and for this purpose the traders organised armies of brigands, and formed chains of stations, of about 300 men each, throughout their districts. Raids were made on native tribes, who were obliged to submit, fly the country, or ally themselves to the slave hunters, to be used against other tribes; and anarchy prevailed throughout the country.

In order to carry out the reforms, it was necessary to annex the Nile Basin, to establish a sound government and commerce, and to open the Equatorial Lakes to steam navigation. The Khedive issued a firman to Sir S. Baker on 1st April, 1869, whereby he gave him absolute and supreme power over all the country south of Gondokoro. *1869.*

Baker left Suez for Suakin in December, 1869, and proceeded to Khartum, where the expedition was fitted out. He experienced much opposition from Egyptian officials, who were all more or less implicated in the slave trade. He also made the discovery that the very provinces he was about to annex were already leased by the Governor-General of the Sudan to a notorious slave-trader, named Ahmed Sheikh Aga, whose son-in-law and partner, Abu Saoud, was a still more notorious character.

Another expedition was being fitted out, at the same time, to Bahr el Ghazal, for the purpose of establishing a settlement at some copper mines on the frontier of Darfur.

In February, 1870, Baker left Khartum, and after, with great difficulty, exploring the navigation of the White

Annexation of Gondokoro, May 26th, 1871.

Nile, arrived at Gondokoro, and formerly annexed this station, as "Ismailia," on May 26th, 1871. In January, 1872, he left Gondokoro for the south, and on the 14th May of the same year, at Massindi, proclaimed Unyoro an Egyptian province. He organised military posts such as Massindi, Foweira, Fatiko, &c., and entered on friendly terms with M'tesa, the King of Uganda, thus establishing the Khedive's rule to within 2 degrees of the Equator. He dealt the slave trade a heavy blow by putting a stop to it in the annexed territory, as well as on the Nile, so that all exit for the traffic in the direction of Khartum would have been closed if the Egyptian officials could have been trusted.

Unyoro annexed, 14th May, 1872.

In August, 1873, Baker returned to Cairo, and the Khedive put the Government of the Sudan on a fresh footing, by dividing it into provinces under responsible governors, more or less independent of the Governor of Khartum. Thus Yusuf Effendi was made Governor of Fashoda, Ismail Yacub Pasha of Khartum, and Hussein Kalifa of Berber.

Baker returns to Cairo, August, 1873.

In 1871 the railway scheme was again taken up; Mr. Fowler was employed by the Khedive to make careful surveys, and the result was an elaborately prepared project for making a line from Wadi Halfa, *viâ* Shendi, to Khartum, with a plan for the passage of the 1st Cataract. Such a line would have been of vast importance in opening up the trade of Central Africa.

1871. Railway scheme again taken up, careful surveys made.

At the close of Sir Samuel Baker's expedition, the Khedive, still anxious to consolidate his Empire, appointed Colonel Gordon, R.E., to carry on the work. Gordon arrived in Cairo early in 1874, and left for the scenes of his future operations on 21st February. His appointed task was to continue the reconnaissance of the Upper Nile, to establish a Government, and to destroy the slave trade. Accompanying him were Lieut.-Colonel Long, an American officer in the service of the Khedive, Lieut. Hassan Wussif, and a number of European civil employés. It was arranged that the territory over which the Governor-General of the Sudan now ruled was to be limited to the south by Fashoda; Gordon to be Governor-General of the Equatorial provinces of the Nile, and the respective headquarters to be at Khartum and Gondokoro.

1874. Colonel Gordon appointed Governor of Equatorial Provinces.

Gordon left Khartum in March, 1874, and reached

Gordon Appointed. 149

Gondokoro the 15th of the following month, where he was cordially received by the Commandant, Raouf Bey. He found that the provinces in question were merely nominally under Egyptian control, there being but two garrisons, one at Gondokoro consisting of 450 men, 150 of whom were Egyptian soldiers, and a second at Fatiko of 200 Sudan soldiers. His first steps were to occupy Bohr, an important position north of Gondokoro, and to send Colonel Long on an expedition to M'tesa, King of Uganda. He then in June, 1874, proceeded to break up three large slave-trading stations on the Bahr el Zeraf, and established a strong post at Sobat, so situated as to be able to arrest all illegal traffic on the river. The liberated slaves he, in accordance with their own option, planted at Sobat, and encouraged them to turn their attention to agriculture, it being one of his ideas that most of the wars between tribes were caused by the great deficiency of food. *(Slave stations broken up, 1874.)*

During the summer of 1874, Raouf Bey returned to Cairo, and was given the command of the Harrar country. Gordon sent Gessi about the same time to make an inspection along the Bahr el Ghazal.

Abu Saud, notorious in Baker's time, had accompanied Gordon from Cairo. The latter, though aware of his character, knew him to be a man of great influence among the slave-dealing communities, and determined to turn him to account. On first taking over the government at Gondokoro, he made Abu Saud his lieutenant, and employed many of the other slave dealers under him. This, however, was of short duration; Abu soon got beyond himself, and, showing his true character, was speedily dismissed by Gordon; while, towards the end of the year, a clean sweep was made of all the other slave-dealing Dongolese, whose intrigues had seriously hampered Long's expedition.

On 11th September, 1874, 25 chiefs of the tribes round Gondokoro came in to pay homage to Gordon, a remarkable proof of the success of his rule, as up to this they had been at open enmity with the garrisons. *(September, 1874. Submission of chiefs round Gondokoro.)*

In October Yusuf Bey, Governor of Fashoda, intercepted a convoy of 1,600 slaves and 190 head of cattle from the stations of Ratatz and Kutchuk Ali on the Bahr Zeraf.

About this time Gordon was making preparations for his expedition to the lakes. The sections of the steamers, which had been left at Gondokoro by Baker, were sent forward by carriers, to be put together at the Falls of Dufile, beyond which point there is a free passage to the lake Albert Nyanza.

It was decided to establish fortified posts at the following stations:—Laboreh, Dufile, Fatiko, and Foweira; this step was rendered necessary by the hostile attitude shown towards Colonel Long's expedition by the King of Unyoro backed up by slave traders.

<small>1874. Representative sent to M'tesa.</small>
In consequence of the report of Colonel Long, who returned in October, Gordon arranged to send a trustworthy representative * to M'tesa, King of Uganda, who had shown himself to be friendly.

On the 21st November Gondokoro was abandoned as the headquarters in favour of Lado, a more healthy spot a few miles down the river, while another post was established at Regaf, a short distance up the river.

At the close of the year 1874 Gordon reported the organisation of governmental districts along the whole line of his provinces, the chief stations being the following:—

1. *Sobat*, at the junction of the Sobat River with the Nile; garrison, 50 Sudan regulars.
2. *Nasr*, on the Sobat; garrison, 100 Dongolese irregulars.
3. *Rabatshambé* (Shambeh), 30 Sudan regulars, 150 Dongolese irregulars.
4. *Makaraka*, 20 Sudan regulars, 150 Dongolese irregulars.
5. *Bohr*, 10 Sudan regulars, 150 Dongolese irregulars.
6. *Latuka*, 10 Sudan regulars, 100 Dongolese irregulars.
7. *Lado.* Headquarters, 180 Sudan regulars, 50 Egyptian regulars.
8. *Regaf*, 80 Sudan regulars.
9. *Dufile* (Ibrahimieh), 10 Sudan regulars.
10. *Fatiko*, 250 Sudan regulars, 100 Egyptian regulars.
11. *Foweira*, 100 Sudan regulars, 100 Egyptian regulars.

---

* Dr Emin Bey.

Conquest of Darfur.

The results of the nine months' work are summed up by the Egyptian General Staff* as follows :—

1st. The White Nile had been mapped with very considerable accuracy from Khartum to Regaf by Lieutenants C. M. Watson and Chippendall, R.E.

2nd. The slave trade on the White Nile had received a deadly blow.

3rd. Confidence and peace had been restored among the tribes round Gondokoro, who now freely brought in for sale their beef, corn, and ivory.

4th. The work of opening a water communication between Gondokoro and the lakes had been seriously commenced.

5th. Communications had been established with M'tesa and the connection of Lake Victoria with Lake Albert, by way of the Victoria Nile, demonstrated.

6th. Government districts had been formed and secure posts with intercommunication established.

7th. New expeditions were organised and ready to commence.

Conquest of Darfur, 1874.

During the year 1874 an important addition was made to the Egyptian possessions in the shape of the Province of Darfur.

Gordon writes:—" Dar For and Dar Fertit mean *the land of the Fors* and *the land of the Fertits*. The Fors and the Fertits were the original negro inhabitants; then came in the Beduin tribes, who partially conquered the country and made the Fors Mussulmans, giving them a Sultan. The Fors and the Beduin tribes, the one stationary and the other nomadic, live in peace, for their habits are different."

The country of Darfur had never been subjugated, but had been governed by its own Sultans in unbroken succession for more than 400 years. The inhabitants were not of the true negro type, and the numerous wandering Arab tribes paid tribute to the Sultan and formed the bulk of his fighting men. Darfur enjoyed a celebrity not only as a centre of commerce, but also as a large slave

---

* "Provinces of the Equator," published by the Egyptian General Staff.

depôt, a fact which appears from the following correspondence which passed between Bonaparte and Sultan Abd-el-Rahman, surnamed "the Just." During the French Expedition to Egypt, "the Just" wrote to Bonaparte "In the name of God the compassionate, the merciful," saying he was glad to hear that he had conquered the Mamelukes. The reply was as follows:—

"Au Sultan du Darfour, 12 Messidor, an VII, au nom. de Dieu, clément et miséricordieux, il n'y a d'autre Dieu que Dieu! au Sultan du Dâr-fur Abd-el-Rahmân.

"J'ai reçu votre lettre: j'en ai compris le contenu; lorsque votre caravane est arrivée j'étais absent ayant été en Syrie pour punir et détruire nos ennemis. Je vous prie de m'envoyer par la première caravane 2,000 esclaves noirs ayant plus de 16 ans, forts et vigoureux: je les achèterai pour mon compte. Ordonnez votre caravane de venir de suite, de ne pas s'arrêter en route: je donne les ordres pour qu'elle soit protégée partout.

"Le Général-en-Chef BONAPARTE."

Dating from the days of Mehemet Ali's expeditions, Darfur was in constant dread of Egyptian aggression, and the country was practically closed to all Europeans, who were regarded as spies. For many generations Darfur had sent annually a caravan containing ivory, feathers, gum, slaves, &c., to Egypt, bringing back in exchange cloth, beads, firearms, &c. In 1874, the slave trade having been stopped in Egyptian territory, the Governor of the Sudan seized all the slaves belonging to the caravan of that year; this was one of the causes which led to a rupture with the Sultan of Darfur.

In 1869 the power of the slave dealers in the Bahr el Ghazal had become so great that they refused to pay their rentals to the Egyptian Government. Conspicuous among them was a certain Zubehr Rahama, who, according to Dr. Schweinfurth, lived in princely style and was regarded as a kind of king.

Bellal's expedition to Bahr el Ghazal destroyed by Zubehr, 1869.

With the object of re-establishing his authority in the Bahr el Ghazal provinces, and also of conquering Darfur, the Khedive sent a small force under the command of Bellal. This force was destroyed by Zubehr, who became the chief power in the country. The Sultan of Darfur, in the meantime, to meet Bellal's threatened attack, had placed an embargo on corn along his southern frontier. This incensed the slave traders, who drew their supplies from Darfur, and a further cause of quarrel was the invasion of Bahr el Ghazal territory by Darfur troops in pursuit of slaves. Zubehr accordingly prepared for an invasion of the province. The Egyptian Government, seeing the danger of his acquiring fresh strength, determined upon taking the conquest into their own hands, giving out as a pretext that the repeated hostile expeditions of the Sultan had made it necessary to occupy Darfur. Two expeditions were accordingly organised— one from the north under the command of Ismail Yakub Pasha, and one from the south under Zubehr. In one of the ensuing battles the Sultan and two of his sons were killed, and Darfur fell into Egyptian hands. Zubehr was made a pasha, but he claimed a right to be made governor-general of the new province, and his acknowledged power was likely to make him formidable. His request, however, was refused, and though at first he intended to assert his independence, he in the end decided to push his claim at Cairo. Here he was, however, detained, his son Suliman, of whom more hereafter, meanwhile taking his place in the provinces.

Darfur having thus become an Egyptian province, the Khedive sent out two scientific expeditions, composed of staff officers and attachés, to report on the capabilities of the country. These left Cairo on the 5th December, 1874: one, under Colonel Purdy, was to enter Darfur on its northern frontier; the other, under Colonel Colston, by the east from Kordofan. The latter expedition was afterwards commanded by Major Prout, when Colston was incapacitated by sickness. Reports of these expeditions were compiled by the Egyptian General Staff.

Exploration of Darfur and Kordofan, 1874.

Relations with Abyssinia.

The relations between Egypt and Abyssinia have an important bearing on the history of the Sudan, and in future years are likely to exercise a still further influence on this portion of Africa.

The Turks and Arabs have never yet succeeded in subjugating this country, although many attempts have been made to that end. As far back as the sixteenth century the Turks had seized the port of Zula on the Red Sea, and in later times Suakin and Massawa; but, though based on these ports, they could make no headway into the Abyssinian hills, nor even occupy the coast provinces from Massawa to Suakin. During the aggressions of Ismail, son of Mehemet Ali, the Egyptians and Abyssinians came into collision from Kassala to Gallabat, and the Abyssinians were gradually pushed back to the mountains as their boundary, being hemmed in on all sides by Turks, Egyptians, and the tribes of the Galla country.

Massawa transferred to Egypt, 1866.

In 1866 Turkey transferred her interest in Massawa to Egypt in consideration of an increased tribute, and in 1867 the Khedive claimed authority as far as Zula, which is situated in Annesley Bay. Early in 1868 the English expedition to Abyssinia took place, and the Khedive, wishing for the countenance of England in his present and possible future encroachments on the Red Sea coast, did all in his power to assist the undertaking. Egyptian troops were offered to the British Government, though not accepted, and Kassala and Gallabat were spoken of as possible bases of operations. All this did not tend towards creating a good feeling between Egypt and Abyssinia.

English expedition, 1868.

When the Khedive, Ismail Pasha, was arranging his Sudan railway scheme, he proposed to make a branch line to Massawa, which would necessarily pass through the province of Bogos.

The Khedive claimed that Bogos had been conquered by Mehemet Ali, though as a matter of fact the borderland only had been held by the Egyptians, whilst the Abyssinians denied that they had ever relinquished their rights to the territory. Border war had been maintained till Said Pasha, the former Khedive, had withdrawn his troops, and Bogos for many years had remained neutral ground.

In the summer of 1874 there was a certain Swiss resident at Massawa named Munzinger, who acted as Consul for both England and France. Seizing the opportunity of the King of Abyssinia being at war with the Gallas, the Egyptian Government employed Munzinger to occupy Keren, the capital of Bogos, with 1,500 men.

Keren, capital of Bogos,

About the same time, Egypt also acquired the territory of Ailet, a province lying between Hamasîn and Massawa, by the treachery of the Governor, who sold it to the Khedive. [occupied, 1874.]

Against these acts the King appealed to Europe, and especially to England, sending as his envoy Colonel Kirkman, a Scotchman, then in the service of King Johannes, but who had formerly been with Gordon in China. This mission had no practical result, and the relations between Abyssinia and Egypt were more strained than ever.

In 1875 the Khedive purchased from the Sultan, for about £15,000 a year additional tribute, the port of Zeila, the base from which for many centuries Turk and Arab had unsuccessfully attacked Abyssinia; and in fact acquired at the same time all the Sultan's nominal rights to the coast country from near Tajureh to a point on the Indian Ocean, including Berbereh, the transfer actually taking place in autumn, 1875. [Port of Zeila purchased by Egypt, 1875.]

ANNEXATION OF HARRAR, 1874.

The province of Harrar was annexed by an expedition under Raouf Pasha, whom, it may be remembered, Gordon had relieved at Gondokoro in 1874. After the death of Emir Ahmed, Sultan of Harrar, mentioned by the traveller Burton, the inhabitants made Khalifa Citra Emir. He was deposed after a three days' reign by Mohammed; the latter oppressed his subjects, favouring the Galla tribes, and bullying the Mussulmans. The people asked the Khedive to take possession, and in the year 1874 Raouf Pasha, being sent up for the purpose, met with little opposition. He began his government by the unnecessary act of causing the Sultan to be strangled. The Sultan's son went to Cairo to complain, but nothing was done. [Harrar annexed, 1874.]

GORDON'S EXPEDITION TO THE LAKES, 1875.

Early in 1875 Gordon heard ill reports of Kabarega, King of Unyoro, who, with the old slave traders, was meditating treachery. He had already cleared his province of all these traders on whom he could lay hands, but 50 of them had escaped him, and taken themselves to the chief above mentioned. Rionga, Kabarega's rival, now received Gordon's support. [1875.]

From the experience gained, it became evident to Colonel Gordon that, in order to open up the Equatorial provinces, an outlet to the eastern coast must be made. The Nile was found to be impracticable as a waterway, owing to the numerous rapids, the obstruction formed by floating masses of vegetation (*sudd*), and the scarcity of wood. And as Gordon writes from Lado: "The only valuable parts of the country are the highlands near M'tesa, while all south of this (Lado) and Khartum is wretched marsh."

1875. In January, 1875, Gordon proposed to the Khedive that he should establish a station at Mombasa Bay, 250 miles north of Zanzibar, and also take Formosa Bay, or rather a point, where the Tana and Ozy debouch, to the north of it. In making this proposition he was under the impression that the Tana was navigable as far as Mount Kenia, and that Lake Baringo was connected with the Victoria Nyanza, neither of which suppositions are true. The Khedive on his side proposed the mouth of the Juba as a base, and fitted out an expedition for the purpose of occupying it, of which more hereafter.

Gordon now set himself to transport a steamer from Lado to the lakes. The difficulties he had to contend with were very great, including the hostility of the border tribes, the obstacles to navigation, and, above all, the useless material of which the Egyptian troops were composed. The heavy parts of the steamer had to be carried separately in large Nile boats (nuggers) to Dufile Falls, above which and up to the lakes the river is navigable. As he advanced, stations were established along the west bank of the river. This bank was more secure from attack by natives, as the mountains came within eight miles of it, and limited the sphere of their operations; while on the east bank the Bari tribe was very hostile. A party under Linant, one of Gordon's officers, was here surprised and massacred.

As regards the finances of the expedition, Gordon writes from Muggi, in August, 1874:—"In a year he (the Khedive) has had £48,000 from the province, and I have spent, say, £20,000 at the outside, and have £60,000 worth of ivory here." In September, he says that he was entirely independent of the Sudan Government as regards supplies, and could raise them from his own resources. In this month, parties were sent out to levy taxes in the shape of cattle on the hostile tribes, which had a salutary effect in keeping them quiet.

During Gordon's absence, the Shillûk tribes in the neighbourhood of Fashoda rose in rebellion against the oppression of the Government, and, had it not been for the presence of Gessi there at the time, Fashoda would probably have been lost. Gessi was an Italian adventurer of great force of character; he joined Gordon's staff in the summer of 1874, having, during the Crimean war, acted as interpreter to British troops. *Gessi Pasha.*

The steamer reached Labore in December, great difficulties having been met with in getting the boats conveying it up the rapids.

Juba River Expedition, 1875.

In the autumn of 1875 the Khedive, having long had under consideration the advantage of opening up a line of communication from the Indian Ocean to the central provinces, sent out what is known as the Juba River Expedition. The command was given to McKillop Pasha (an English naval officer who died in 1879), and he was accompanied by Colonels Ward and Long, the former to survey the harbours along the coast and the latter to command an inland expedition. Colonel Gordon was to co-operate from the direction of Victoria Nyanza. *The Juba River Expedition, 1875.*

The anchorage at the mouth of the Juba River having been found inferior, the Expedition ran several miles further south to Port Durnford, and the harbour of Kismayu; but here they encroached on the territory of the Sultan of Zanzibar. Several interests now clashed with the success of the enterprise. The British Government were bound more or less to the Sultan by treaties concerning the slave trade. The merchants of Zanzibar became alarmed for their equatorial trade, and the people of Aden for their supplies from the Somalis, who had been independent till Egypt had acquired a portion of their territory and levied taxes at their ports. The result was that, at the instance of Great Britain, the Egyptian Expedition was given up, but, on the other hand, the Khedive's authority along the coast, as far as about the 10th degree of north latitude, was tacitly acknowledged.

Abyssinian War, 1875-76.

Ismail Pasha was thus encouraged to think that he was entitled to the whole of the Red Sea coast, and could resist any pretensions of the Abyssinians to a port; while England believed that she had erected a safeguard against European settlement on the coast, and had opened the way to a Slave Treaty with Egypt.

WAR WITH ABYSSINIA, 1875-1876.

Abyssinia. Arendrup's Expedition, 1875.

During the same period other important events were passing in Abyssinia. Soon after the acquisition of the Port of Zeila by the Khedive, an Egyptian force was despatched to Massawa under Colonel Arendrup, a Danish officer in the Egyptian service. King Johannes had lately formed a new province (Ginda), which included the seaboard from the head of Annesley Bay to Amphilia Bay and the Shoho, the Port of Zula, and the district of Ginda lying south of Ailet. This he had done to ensure the Port of Zula to Abyssinia, and he made Kirkman Governor of the new province, giving him the freehold for life. Kirkman accordingly had established his headquarters at Ginda, and ran up the British flag. In October, 1875, Arendrup's force, having landed at Massawa, proceeded to Ginda and took possession of it, and soon afterwards moved on Adua, the capital of Abyssinia.

Destruction of Egyptian Army, 11.11.75.

King John, however, having collected a large force, surprised and totally annihilated the Egyptian army at Gundet, on the 11th of November. On the news reaching Cairo, another expedition on a larger scale was immediately organised, and the chief command given to Ratib Pasha, who was accompanied by Prince Hassan and several American officers in the service of the Khedive. The headquarters arrived at Massawa about the middle of December.

Second expedition fitted out, December, 1875.

Owing, however, to the disorganised state of the Staff, and the difficulties of transport, the army did not get under way till the middle of January, 1876, and, after tedious marches, it arrived at the Kaya Khor Pass, near which place, at Gura, it was met and defeated by King John on 7th March.

Defeat of the Egyptians, 7th March, 1876.

The Egyptians retired into a fort they had constructed at Kaya Khor, where, during the next two days, they were assailed by the Abyssinians. On the 11th of March, however, King John withdrew his forces, and peace negotiations were entered upon. The Egyptian army commenced its return march for Massawa on the 19th April.

Ratib now returned to Cairo, leaving Osman Pasha in command at Massawa.

Walad* Mikael, a former Governor of the Hamasîn, and hereditary ruler of Hamasîn and Bogos, who had joined the Egyptians during the campaign, now occupied himself in making a raid against the Hamasîn territory of Abyssinia, which he laid waste in all directions. He then retired into Bogos and remained for some time at the Senhît Fort under protection of the Egyptians, who kept him as a menace to King John. The latter employed another chief, Shella Khan Alula, to watch him and to retaliate by ravaging the Bogos and Ailet countries. Menelik, King of Shoa, meanwhile had marched against King John, under the impression that he was worsted by the Egyptians, but he now returned to his own country.

The peace negotiations had come to an abrupt termination on account of the proceedings of Mikael, but in June, 1876, the King sent an envoy to Cairo to endeavour to have the boundary fixed, to secure certain privileges for Abyssinia at the Port of Massawa, and to obtain an Abuna (high priest) to fill the place of one who had died; offering at the same time the surrender of Hamasîn if Walad Mikael was given up to him. The King's representative was retained at Cairo, on one pretext or another, till December, when he was released through the influence of the British Consul.

Gordon's Operations, 1876–1879.

Early in 1876, Gordon made preparations for Gessi to proceed to Lake Albert Nyanza with two lifeboats, while he himself proceeded towards Lake Victoria.

He had now surveyed the river from Khartum to Dufile, and from Foweira to Mruli. Gessi started in March, and succeeded in circumnavigating the lake in nine days, finding it to be only 140 miles long and 50 miles wide. The natives showed themselves hostile, and the west coast was inaccessible.

---

* Or Wolda.

In January, Gordon had given up all idea of forming an expedition to meet that proposed from the Juba river; his reasons were that his troops were utterly untrustworthy and unfitted for such a task.

In July the steamer was at length put together above the Dufile Falls, and the passage cleared to the Albert Lake.

A treaty was made with M'tesa recognising his independence, and Dr. Emin Effendi,* a German by extraction, was sent to him as Gordon's representative.

<small>Gordon leaves for England, October, 1876.</small>
In October Gordon left for Khartum and for England, having handed over the government of his province to Colonel Prout. He had during the three years successfully checked the slave trade in the Equatorial provinces, and established the basis of a sound government, if such could be found under Egyptian rule. That he could not entirely suppress the slave trade was due to its huge ramifications, the despicable quality of his troops, and the resistance offered to all his endeavours by the government of the Sudan under Ismail Yakub Pasha.

<small>Gordon returns to Egypt, January, 1877.</small>
In February, 1877, Gordon, under pressure, returned to Egypt, and the Khedive made him Governor-General of the Sudan, uniting in one great province the Sudan, the Equatorial provinces, and the Red Sea provinces; thus giving him a district some 1,640 miles in length by an average of 660 in breadth, with three Vakîls (deputy governors) for Sudan proper, Darfur, and the Red Sea provinces respectively. The Khedive drew his attention specially to the suppression of the slave trade and the improvement of the communications, and gave him powers to negotiate with Abyssinia in order to end the disputes with King John.

<small>Gordon goes to Abyssinia, 1877.</small>
Gordon at once proceeded, *viâ* Massawa, to the Abyssinian frontier to make a treaty, if possible, with the King. He found that there was no hope of bringing the matter to a satisfactory result till a stop was put to the raids of Walad el Mikael. Just now a large portion of Gordon's troops were withdrawn for service in the Turco-Russian war, and it was useless for him to think of using force against Mikael, while the news of a serious revolt in Darfur required his presence elsewhere. He therefore agreed to supply Walad el Mikael with money and provisions, on

---

* Edward Schnitzer.

condition that he gave up his attacks on Abyssinia. King John, taking advantage of this temporary respite, proceeded to attack Menelik, King of Shoa.

Gordon having visited Bogos, Kassala, Gedaref, and Sennâr, proceeded to Khartum; here he spent some time in carrying out reforms, among others in giving back to the Ulemas their ancient privileges of which they had been deprived by the late Governor, Ismail Yakub Pasha. In May, however, he found himself obliged to start for Darfur.

Harûn, a relative of the late Sultan of Darfur, and a claimant to the throne, took advantage of the discontent caused by the misgovernment of the province, to raise a revolt in February, 1877. He had a very large number of men with him, as the Beduin tribes, who had not helped the Sultan when Darfur was conquered in 1874, now joined his standard. 1877.

These tribes were semi-independent under their own Sheikhs, and each of them could put from 2,000 to 6,000 horse or camel-men into the field. They were largely engaged in the slave trade, making raids on the negro tribes to the south, or buying slaves from other Beduin tribes who lived out of range to the west. Though the traffic of the large slave caravans had ceased, yet there was still an extensive trade carried on by small dealers, which it was impossible to put down.

The Governor of Darfur at this time was Hassan Hilmi Pasha, who showed no energy, as up to May he had failed to render assistance to the stations of El Fasher, Dara, Kolkol, and Kebkebieh, where the followers of Harûn had hemmed in the Egyptian garrisons. A force had, it is true, been sent from Foga for the purpose, but seemed unable to accomplish the task.

Gordon arrived himself at Foga on the 7th June, having dismissed, before his departure from Khartum, Halid Pasha, who had been sent to him as second in command. Gordon arrives in Darfur, June, 1877.

In addition to the revolt in Darfur, Suliman, son of Zubehr, was now at the head of the slave dealers to the south, and, having a large force at his command, was holding a threatening attitude. Shakka was his headquarters, and the nest of the slave trade in that part. Gordon, considering the country was scarcely worth keeping, determined to call in all the outlying stations of Darfur, and merely maintain garrisons along the trunk road through El Fasher. Harûn was at Tanné, and Gordon intended to move against him with the force at his disposal, reinforced by the garrisons of Towaisha, Dara, and Kadjmur, in all about 3,000 men. In July he was at Dara, and Harûn retreated to Tura, whence he ravaged the country to the north, but, seeing Gordon was too strong for him, disappeared for the time.

<small>Meeting with Suliman, August, 1877.</small>

Gordon was at El Fasher in August, but soon after left for Dara, where he heard that the slave dealers were gathering in force. Here he met Suliman and ordered him to lay down his arms; after some hesitation Suliman left a large number of his men with Gordon and returned to Shakka; to this place Gordon followed him about the middle of September, and sent him to Bahr el Ghazal, while the other chiefs he dismissed to various places. The slave trade was thus broken up for the time being in this direction, and very large numbers of slaves had been liberated. There were, however, upwards of 4,000 more slave hunters to be dealt with in the Bahr el Ghazal, but Idris, the chief of these, was friendly to Gordon.

<small>Mikael again giving trouble, 1877.</small>

Gordon now returned to Khartum, viâ El Obeid, and proceeded immediately to Bogos, where he heard that Mikael had resumed hostilities. In March, Gordon had proposed to King Johannes that Egypt should retain Bogos, but be answerable for the conduct of Mikael. Now, however, seeing that the latter was not to be trusted, he proposed to King Johannes to join him in seizing and sending him to Cairo. To this Gordon received no answer, and Mikael continued his aggressive action.

On December 26th Gordon writes:—"I am now waiting for a letter from Ras Barion, the frontier General .... I want to get Johannes to give a pardon to Walad el Mikael's men, in order that, if I have to attack them, I may be able to give them the chance of getting away. If I attack them now, with Abyssinia closed to them, they would fight desperately."

<small>Visit of Gordon to Harrar, and dismissal of Raouf Pasha, the Governor, April, 1878.</small>

At the end of the year Gordon, getting no satisfaction, returned to Khartum by Suakin and Berber, and, having paid a visit to Cairo, again started for the Red Sea provinces. Having touched at Zeila, he went on in April, 1878, to Harrar. Here he found Raouf, the Governor, had been guilty, not only of oppression, but also of illegal trading on his own account, and immediately dismissed him.

Fresh trouble now arose on the Abyssinian frontier. In March, Walad Mikael attacked, defeated, and killed Johannes's general, Ras Barion, and got possession of Gordon's letters, which revealed his real intentions. Mikael had been enabled to make this raid by the assistance rendered to him by Osman Pasha, Gordon's Vakil, who supplied him with ammunition, and in addition received a congratulatory letter from the Khedive's Minister of War, urging him to press on his conquest. However, he did not follow this advice, and before long came to terms with the King, and all seemed quiet for a time, though further troubles were soon to crop up.

In July, 1878, Gordon heard of the revolt of Suliman, Zubehr's son, and despatched an expedition under Gessi to put it down. The history of Gessi's campaign will be narrated later on.

The railway scheme at this time occupied the Governor-General's attention. He considered that the natural outlet for the Sudan trade was from Berber to Suakin, and that the Nile railway idea was visionary. Under Ismail Pasha the work had been commenced, but had come to a standstill in 1877, after an expenditure of some £450,000, and the completion of about 50 miles of line from Wadi Halfa southward. Gordon's proposal was to utilise the river where navigable, for small steamers, and to lay tramways in the intervening spaces. The Controllers, however, did not take up his scheme, and the other affairs of his Government prevented him from giving further attention to the subject.

At this time the operations for stopping the slave trade were in active progress, as shown by the fact that within two months 14 caravans had been taken.

Towards the end of 1878, the Khedive determined to take the Harrar and Zeila districts out of Gordon's control.

In December, Walad Mikael started to make his submission to King Johannes, and the latter entered into further negotiations with Gordon about the frontier.

1878.

One of the King's demands was for an Abuna, or Archbishop. An Abuna was always obtained from the Coptic

Church at Alexandria, and was the only person in Abyssinia who could ordain priests.

Gordon had some difficulty just then as to the disposal of 1,300 slave soldiers ("Bazingers") who had remained faithful to the Government, and finally decided on sending them under Nuer Bey Angara, their chief, accompanied by two Europeans, to a zone of country between Wadai and Darfur. These soldiers had been originally kidnapped by Zubehr and trained to arms.

Though Gordon had pointed out that the destruction of Zubehr's force was the turning point in the slave trade question, he could get no assistance from Cairo.

The Slave Convention of August 4th, 1877.
On August 4th, 1877, a Convention had been concluded between Great Britain and Egypt, by which all public traffic in slaves was at once prohibited, while the private trade in Egypt was to be suppressed in 1884, and in the Sudan in 1889. Although it was well known that Zubehr was mainly responsible for the slave trade of the past 10 years, yet he was now at Cairo being treated as an honoured guest, and Nubar Pasha even offered to send him to assist Gordon. The latter, however, declined the offer, and occupied himself by appointing European Vakîls to all the frontier posts.

Gordon starts for Kordofan, March, 1879.
In March, 1879, Gordon set out for Kordofan. Not only was the revolt in full vigour in Bahr el Ghazal, but there were also risings in Darfur and Kordofan. In the former, Harûn had once more appeared on the scene, and in the latter, the insurgents were led by Sabahi, formerly one of Zubehr's chiefs, who had taken to slave dealing on his own account, had murdered the governor whom Gordon left at Edowa, and gone to the hills where the Egyptian troops under Hassan Hilmi Pasha were making no efforts to attack him.

Gordon's reasons for undertaking his present expeditions were to help Gessi, to prevent partisans of Zubehr in Kordofan sending aid to the slave dealers, to cut off runaways, and to hinder Zubehr's bands breaking into Darfur, and joining Harûn. At the end of March, he went to Edowa, from which station Sabahi with 400 men was only four days distant. Many captures of slave caravans now took place, the total number captured since June, 1878, being 63. Shakka was reached on 7th April, where a message was received from Gessi asking for more troops and ammunition. Gordon now decided that it would be prudent to reinstate the Sultan's family in Darfur, in the person of the son of Sultan Ibrahim, and telegraphed to the Khedive to send him down, as, at that time, he was kept at Cairo. In December, 1877, Gordon had found, imprisoned at Suakin, an ex-Vizier of Darfur; he had liberated him and sent him back to the province. Now he appointed him Regent, until the son of the deceased Sultan arrived from Cairo, and wrote to Harûn pointing out the uselessness of his further opposition, and inviting him to come in and assist to establish the new Sultan. In a letter written at this time he makes the following observation:—" If the liberation of slaves takes place in 1884 [in Egypt proper], and the present system of government goes on, there cannot fail to be a revolt of the whole country . . . . It is rather amusing to think that the people of Cairo are quite oblivious that in 1884 their revenue will fall to one-half, and that the country will need more troops to keep it quiet. Seven-eighths of the population of the Sudan are slaves, and the loss of revenue in 1889 (the date fixed for the liberation of the slaves in Egypt's outlying territories) will be more than two-thirds, if it is ever carried out."

Gordon, leaving Shakka in April, went by Kalaka, Dara, El Fasher, to Kolkol, which he reached on 26th May; here he relieved the garrison, and returned to El Fasher. At the latter place he heard from Gessi of the capture of Suliman's stronghold, and was about to start for Khartum, when learning that a force of Zubehr's men was *en route* for Darfur, he returned to Towaisha, and, on June 25th, he met Gessi, who informed him that the last of the rebel bands had been crushed. Leaving Gessi to follow up Suliman, Gordon now left for Khartum. _{Gordon meets Gessi, June 25th, 1879.}

Gessi's Campaign, 1878.*

Before Zubehr had left for Cairo to push his claims to the Governorship of Darfur, he had made his officers swear that if, during his absence, he sent them word to conform to the arrangements he had made under a certain tree, then they were to revolt. He accordingly did send them _{Revolt instigated by Zubehr, 1878.}

---

* "Colonel Gordon in Central Africa," p. 371.

orders on finding that his claims were not attended to. The extent of the insurrection was much larger than generally supposed; the chief slave dealers had in their plans apportioned out the provinces of the Sudan among themselves, and even gave out that they would not stop short of Cairo. They were backed up by numerous Arab tribes, and were powerful enough to tax the whole strength of Egypt. It was from the Arabs that most of the slave hunters were drawn, and they looked with scorn and hatred on the Egyptian rule.

Colonel Gordon wrote:—"There is no doubt that if the Governments of France and England do not pay more attention to the Sudan—if they do not establish at Khartum a branch of the mixed tribunals, and see that justice is done, the disruption of the Sudan from Cairo is only a question of time. This disruption, moreover, will not end the troubles, for the Sudanese, through their allies in Lower Egypt—the black soldiers, I mean—will carry on their efforts in Cairo itself. Now, these black soldiers are the only troops in the Egyptian service worth anything."

July, 1878, expedition organised by Gessi.

In July, 1878, Gordon hearing that the son of Zubehr (Suliman) had seized the province of Bahr el Ghazal, at once sent up an expedition commanded by Gessi.

Gessi started up the river, and on his way met with many slave nuggers, and even Government steamers, plying the slave trade under the eyes and with the connivance of the Egyptian Vakils. He first went to (Rabat) Shambeh to collect reinforcements, and then struck off in the direction of Rumbek on the River Rohl. His march was greatly impeded by the floods, and it was not till the first week in September that he reached the above-named place. Here he heard of the open revolt of Suliman, who had surprised and massacred the troops at Dem Idris, and was laying the country waste in all directions. The Arabs now began to join Suliman in large numbers, and his army soon numbered about 6,000 men. Gessi in the meantime had but 300 regulars, 2 guns, and 700 irregular troops; his communication with Khartum was almost closed by the *sudd* in the river, which, moreover, together with the rains, caused the whole surrounding country to be flooded and made marching impossible. He accordingly fortified himself at Rumbek till November.

Gessi's Campaign.

He occupied the time in regenerating the province, which he found labouring under gross abuses and a staff of corrupt officials.

He was at length able to leave Rumbek on the 17th November, and, after having met with some hostility from the natives on the River Jur, arrived at the Wau on 5th December, where he established a station. He found Suliman had carried off upwards of 10,000 women and children, and the inhabitants about Wau were greatly incensed against the slave dealers. Having received reinforcements and been joined by a friendly Sheikh, Gessi marched for Dem Idris, which he reached about the middle of December. Suliman was on his way towards Shakka, thinking himself protected by the floods from an attack from the south, but hearing of Gessi's arrival at Rumbek he at once turned to attack him with 10,000 men. The attack took place on the 28th December, but was repulsed with great loss after severe fighting. On 12th January, 1879, Suliman, having been reinforced, again assaulted Gessi's post, and after two days' heavy fighting was again driven back. Gessi in the meantime was running very short of ammunition, but in spite of this repulsed a third attack on the 28th and 29th of January. On 11th March, having received some ammunition, he attacked the stronghold of Suliman, which was constructed of wooden huts and barricades made of trunks of trees. Having set fire to the whole by means of rockets, he met and utterly routed the brigands as they sallied out, but had not sufficient ammunition to pursue them. By the beginning of February, Gessi had cleared off many of the slave dealers, and had liberated more than 10,000 of their captives; the result being that confidence was being rapidly restored, and the headmen of tribes were giving their allegiance to the Government.

On 1st May Gessi, having received further reinforcements, marched on Dem Suliman, which he took by assault three days later, capturing much booty. Suliman himself escaped, and took refuge in a village some distance off. On the 9th May Gessi, with 600 men, started in pursuit, and after nine days' absence returned to Dem Suliman in triumph, having taken many of the slave dealers, although Suliman, with Rabeh and Sultan Idris, two noted leaders, had escaped.

marginalia: November, 1879. Suliman attacks Gessi, 28th December, 1879. Second attack, 12th January, 1879. Third attack, 28th and 29th January, 1879. Gessi attacks Suliman, 11th March. Dem Suliman taken by Gessi, 4th May, 1880.

Suliman captured, 15th July, 1880.

Though much had been done, the revolt was not, as Gessi thought, completely crushed, and in a few weeks, hearing that Suliman was meditating a junction with Harûn, he at once went again in pursuit. On the night of the 15th July he surprised the enemy, and although he had only 290 men to their 700, he contrived to conceal the fact, and induced Suliman to lay down his arms. Fearing that, by plotting with the rebel Abdulgassin, who was at no great distance, the prisoners might escape, he shot the 11 ringleaders, including Suliman, and dismissed their men to their new countries. Gessi had now broken the neck of the revolt, and, aided by the tribes whose families he had freed from slavery, he hunted down the remaining bands. Abdulgassin was caught and shot, and only Rabeh escaped to the west, where he eventually carved a kingdom for himself near Lake Chad.

GORDON'S MISSION TO ABYSSINIA, 1879.

In August, Gordon arrived at Cairo and conferred with the new Khedive, Tewfik, on affairs in Abyssinia. Walad Mikael and Johannes's general, Alula, were now plotting a joint attack on Bogos, and Gordon's proposal that he should at once go and endeavour to settle matters with the King, was eagerly accepted by the Khedive.

Gordon goes to Abyssinia, 1879.

He landed at Massawa on 6th September, 1879, and finding that Bogos was practically in the hands of the Abyssinians, started on the 11th to meet Alula. The next day he heard that Alula, by the King's orders, had made a prisoner of Walad el Mikael and all his officers, and that Mikael's son had been killed. On the 16th Gordon reached Gura, the rendezvous, and, at an interview with Alula, requested him to state the complaints of Abyssinia against Egypt. Alula, on the 18th, replied that he had better see the King himself, and Gordon accordingly left the following day for Debra Tabor, near Gondar. He arrived there on the 27th October. On the 28th October, the King stated his claims as follows :—
"You want peace; well, I want retrocession of Metamma, Shangallas, and Bogos, cession of Zeila and Amfila (ports), an Abuna, and a sum of money from one to two million pounds; or, if his Highness likes better than

paying money, then I will take Bogos, Massawa, and the Abuna. I could claim Dongola, Berber, Nubia, and Sennâr, but will not do so. Also I want certain territory near Harrar." Gordon asked him to put these demands in writing, and give the Khedive six months for reply. But the King would give no satisfactory answer. On the 6th November there was another interview. The King had evidently been put up to his first demands by the Greek Consul at Suez, who was with him at the time, and now neither liked to withdraw his demands, nor to put them in writing. After some further delays, the King at length gave Gordon a letter and let him go, which he accordingly did, and started for Gallabat, intending to go to Khartum. Before reaching Gallabat, however, the King had him arrested and brought back through Abyssinia. He reached Massawa, after much privation, on 8th December, and then ended his connection with the Sudan and Abyssinia.

Shortly before his departure he had given up the district Unyoro, and the stations of Mruli, Kodj, Foweira, Keroto, and Magunga were accordingly evacuated by Egyptian troops. Massindi and Kissima had been given up two years before. The Somerset Nile was now the boundary of the Khedive's territory, and new stations were formed to defend it, whilst the province of Makaraka was also incorporated. Dr. Emin Bey had been made Governor of the Equatorial provinces, with his headquarters at Lado, and under him were the three Mudirs of Makaraka, Kiri, and Magunga. Many improvements had been made in these provinces, and Lado was greatly increased in size and importance.

Raouf Pasha was Gordon's successor at Khartum, while a second pasha was given the government of Massawa and the adjacent coast, and a third was appointed to Berbera, Zeila, and the Harrar district. As Gordon pointed out to the Khedive, King Johannes was much too occupied with internal affairs to be able to give further trouble on the border for the present; but in the summer of 1880, the Somalis revolted, and Egyptian troops had to be sent to aid the Governor of Harrar.

Gessi, as Governor of Bahr el Ghazal, was most successful; he had completely stamped out the slave trade, done much to encourage agriculture, and revived to a great extent the ivory trade.

On the departure of Gordon, however, and in the absence of a strong central government, the slave dealers again showed themselves in other parts, and before long, slave caravans were once more on their road to Lower Egypt and the ports of the Red Sea.

Railway scheme again entertained, 1880.

Early in 1880 the railway scheme again seems to have occupied the attention of the Khedive, who then visited the Sudan, and expressed himself strongly in favour of a line from Berber to Suakin.

In September, 1880, Gessi, finding his position intolerable under Raouf Pasha, Governor-General of the Sudan, resigned his post, and, after having suffered great hardships on the way, on account of the steamers being stopped by the *sudd*, he at last reached Khartum; meeting with a cold reception there, he managed to get to Suez,

Gessi's death, 30th April, 1881.

where he soon after died, 30th April, 1881, from the effects of the suffering he had endured. Lupton Bey, an Englishman,* succeeded him in the governorship of Bahr el-Ghazal.

In April, 1882, the Sudan was reorganised on paper, and was to be again under one Governor-General with four subordinate governors for the West Sudan, Central Sudan, East Sudan, and province of Harrar. Schools and seats of justice were to be established, and special arrangements to be made for the suppression of the slave trade.

INSURRECTION OF THE FALSE PROPHET, 1881.

The Mahdi.

The next great cause of disturbance in the Sudan was the appearance of the False Prophet.

For many years the creed of Mohammed has been making immense strides in Central Africa, where it seems to have a peculiar fascination for the native races; and high authorities estimate the number of converts to this religion at from eight to twelve millions. The idea of the regeneration of Islam by force of arms has gained a strong hold over the enthusiasm of these new converts, and on the appearance of the False Prophet in August, 1881, thousands flocked to his standard.

The person in question was a Sheikh named Mohammed

---

* Captain of a Red Sea merchant steamer.

Ahmed, the son of a carpenter, and a native of Dongola. He was born about the year 1848, and educated in a village near Khartum, where he studied religion. In 1870 he became a Sheikh, and, after a short stay at Kaka, near Fashoda, he finally took up his residence at the Island of Abba. Here his influence much increased, and he gradually acquired a great reputation for sanctity, and in time assembled a considerable number of dervishes or holy men around him. He augmented his influence by marrying daughters of the leading Sheikhs of the Baggara, and by his power and tact succeeded in merging together the various tribes.

The principles of his teachings were universal equality, universal law and religion, with a community of goods. All who refuse to credit his mission are to be destroyed, whether Christian, Mohammedan, or Pagan.

* The causes of the rebellion were ascribed to—

1. The venality of the officials, and the oppressive and unjust manner of collecting the taxes.

2. The suppression of the slave trade. Most of the supporters of the Mahdi, more especially the Baggara tribe, owed all their wealth to the traffic in slaves.

3. The military weakness of Egypt. Colonel Stewart did not consider this as any real cause of the rebellion, as he believes the troops in the Sudan would have been sufficient, had they been properly handled.

1881.

In May, 1881, the Mahdi first advanced his claims to being the prophet foretold by Mohammed. <small>May.</small>

In July, Raouf Pasha, then Governor of the Sudan, had his attention drawn to these pretensions. The Mahdi was then living at Marabieh, near the Island of Abba. <small>July.</small>

In August he publicly proclaimed his mission during the Feast of Ramadan, and small parties of troops were sent to dispose of him, but failed to do so. He first showed himself in force in the neighbourhood of Sennâr, and then took refuge in the Shillûk country, finally taking up his position at Jebel Gedîr, about 150 miles north-west of Kaka on the White Nile. <small>August.</small>

A force of 350 regulars, under one Reschid Bey, attacked the Mahdi, but were defeated with loss. <small>9th December.</small>

---

* Report on the War in the Sudan, by Lieut.-Colonel Stewart, 11th Hussars.

1882.	The latter, having recruited his force, began early in spring to threaten the province of Kordofan.
4th March.	Raouf Pasha, Governor of Khartum, was now recalled, and Abd el Kader appointed in his place. Pending the arrival of the latter, Giegler Pasha was temporarily appointed.
April.	In April a concentration of troops was directed on Kaka, and 3,000 men collected there, whereby the garrisons throughout the country were much reduced.

The rebels, taking advantage of this concentration, attacked Sennâr, and had many minor successes in that part of the country, until they were dispersed by Giegler Pasha, who arrived about the middle of May.

May.	
11th May.	Abd el Kader reached Khartum on the 11th May.
14th May.	On the 14th the Egyptian troops were successful in an action near El Obeid, the result of which, however, was unimportant.

Towards the end of May, Yusuf Pasha, Governor of Fashoda, was ordered to march with the force from Kaka against the Mahdi, who was in the mountains at Gedir. After great delays, Yusuf set out with a large disorganised force of several thousand men and swarms of camp-followers; but the rains had begun, and progress was slow.

7th June.	On the 7th June the Egyptian army came face to face with the rebels in a densely wooded country. A zeriba was commenced, and the troops were formed up in hollow square; but the rebels broke in upon them, defeated, and utterly destroyed the whole force.

This crushing defeat placed the Egyptian Government in a critical position, and gave great impetus to the insurrection.

The Mahdi now sent a portion of his army, under Wad el Makashif, across the White Nile by the ford of Abu Zeir, to threaten Sennâr. He remained himself for some weeks at Gedir, though detachments of his following were raiding in Kordofan.

24th June.	On the 24th June the rebels attacked Bara, but were repulsed with heavy loss.
17th June.	On the 17th an attack was made on Om Shanga, in Darfur, but was likewise repulsed; but towards Shakka an Egyptian force of 1,000 men was almost annihilated on the 20th July.
20th July.	

Fighting in 1882.

Many minor engagements were fought upon the lines of communication between Kordofan and Duêm, which resulted in favour of the rebels. _{1882.}

At the beginning of August the Mahdi, with the bulk of his forces, was at Jebel Gedir; a second army was wasting Kordofan; a third stretched along the White Nile from Duêm to Gezirct Abba on the north-west, and from Kaka to Marabieh on the east bank. _{August.}

The rebels were defeated at Bara, and El Obeid was revictualled. _{19th August.}

On the 23rd, Duêm was attacked, but the rebels were here driven back with a loss of 4,500 men; and Makashif, who was advancing on Khartum, was also defeated with heavy loss about the same time. _{23rd August.}

The Mahdi now took the field in person, and advanced on El Obeid. On three successive days he made desperate assaults on the garrison, but on each occasion he was repulsed with great slaughter. The rebels are said to have had 10,000 men killed, while the Egyptian loss is put down at 288. These disasters caused great loss of prestige to the Mahdi, who had never heretofore been defeated when personally leading. _{4th, 5th, 6th September.}

A relief column of about 2,000 men was now sent from Duêm under Ali Bey Satfi, and was directed on Bara. This column had two engagements with the enemy, in the first of which it was successful, but the second time was defeated with a loss of 1,130 men, the survivors making good their retreat to Bara. _{24th September.}

In October Bara was attacked with great determination on two successive days, but the rebels were driven off with great loss. The Mahdi then blockaded both El Obeid and Bara. About this time an expedition under a Sheikh, sent against Duêm, was defeated, and the leader captured and hung at Khartum. _{9th, 10th October.} _{10th November.}

At the end of the year El Obeid had a garrison of 3,000 men, and Bara 2,000; both were reported to be well provisioned. Reinforcements were daily arriving at Khartum.

[From this point it will be necessary to divide off from the main history the events since 1882 in Darfur (p. 185), the Eastern Sudan (p. 188), and Bahr el Ghazal (p. 195).]

CHAPTER II.

EVENTS ON THE NILE FROM 1882 ONWARDS.

1883.

In December, 1882, Colonel Stewart (11th Hussars) arrived at Khartum with orders to report on the situation. His valuable report,* dated 9th February, 1883, went thoroughly into the question of finance and administration, and recommended drastic reforms, stating that the Egyptians by themselves were totally incapable of governing such a huge tract as the Sudan.

Fall of El Obeid, 17th January, 1883.

Almost the first event of 1883 was the fall of El Obeid, on the 17th January. For six months Mohamed Pasha Said had held out, but was eventually obliged by famine to capitulate. The gallant commander was shortly afterwards killed by his captors, and the Mahdi transferred his headquarters to the town.

Meanwhile Abd el Kader Pasha, Governor of Khartum, was doing his best to suppress the rebellion in the angle between the White and Blue Niles, and on the 24th February he beat the Emir Ahmed el Makashif at Meshra ed Dai, and raised the siege of Sennâr town for a time. In response to his former appeal to Cairo for reinforcements troops were being collected, and Hicks Pasha was sent with a crowd of some 10,000, mostly undrilled, Egyptians to his support, arriving in Khartum, *viâ* Suakin and Berber, on the 4th March.

Hicks arrives.

Abd el Kader was, shortly before Hicks's arrival, superseded by Ala ed Din Pasha.

Battle of Marabieh.

After a strong reconnaissance in force up the White Nile, during which Makashif was heavily defeated and killed at Marabieh on the 29th April, Hicks began preparations for an advance into Kordofan on a large scale. He started in September from Duêm with about 8,200 men, marching on El Obeid *viâ* Khor Abu Habl, this

---

* Foreign Office Bluebook, Egypt, No. 11, 1883.

route having been recommended to him as holding much water. The Mahdi, informed of their approach, collected some 40,000 men and encamped in the forest of Shekan.

Misled and betrayed by their guides, and suffering terribly from want of water, Hicks's force advanced into the forest on the 5th November, was set upon by the enemy in overwhelming numbers and annihilated, some 300 only escaping death.

Annihilation of Hicks's Expedition, 5th November, 1883.

The news of this disaster naturally raised the Mahdi's influence to the highest pitch, and produced a corresponding depression on the Egyptian side. At Khartum, which had been virtually in a state of siege since July, there was a panic, but De Coetlogon (left by Hicks with the depôt), Power, Herbin, and Hansal (British, French, and Austrian Consuls respectively), collected food and outlying garrisons, and strengthened the defences by the end of the year. Sennâr was meanwhile again besieged.

The effect of Hicks's disaster on the Home Government was that it was decided that the Sudan should be abandoned and the garrisons evacuated. General Gordon was chosen as the man to carry out this difficult task, and he, accompanied by Colonel Stewart, arrived in Khartum on the 18th February, just a month after the proclamation in that town of the Government's intentions.

1884. Gordon arrives.

Gordon was enthusiastically received at Khartum, and proclaimed, in addition to the foregoing, that the suppression of the slave trade by Egyptian means was now abolished, and that the Sudan was now independent, with himself as Governor-General. A large exodus northward consequently took place.

Gordon quickly came to the conclusion that if the Sudan was evacuated, the only man capable of keeping it in order after the Egyptians had retired would be Zubehr Pasha. His request, however, was refused by the Government, so Gordon resolved to hold Khartum at all costs and crush the enemy if possible, that being in his opinion the only method of securing the evacuation of the garrisons with safety and honour.

Meanwhile the flood of Mahdism was spreading northwards, and after a fruitless attempt—owing to the rising of the Robatab tribe—on the part of Captain Kitchener and Lieutenant Rundle to communicate with and assist Hussein Pasha Khalifa, Governor of Berber, this town

Fall of Berber, 20th May, 1884.

was attacked, and, after a certain amount of resistance, taken by the enemy on the 20th May. Captain Kitchener's efforts, however, in negotiating with the Bishárîn and Ababdeh in the Korosko-Abu Hamed desert with a view to stopping an advance through this desert were successful, and a reconnaissance on the left bank of the Nile along the Arbaîn route from Assiut to Sakiyet el Abd by Lieut.-Colonel Colvile and Lieut. Stuart-Wortley proved that the water supply along that route was absolutely insufficient for the advance of an enemy in this direction. It was therefore certain that if an advance northwards took place, it could only come by the Nile, and subsequent events have proved the correctness of this supposition.

Halfa and Korosko were fortified about this time, and English troops sent up to Assuan.

Action at Debbeh.

In June, Heddai, victor of Berber, advanced downstream in the direction of the Dongola province, but was beaten at Debbeh (5.7.84) by a force of Bashi Bazuks, and again at Tani. Mustafa Pasha Yawer, Mudir of Dongola, gave rise to some anxiety by his doubtful and temporising action with regard to the enemy, but these successes appear to have decided his line of action.

Battle at Korti, 11th September, 1884.

On the 1st September he advanced with 400 men against Heddai, who had been reinforced by Mohamed Mahmud to the total number of 3,000, and in a smart action close to Korti totally defeated the Emirs, killing them both. Captain Kitchener, who had been sent to report on the Mudir, now pushed on, and entered into negotiations with the great Kababish tribe and their Sheikh Saleh for assistance in the forthcoming Nile expedition which had just been decided on for the relief of Gordon.

Gordon relief expedition.

This expedition was put in hand in the beginning of August, and the command of it given to Lord Wolseley. It was composed of 9 battalions,* a camel corps of 4 "regiments,"† and the 19th Hussars, besides light artillery and other details. The major portion was despatched up the

---

* 1st battalions R.I., Sussex, S. Stafford, Black Watch, West Kent, Gordon Highlanders, Cameron Highlanders; 2nd battalions D.C.L.I. and Essex.

† Drawn from heavy cavalry, light cavalry, brigade of guards, and mounted infantry.

Nile in whaleboats, and it concentrated eventually in December at Korti.

During the advance of the expedition, Gordon employed every means to keep the enemy at a distance. On the 29th and 31st August his "fighting Pasha," Mohamed Ali Pasha, defeated Emir Abd el Kader at Gereif and Sheikh el Obeid at Halfaya respectively, but five days afterwards was heavily defeated and killed by the latter at Om Dubban, whither he had followed him after a third victory at El Eilafun. *Fighting round Khartum.*

This defeat was a heavy blow to Khartum, and on the 10th September Gordon sent Stewart, Power, Herbin, and some Greeks downstream on the "Abbas" steamer to give an account of the state of affairs to the authorities. These officers were decoyed ashore and murdered on the 18th near Hebbeh, at the head of the Fourth Cataract. *Murder of Colonel Stewart, &c.*

On the 29th September Gordon sent three steamers down to Shendi to meet the British expedition, and these* remained on the river under the command of Nushi Pasha, fighting and reconnoitring, until the 21st January, when the British desert column met them near Metemma.

After the defeat near El Eilafun, the Mahdi summoned all the tribes to the attack of Khartum, and this city was closely invested. Omdurman, held by Faragallah Pasha, was repeatedly attacked, and was obliged by famine, on the fifth day of the New Year, to surrender.

The garrison of Khartum was now getting weaker and weaker through famine, and though Gordon despatched cheery messages to say he "could hold out for years," he knew it would be all over with Khartum if the expedition did not arrive in time.

On the 28th December a river column of 4 battalions,† 1 squadron, and details was sent upstream from Korti, under Major-General Earle, with the object of reaching Abu Hamed, communicating thence (for supplies) with Korosko (Major Rundle), and pushing on to seize Berber. *River column.*

On the 30th December a desert column, chiefly composed of camel corps, total about 1,100 fighting men, left *Desert column.*

---

* The "Tel Howeiya," "Bordein," "Mansura," and, subsequently, the "Safieh."

† S. Stafford, Black Watch, D.C.L.I., Gordons.

Fall of Khartum.

Korti to occupy Gakdul Wells, over halfway to Metemma. This done, Sir Herbert Stewart (in command) sent back for more troops and supplies, and the column, increased to about 1,800 fighting men, left Gakdul on the 14th January, 1885. On the 17th, a force of about 11,000 of the enemy, under Abu Safia (or Abd el Mejid ?) was encountered and heavily defeated near Abu Klea Wells, and the column pushed on to the Nile, which it reached, after another stiff fight near Abu Kru, on the evening of the 19th. On this day Sir H. Stewart was mortally wounded.

margin: 1885. Battle of Abu Klea, 17th January, 1885.

On the 21st, a reconnaissance in force of Metemma was carried out. Gordon's four steamers arrived during the action, and, Colonel Sir C. Wilson now in command, after proceeding next day on a reconnaissance towards Shendi, left Gubat on the morning of the 24th with two steamers for Khartum.

On arriving there at noon on the 28th, Khartum was found to have fallen $2\frac{1}{4}$ days previously, the town having been taken by assault, and Gordon having been killed, just before dawn on the 26th. The two steamers were both wrecked in the Sixth Cataract on the way back, and Sir C. Wilson and his party were only extricated by Lord C. Beresford (on a third steamer) after a hard fight with a shore battery* near the mouth of the cataract.

margin: Fall of Khartum.

The desert column, now under Sir R. Buller, short in transport and in numbers, retired to Abu Klea, at which point they beat off the pursuing enemy (16th February), and eventually reached Korti during March.

The river column had meanwhile ascended the Fourth Cataract with extreme difficulty, and met the enemy near Kirbekan. Here a decisive action was fought (10th March), in which the Mahdists were thoroughly beaten, but General Earle was killed. The command devolved on Brigadier-General H. Brackenbury, and the column reached Huella (or Khulla), within 30 miles of Abu Hamed, on the 23rd February, having destroyed the village of Stewart's murderers on the way.

margin: Battle of Kirbekan.

Here orders were received to turn back, and the column retired, reaching Merowe on the 5th March.

---

* One of whose shots burst the boiler of the steamer.

When the news of the fall of Khartum reached England, it was first determined to operate on the Sudan from the Suakin side, and a British expedition was sent there, together with a force of navvies to construct a railway to Berber (*v.* p. 189). Preparations were also begun for another Nile campaign in the autumn, and the troops of the late expedition were encamped for the summer along the river.

After some months the Government decided to proceed no further with the Sudan operations, and the whole force was withdrawn, leaving the country unoccupied south of Kosheh. A temporary native Government was established at Dongola, but it proved of no value, and fell to pieces on the advance of the enemy. Retirement of expedition, June, 1885.

The Mahdists pushed gradually forward, and by the end of November came into touch with our frontier field force, now composed of 1,700 British and 1,500 Egyptian troops. A harassing month of skirmishes ensued, which was put an end to by the decisive victory of our troops, under Sir F. Stephenson, at Ginnis, on the 30th December. Abdul Mejid was wounded, and the enemy's losses amounted to 800 out of 6,000. Battle of Ginnis, 30th December, 1885.

Meanwhile the Mahdi was dead. He had been poisoned by a woman, and died on the 22nd June. Before his death, he had nominated four Khalifas to succeed him in order, and had also sketched out a broad plan for the invasion of Egypt. Death of the Mahdi. The Khalifas.

The first of the Khalifas, Abdullah Ibn es Sayid Hamadallah et Tuaishi, a Baggara of the Taaisha tribe (as his name implies), succeeded the Mahdi, and consolidated his position (which he still occupies) by tyranny, cunning, and crime.

The second Khalifa, Ali wad Helu, is a Sheikh of the Degheim and Kenana Arabs.* He is fanatical and religious, but his quarrels with Abdullah have not disposed him in his favour.

The third Khalifaship, which was offered to and refused by the Sheikh es Senussi, was filled by one Adam wad el Oweysir, but appears to have lapsed. The fourth Khalifa is Mohamed esh Sherif, son-in-law of the Mahdi. His

---

* Originally from Sennâr; horse-breeding tribes.

men having been mostly killed under Wad en Nejumi, at Toski, he has been often imprisoned by Abdullah, and is of comparatively small account. He is, however, considered to be, strictly speaking, next in succession to Abdullah.

1886. During 1886 the frontier of Egypt was withdrawn to Wadi Halfa, and the enemy, checked but not daunted by the fight at Ginnis, worried and raided and tore up the railway to their heart's content. Numerous small skirmishes occurred, but no serious fighting was destined to take place for another three years.

Although the Khalifa was anxious to carry out at once his plans for the invasion of Egypt, he was prevented by three causes: first, a revolt in Darfur and Kordofan (*v.* p. 186); secondly, attacks by the Abyssinians (*v.* p. 191); thirdly, attacks by the Kababish.

1887. Action at Sarras. During 1887 the only fighting of importance on the Nile was Colonel Chermside's action of the 28th April, in which Nur el Kauzi and 200 Arabs were killed at Sarras. A misfortune, however, occurred in the defeat and death, at Mahbass Wells, of Sheikh Saleh and many of his Kababish, who had repeatedly, by harassing their left flank, prevented Mahdist reinforcements from coming down the river. This great tribe was now split up and hunted down by the enemy until it was almost annihilated.

About this time Charles Neufeld, a German merchant, was captured in the desert and sent to Omdurman, where he still is.

1888. The small English force was now (4.1.88) withdrawn from the frontier, and the task of defending it devolved entirely on the Egyptian Army. A glance at the history and constitution of the latter will not be out of place here.

The Egyptian army. After the defeat of Arabi and his army in 1882, Sir Evelyn Wood, aided by a small but competent staff of officers, began the formation of a new Egyptian Army. By January, 1883, it consisted of 8 Egyptian battalions (forming 2 brigades, the first under British and the second under native officers), 1 regiment of cavalry, and 4 batteries of artillery.

The IXth Sudanese battalion was raised at Suakin in May, 1884, and in March, 1885, Sir Francis Grenfell became Sirdar.* The remaining battalions were raised as follows:—

Xth Sudanese, January, 1886.
XIth Sudanese, January, 1887 (formed from the Reserve).
XIIth Sudanese, November, 1888.
XIIIth Sudanese, June, 1886.
XIVth Sudanese, March, 1896.
15th Egyptian, March, 1896 (formed from the Reserve).
16th Egyptian, March, 1896 (formed from the Reserve).
17th Egyptian, 1896 and 1897.
18th Egyptian, 1897 (not complete).

Besides the above, there are now 10 squadrons of cavalry, 5 batteries artillery, 8 companies of camel corps, 3 companies garrison artillery, &c., besides 13 gunboats.

At the end of 1888 the Khalifa made great preparations for the invasion, and a large force was collected under Wad en Nejumi. *Invasion by Wad en Nejumi.*

By the end of May, 1889, Nejumi had reached Sakyet el Abd with some 4,000 fighting men and 7,000 camp followers, the Egyptian frontier force being then about 2,000 men. *1889.*

On the 2nd July, Colonel Wodehouse, O.C.F.F.F., engaged the enemy at Argîn,† and, although with much inferior numbers, advanced with determination to the attack, and inflicted a loss of 1,400. *Battle Argin.*

A British brigade was now being sent upstream, but General Grenfell, finding Nejumi advancing very quickly, determined to attack him without waiting for English troops.‡ He stopped him at Toski,§ on the 3rd August, and with 2 Egyptian and 4 Sudanese battalions (besides cavalry and artillery) routed him completely. Wad en Nejumi was killed, and his forces were practically destroyed. Thus ended the Mahdi's dream of the conquest of the world. *Battle Toski, 3rd August 1889.*

---

* Sir H. Kitchener succeeded as Sirdar in the spring of 1892.
† Three miles north of Wadi Halfa, on the left bank.
‡ One squadron of the 20th Hussars was the only British force present.
§ Twenty miles north of Abu Simbel.

1890.

The victory of Toski had the effect of crushing for several years any important movement northwards on the part of the Dervishes, and the recapture of Tokar in February, 1891 (*v.* p. 192), caused the Khalifa still more to draw in his horns.

1891.

The Shillûks were meanwhile giving the Dervishes considerable trouble in the neighbourhood of Fashoda, and in 1891 Zeki Tumal was sent against them; two steamers had stuck in the *sudd* in the winter of 1888, and had been taken by the Shillûks, and desperate efforts were made by the Dervishes to effect their recapture (*v.* p. 198).

In August, 1891, the Nuer were used as allies by the Dervishes, and succeeded in killing the Sultan of the Shillûks. Soon afterwards, however, the Nuer turned against their allies and expelled them from the country south of Fashoda, whilst the Shillûks inflicted a severe defeat on their enemy near Fashoda, in December, 1891, and again in January, 1893. The war was waged with indecisive results till 1894, when the Dervishes finally crushed the Shillûks and murdered their Queen. Since then the Dervishes have had a small tax-collecting outpost at Fashoda, and the riverain tribes have remained fairly quiet.

During 1891 the Khalifa, alarmed at a rumour of an Egyptian advance, expressed himself as desirous for peace, but in December of that year he showed his true hand. He had long been aiming at making the Khalifate a hereditary succession, and, finding an excuse for quarrelling with the Khalifa Sherif, he threw him into prison and loaded him with chains.* He would, no doubt, have liked to do the same with the remaining Khalifa, Ali wad Helu, but the latter Sheikh had too powerful a following of Degheim and Kenana, and Abdullah desisted. At the same time, however, he effected a clean sweep of all disaffected Emirs, and, by executing some and exiling the majority, he succeeded in consolidating his own dominion. His nearest relations are his brother, Yakub, and his son, Osman Sheikh ed·Din; of these two he intends his son to succeed him.

---

* The Khalifa Sherif was not released till July, 1895.

Dongola Expedition, 1896.

In 1892 raids recommenced on the frontier, and in December a serious raid was only stopped by a fierce fight at Ambigol, in which Bimbashi Pyne was killed, together with 26 of his men. *(1892.)*

In July, 1893, another big raid was made by Osman Azrak on the oasis of Beris, and 11 natives were taken prisoners. As the Khargeh, Beris, and Dakhleh oases were thus threatened, posts were established at these places. In November the Dervishes raided Murrat Wells and killed Saleh Bey, Sheikh of the Ababdeh. *(1893.)*

In 1894 little occurred of importance on the Nile, though the year was memorable for the capture of Kassala by the Italians (*v.* p. 193). *(1894.)*

In the beginning of 1895 Shebb oasis was attacked, but the raiders were repulsed, and at the end of the year an attack was made on Adendan, a village north of Halfa. These raids, however, were soon to be avenged, for in March, 1896, it was determined to retake Dongola, and the Egyptian Army was concentrated along the frontier by the end of that month. *(1895.) (1896.)*

Reference must here be made to the successful escapes of three Europeans from Omdurman: Father Ohrwalder in December, 1891; Father Rossignoli in October, 1894; and Slatin Bey in February, 1895. These gave most valuable accounts of affairs at Omdurman, and besides corroborating information already gained, the latter, in particular, threw a vivid light on the state of the Dervish power. *(Escapes from Omdurman.)*

On 20th March (1896), an advanced Sudanese brigade occupied Akasheh, and on the 1st May a cavalry skirmish with the enemy took place near this spot. The railway was quickly pushed on across the Batn el Hagar, and on the 7th June the Sirdar surprised and almost annihilated the Dervish garrison at Firket, pushing his cavalry on to Suarda. Cholera now travelled up the river from Cairo, and for 10 days caused considerable casualties. The railway meanwhile reached Kosheh on the 4th August, and the Egyptian forces pushed on to the Dongola Province. At Hafir the enemy were in force, but (19th September) were driven out by gunboats and artillery, and on the 23rd of the same month the army marched into Dongola, the enemy, under Wad Bishara, refusing to meet them in the open, and bolting southwards in a disorganised rabble. The retreat was quickly turned into *(Egyptian advance.) (Battle of Firket, 7th June, 1896.) (Cholera.) (Occupation of Dongola, 23rd September, 1896.)*

a rout by the pursuing troops, and the river was occupied up to Merowe.

1897. Capture of Abu Hamed, 7th August, 1897.
1897 began by completing the railway to Kerma (which it reached on the 4th May), and by starting a new railway from Halfa to Abu Hamed across the Korosko Desert. Abu Hamed was taken after a sharp fight on the 7th August by a flying column under Major-General Hunter, and Berber was occupied by friendlies on the last day of that month, the Dervishes evacuating it at our approach. The occupation was quickly confirmed by the regular troops (6th September), and four gunboats were dragged, under circumstances of exceptional difficulty, up the Fourth Cataract (August).

Occupation of Berber, 6th September, 1897.

The army was then placed in occupation of the river from the Atbara to Dongola, but, in consequence of the intention of the enemy to recapture Berber, it was concentrated about this place in January, 1898. The railway meanwhile reached Abu Hamed on the 4th November, 1897, and was pushed forward along the right bank towards Berber.

1898.

In March a British brigade was despatched to reinforce the Egyptian troops, and the army moved up the Atbara to intercept Mahmud, who, with Osman Digna and a large force, was making for Berber.

Battle of the Atbara, 8th April, 1898.
The resulting battle of the Atbara (8th April) and total destruction of Mahmud's force must still be fresh in the reader's mind. During the spring and summer further preparations were made for the final destruction, with the help of two British brigades, of the Khalifa's power.

CHAPTER III.

DARFUR AND KORDOFAN FROM 1882 ONWARDS.

The flame of the Mahdi's rebellion quickly reached Darfur in 1882, and the prophet lost no time in attacking the Government posts, which were at that time, it will be remembered, under Slatin Bey. Madibbo, insurgent Sheikh of the Rizighat, attacked and occupied Shakka in July, but on following up his success was met by Slatin at Injeleila, near Darra, and twice heavily beaten by him. Slatin then retired to El Fasher to concentrate, and succeeded in repulsing the enemy from Om Shanga.

Early in 1883 a message was sent to Slatin from Khartum, ordering him to nominate a local Sultan as King of Darfur, and to retire on Khartum. The message, however, never reached Slatin. The tide of Mahdism gradually flooded Darfur, in spite of Slatin's gallant efforts to stem it. He fought 27 battles in various parts of his province, but his own troops by degrees fell away from him, themselves infected with the new faith. After certain proof had been adduced of the disaster to Hicks's expedition, the last remnant of loyalty flickered out from Slatin's troops, and the Bey found himself obliged to surrender at Dara in December. He was sent to El Obeid under the name of the Emir Abd el Kader, and thence to Omdurman, where he remained a prisoner until his escape in 1895. *Surrender of Slatin.*

Zogal, formerly Mudir of Dara, was now appointed Dervish Emir of the province. His first act was to take El Fasher, a garrison of 1,000 men and 10 guns, still holding out under Said Bey Guma, and, this accomplished* (15th January, 1884), he devoted his time to reducing Jebel Marra, where the loyal hill population gave him considerable trouble. *Zogal made Emir.*

On the death of the Mahdi in June, 1885, Madibbo and

---

* By filling up the wells whence the garrison drew water.

his Rizighat revolted against the authority of the Khalifa. Karamalla, Emir of Bahr el Ghazal, thereupon advanced against him and defeated him. Madibbo fled to the Beni Helba Arabs, who protected him, but he was eventually caught, taken to El Obeid and executed.

Zogal had several times been suspected of too great independence and he was often summoned to Omdurman. At first he had refused, but in the end he went and was imprisoned on his arrival, being liberated shortly afterwards. He did not return to Darfur.

Yusef, Emir of Darfur. Sultan Yusef succeeded him as Emir of Darfur, but on Karamalla and Ketenbur (the latter being Karamalla's trusted General) raiding from Bahr el Ghazal on to Darfur territory, Yusef protested strongly, and the quarrel developed rapidly into war.

1887. In May, 1887, Sultan Zayid, the black ruler of Jebel Marra, came to Yusef's assistance and beat Ketenbur, with great slaughter, near El Towaish. Karamalla then withdrew to Injeleila, entrenched himself there, and sent to Omdurman for reinforcements. Osman wad Adam (Ganu), sent to his assistance with a large force, reached Shakka, encountered the Darfurians near Dara, and forced them back (26th December). A second battle was even more disastrous, for Osman Ganu routed Zayid **Death of Yusef and Zayid.** completely and entered El Fasher. The two Sultans fled to the hills, but were shortly killed. Hereupon the brothers of Yusef appealed to the Sultan of Borgu for help against Osman. The Sultan applied to the Senussi for advice; but the Sheikh refused to interest himself in the matter unless he were attacked by the Mahdists, **1888. Abu Gemaizeh.** so the Sultan of Borgu declined. The Darfurian chiefs, however, found a ready ally in the shape of Abu Gemaizeh, Sheikh of the Masalit Arabs, and the rising against the Mahdists began to swell in numbers. Wild rumours spread over the Sudan of the advent to power of a great Anti-Mahdi, but although the latter destroyed nearly half of Osman Adam's force (October, 1888) at Kebkebieh, his forces were themselves destroyed in a fierce battle **1889.** fought close to El Fasher on the 22nd February, 1889. Abu Gemaizeh died next day, and the movement, which had at one time threatened to assume immense proportions, expired by itself. Thus for some time to come the Dervish power was again supreme in Darfur.

During these years Kordofan had been, more from necessity than from choice, passively Mahdist, and submitted peacefully to the Dervish yoke.

In 1891 Kordofan and Darfur became again disturbed, and various ineffectual risings took place. Sultan Abbas succeeded in turning the Dervishes out of the Jebel Marra district and governed in his brother, Yusef's, stead; but the Khalifa appears about this time to have considered Darfur as too far off for active interference, and seems to have acquiesced in this state of things. _{1891.}

In April, 1892, some Degheim and Kenana Arabs in Kordofan became dissatisfied with Abdullah's reign and deserted, but the Khalifa took no notice, finding probably that dealing with the men of a prospective successor, Ali wad Helu, was too delicate a matter in which to take a strong line. _{1892.}

A year afterwards a certain western Saint of Sokoto, Abu Naal, Muzil el Muhan, collected many followers, and for a time was considered as directly threatening the Khalifa's power. His advance, however, was chiefly confined to the despatch of abusive letters, and the movement died out by itself by the end of 1893. ₁₈₉₃

Since that date Kordofan and Darfur have been uneasy under the Khalifa's hand, and Mahmud, the captive of the Atbara, was for several years engaged with much success in suppressing insurrections in Kordofan. At the present moment, however, the only Dervish garrisons in Kordofan are at El Obeid and Bara,* whilst Darfur has, with the exception of a small and hemmed-in garrison at El Fasher, been evacuated by the Mahdists. The people of both these provinces are heartily sick of Dervish misrule, and would welcome with joy a change of masters.

---

* These are recently reported to have been annihilated by the Kordofanis.

CHAPTER IV.

EVENTS IN THE EASTERN SUDAN SINCE 1883.

1883.

Suakin reverses.

El Teb, 4th February, 1884.

Fall of Sinkat.

British expedition. El Teb, 29th February, 1884.

Tamai, 13th March, 1884.

The Mahdist rising in the Eastern Sudan began towards the middle of 1883, when Osman Digna collected the powerful Hadendoa and other tribes and invested Suakin. The outlying Egyptian garrisons in these parts included Sinkat, Tokar, Kassala, Gera, Gedaref, Gallabat, and one or two smaller posts in Northern Abyssinia, and by the end of the year they were mostly besieged by the enemy.

In October, 1883, a reinforcing party for Sinkat was cut off by the enemy, and on the 4th November a party intended for Tokar met with the same fate, Commander L. Moncrieff, R.N., being among the killed. Reinforcements from Cairo—2,620 men, mostly constabulary—were despatched under Colonel Valentine Baker, but before he reached Suakin another disaster occurred on the 2nd December, by which nearly 700 men were cut to pieces near Tamanib. Baker started in January, 1884, to relieve Tokar, but on arriving at El Teb his force of 3,700 men was attacked by 1,200 Arabs. His troops behaved like sheep; they were seized with panic, made no resistance, and were butchered to the number of 2,300, Baker and most of his English officers escaping with the utmost difficulty. 3,000 rifles and four Krupp guns fell into the enemy's hands (4th February).

On the 8th February Tewfik, commander of Sinkat, spiked his guns and fought his way out, but he and the whole of his gallant garrison were cut to pieces.

General Graham was thereupon sent with a small British expedition of 4,000 to relieve Tokar, and having gained a brilliant victory at El Teb (29th February) succeeded in his task, and sent 600 of the Suakin Egyptian garrison back to Cairo. On the 13th March Graham advanced again, and, beating the enemy thoroughly at Tamai, swept them back into the hills. The idea was then mooted of a dash across to Berber, but it was eventually dropped, and Graham's troops retired, Major Chermside being appointed Governor-General at Suakin.

In April the garrison of Gedaref made terms with the enemy and surrendered. *Fall of Gedaref.*

In order to evacuate Kassala and Amadib, the help of King John of Abyssinia was now called in, and in June Admiral Sir W. Hewett, R.N., and Mason Bey, visited him and concluded a treaty to this effect, by which he was to have Bogos and Keren if he succeeded in his task. Later on he agreed also to relieve Gera and Gallabat. *Abyssinian Mission.*

Kassala had been besieged since November, 1883, and was beginning to feel hard pressed. Its garrison consisted of 1,600 regulars and 2,300 irregulars, including a force of Bashi-Bazuks, under the command of Ahmed Bey Iffat; the Beni Amer and Homran tribes in the neighbourhood were also loyal.

In August Mason Bey, now Governor of Massawa, ordered Ahmed Bey Iffat to retire, but this was found to be impossible, as more than half the garrison was composed of natives of the district. John now proposed to relieve Kassala, but he was told that the case of Galabat was more urgent; he therefore began his preparations, and Bogos was handed over to him on the 12th September.

During this latter month Great Britain took over Berbera and Zeila from Egypt, and in November Harrar was handed over to the natives and the evacuation began. 6,500 of the garrison were sent down to the coast without incident, and under the auspices of Majors Hunter and Heath, a new government was established under the native Emir Abdullahi Mohamed Abd esh Shakur. *Evacuation of Berbera, Zeila, and Harrar.*

1885.

[Harrar, it may be noted here, remained under its Emir till the beginning of 1887, when Abdullahi was decisively defeated at Chalanko by Menelik, and the town occupied by the Abyssinians.]

On the fall of Khartum becoming known, another British expedition, assisted by Indian and Australian troops, was despatched to Suakin under the command of General Graham. Its objects were to crush Osman Digna, to occupy the Hadendoa country, to make a railway towards Berber (at all events as far as Ariab), and *Second British expedition.*

to prepare for the opening of the Suakin-Berber road when the Nile Column had captured Berber.

The expedition, numbering 13,000 men, arrived at Suakin on and about the 12th March, and remained for a couple of months. During this time it fought several actions at Hashin (20th March), Tofrek (McNeill's zeriba, 22nd March), and Tamai (3rd April), but none of these were decisive. The railway was carried as far as Otao, but on the retirement of the expedition (17th May) it was abandoned.

Tofrek, 22nd March, 1885.

At the end of November, 1884, the garrison of Gallabat joined hands with the Abyssinians, and decisively beat the Mahdists. They were definitely relieved in February, 1885, and retired to Massawa *via* Abyssinia. Amadib and Gera were also relieved, in April and July, 1885, respectively, and the garrison at Senhit handed over their post to Abyssinia on the 19th April.

Relief of Gallabat, Amadib, Gera, and Senhit.

Colonel Chermside now wrote pressing letters to John, urging him to relieve Kassala at once, and promising 10,000 rifles in the event of his success; Ras Alula, John's most valiant general, therefore began to move in September. Meanwhile, however, the gallant garrison had been starved into submission, and the town fell on the 30th July.

Fall of Kassala, 30th July, 1885.

Osman Digna came towards Kassala in August, but the Abyssinians and Beni Amer attacked him with great determination at Kufit (23rd September) and utterly routed him, killing 3,000 of his men.

Kufit, 23rd September, 1885.

Egypt had on the 6th February handed over Massawa to the Italians, at which the Abyssinians, deeming it an infraction of the Hewett treaty, were seriously annoyed In consequence Ras Alula refused, after the fight at Kufit, to resume operations against the Mahdists, and retired.

1886.

In the beginning of 1886 Osman Digna once more tried to stir up strife in the neighbourhood of Suakin. The tribes, however, did not greet him cordially, and the attitude of the Amarar, Ashraf, and Habab was doubtful. As the year wore on, the Amarar fought against Digna, shut him up in Tamai, and beat him there (6th September). As the Beni Amer, Bisharin, &c., were showing signs of coming in, Osman Digna escaped and took refuge in the rich delta of Tokar. Here he remained quiet for another year.

In June, 1887, the Abyssinians under Ras Adal advanced into Gallabat and beat the Dervishes under Wad Arbab, killing the latter. On reinforcements being sent by the Khalifa, under Yunes ed Degheim, Ras Adal announced his intention of invading the Sudan with a large army. Abdullah responded by sending 87,000 men, under Abu Angar and Zeki Tunial, against Adal, and a great battle was fought in August, 1887, at Debra Sin, 30 miles from Gondar. The Abyssinian army was routed completely, and the Dervishes entered and sacked Gondar. A slight side-issue arose for the moment in the shape of one Nebi Isa, a prophet, who arose at Gallabat in Abu Angar's rear, but although many Dervishes, including Yunes, believed in him, as opposed to the Khalifa, Abu Angar quickly put a stop to the rising by capturing and hanging the prophet. Other risings occurred on the Blue Nile, among the Rufa'a and other tribes, but they were soon suppressed.

At the end of the year Osman Digna advanced again and besieged Suakin. He was, however, beaten in detail and fell back on Handub. The latter place was attacked by Colonel Kitchener with some irregulars on the 17th January, 1888, but the attack did not succeed, and Colonel Kitchener received a serious wound in the face.

Fighting continued at intervals during the whole year round Suakin. Abu Girgeh arrived, but retired again. At last reinforcements were sent from Cairo, including a British battalion, and Sir Francis Grenfell took command. A decisive action ensued just outside the walls of Suakin (battle of Gemaizeh, 20th December, 1888), in which the enemy were completely defeated. In the following year a certain amount of local fighting went on near the town, but the tribes were becoming exhausted, and Osman was losing some of his influence.

King John of Abyssinia was meanwhile vowing vengeance for the defeat at Debra Sin, and in April of 1888 a sham Abyssinian deputation visited Omdurman, nominally to bring the submission of Ras Adal, but in reality to spy out the land. Abu Angar advanced again, and was at first successful, but in July Ras Adal smote him hip and thigh, and the Dervish general died in the following January, whilst Ras Adal became King of Gojam, under the name of Tekla Haimánot. King John was now determined to capture Gallabat and advance on Omdurman; he therefore left Gondar at the end of February, and advanced against Matamma, the capital of Gallabat. Zeki Tumal had fortified this town, and held it with 60,000 men; but the Abyssinians surrounded and overwhelmed them (9th March). During the last stage of the fight, however, King John was killed by a stray bullet, whereupon his army retired at once. The Dervishes harassed their retreat and captured the body of their monarch, so to all intents the result amounted to an Abyssinian reverse.

On hearing of this, John's rival, Menelik of Shoa, seized the throne and proclaimed himself Negus Nagasti, shortly afterwards making a treaty of friendship with the Italians.

During 1890 Handub was still occupied by the enemy, but in the first days of 1891 Colonel Holled Smith, then Governor, attacked and occupied it during the absence of Osman Digna (27th January). He then followed up his advantage by seizing Trinkitat and Teb, and on the 19th February, after a sharp fight with the enemy at Tokar, he occupied the ruins of that town and the village of Afafit, and drove Osman Digna back to Temrin.

This action and its results were a heavy and, as it proved, a final blow to the Dervish power in the direction of Suakin. Trade was reopened between Suakin and Berber in the summer of 1891, and although Osman Digna threatened reprisals, the tribes were getting tired of Mahdist rule, and refused to respond to his overtures. Raids occurred on a small scale near Tokar and Sinkat during 1892 and 1893, but led to no definite action.

Meanwhile the Italians had been steadily increasing their sphere of operations from Massawa, and by a protocol of the 15th April, 1891, had defined the northern frontier of their new colony of Eritrea as starting from Ras Kasar on the Red Sea coast, and thence proceeding in a south-westerly direction to the Atbara, passing east of Kassala. A further proviso enabled the Italians to take and occupy Kassala (if they could), with a small section of Egyptian territory, on condition that they were to hand it over to Egypt if required.

During 1893 the Dervishes, alarmed at the growth of the Italian power, determined to invade Eritrea, and a

Re-occupation of Kassala.

strong force proceeded eastwards from Kassala (then under the command of Mussaid, who had superseded Abu Girgeh in 1891) with that object. The Dervish force of about 12,000, under Ahmed Ali, arrived at Kassala in November, and pushed forward towards Agordat, an Italian post more than half-way to Massawa. Here Colonel Arimondi, with a native force of only a little over 2,000 men, with 42 officers, met them and inflicted a severe defeat on them (21.12.93), killing Ahmed Ali and routing the force completely. *Battle of Agordat, 21st December, 1893.*

In the following July, Colonel Baratieri, with 2,510 men, made a fine forced march from Agordat, and surprised and took Kassala on the 17th of that month. He thereupon commenced fortifying it, and the town was successfully held by the Italians for nearly two and a half years. The Khalifa was furious, and ordered Ahmed Fedil and Osman Digna to retake it. Nothing, however, was done till the 18th March, 1896, when the Dervishes, in consequence of the severe defeat of the Italians by the Abyssinians at Adua on the 1st of that month, attacked Sabderat and were repulsed. Subsequently, on the 2nd and 3rd April, they fought two severely contested actions at Mokram and Tukruf, just outside Kassala, but on both occasions they were decisively beaten by the Italians under Colonel Stevani, and were forced to retreat. *1894. Capture of Kassala, 17th July, 1894. 1895. 1896. Mokram and Tukruf, April, 1896.*

The only event of importance that took place at Suakin in 1896 was the arrival of an Indian brigade in May to replace the Egyptian garrison called to the Nile, and to act as a menace to the Khalifa from the Eastern Sudan. No opportunity for fighting occurred, and the Indians left for home in December. *Indian brigade, 1896.*

In consequence of the occupation of Berber in September, 1897, the Suakin-Berber road was once more opened for trade and transport, and the 4th Egyptian Battalion passed over it in security in the last days of the year. *1897.*

On the 25th December, 1897, the town of Kassala was taken over by Egypt, and garrisoned by the 16th Battalion, &c., under Colonel Parsons. The Sheikh El Morgani was brought from Suakin to the holy place of his ancestors, the Khatmieh, just outside Kassala, and this act had the result of still further alienating Dervish *Kassala re-occupied by Egypt.*

influence from the neighbourhood. The successful actions by the friendlies at Osobri, Gos Rejeb, El Fasher, and Es Safiyeh will still be fresh in the mind of the reader. The garrison of Kassala rendered valuable assistance in destroying the remnants of the fugitives from the battle of the Atbara last April, and Osman Digna himself only just escaped capture by a force of friendlies under Major Benson.

CHAPTER V.

BAHR EL GHAZAL AND EQUATORIA SINCE 1882.

IN the Bahr el Ghazal the first outbreak in favour of Mahdism occurred at Liffi, on the 18th August, 1882. The people had long been suffering under the cruelty and injustice of their "Danagla" rulers sent from Khartum, and part of the Dinka tribe rose readily under Sheikh Jango to upset the Egyptian Government. Lupton Bey, however, was equal to the occasion, and, advancing from Dem Zubehr (Dem Suliman), towards the end of 1882, he defeated Jango with considerable slaughter at Tel Gauna. 1882.
Lupton defeats the Dinkas.

Jango returned with some of the Emir Madibbo's men early in 1883, but was beaten again near Liffi. In September, however, he attacked Rufai Aga, Lupton's captain, at Dembo, and massacred him and all his men. The Dinkas then revolted *en masse*, and blocked the road to Meshra er Rek and the north, and Lupton, short of ammunition, retired to Dem Zubehr. The last communication from Khartum was brought by a steamer, which arrived thence at Er Rek on the 15th August, and Lupton was thenceforth isolated. 1883.

On Karamalla's appointment as Emir of Bahr el Ghazal, he summoned Lupton to surrender, and this the latter, after gallantly fighting for 18 months, was obliged, by the defection of his troops, to do (21.4.84). He was christened Emir Abdullah and sent to Omdurman, where he died on the 17th July, 1888. Surrender of Lupton, 1884.

Thus the last vestige of Egyptian authority disappeared in the Bahr el Ghazal.

The Equatorial province meanwhile, which extended from the Albert Nyanza to Lado (its capital), and included (since 1881) the provinces of Bor and Rohl, and the northern part of Unyoro, was under the charge of Emin Bey (Edward Schnitzer, born 1840), who had been Emin and his province.

placed there by Gordon in 1879. His forces in 1882 consisted of two battalions (about 1,300) of Egyptian and Sudanese troops, and 3,000 irregulars, distributed amongst 40 to 50 stations. This province was, by the end of 1882, practically the only Egyptian territory south of Khartum which was not in sympathy with the Mahdi.

Karamalla, in May (27th), 1884, summoned Emin to surrender. The latter, whose men were greatly scattered and, by this time, considerably disaffected, agreed to send a deputation to surrender, but, meanwhile, held out at Lado and Amadi, hoping for reinforcements. Amadi fell in March, 1885, and on the 18th April Karamalla arrived within three days of Lado and informed Emin of the fall of Khartum. Emin thereupon determined to retire south to Wadelai, giving up the more northerly posts.

1885.

Karamalla shortly afterwards was obliged to fall back owing to disturbances in the Bahr el Ghazal caused by several Emirs refusing to recognise the Khalifa Abdullah as successor of the Mahdi, and Emin retired to Wadelai to open friendly relations with Kabarega, King of Unyoro. Meanwhile Lado and Regaf were attacked by negro tribes in the district but held out.

1886.

On the 26th February, 1886, Emin received, through the assistance of Kabarega, letters from Cairo, *viâ* Zanzibar, in which he was informed by Nubar Pasha (dated 2.11.85) that the Sudan was abandoned, and he "might take any steps he liked should he decide to leave the country." Dr. Junker, who had been, off and on, with Emin since January, 1884, started for Zanzibar, *viâ* Uganda, in January, 1886, and his representations in Europe had the effect of starting the Emin Relief Expedition.

1887.

During 1886 and 1887 a mutinous spirit had been brewing amongst Emin's troops, who wished to retire northwards instead of southwards. On the 15th December, 1887, the advanced guard of Stanley's expedition arrived on the Albert Nyanza, but, not hearing any news of Emin, went back for their boat, which had been left at Kilonga Longa's. Kabarega now, to whom Emin had sent Casati* to keep open communications with Zanzibar, on hearing that Stanley had fought and defeated the Mazamboni, his allies, changed his friendly attitude to

Stanley's relief expedition.

* An Italian officer who had been sent out to assist Gessi Pasha and remained on to explore.

Emin, thinking that the latter had sent for Stanley to invade his (Kabarega's) country. He therefore treated Casati outrageously and expelled him with the greatest ignominy.

Stanley and Emin eventually met at Nsabé (Kavalli's) on 29th April, 1888, and thereupon reports of a great invading White Pasha spread to Omdurman, with the result that the Khalifa in July sent up thence three steamers, six barges, and 4,000 troops to annihilate him. Stanley went back again on 24th May to pick up his rear guard, leaving Mounteney Jephson and a small escort with Emin, to escort him round his province and settle whether he should retire or not. The Khedive's "orders," which Stanley brought with him, were to the effect that Emin and his men might come back with Stanley, or stay on at their own risk. {1888.}

The garrisons in the south said they would go with Emin, but the troops at Labore mutinied, and a general revolt broke out, headed by Fadl el Maula, Governor of Fabbo; thus, on arriving at Dufile, Emin and Jephson were practically made prisoners (18.8.88). On the 15th October news arrived that the above-mentioned Mahdists, in barges, were at hand, and two days afterwards three messengers arrived from Omar Saleh, the Mahdist commander, to summon Emin to surrender. The mutineers now released Emin and decided to fight, and during November and December continuous fighting went on between Lado and Dufile. Regaf was taken by the Dervishes on 15th November, and much loot, several prisoners and captured despatches, ammunition, tarbûshes, and flags, were sent by Omar to Omdurman, whence a portion was forwarded through Osman Digna to General Grenfell at Suakin. This gave rise to all sorts of surmises in Egypt as to the fate of Emin and Stanley. {Arrival of Dervishes. Fall of Regaf.}

During December, Emin's mutinous troops kept the Dervishes at bay between Wadelai and Regaf, and eventually severely defeated them, driving them back to Regaf. They did not, however, follow up their victory, and, under the leadership of Fadl el Maula Bey, remained in and about Wadelai, whilst the Dervishes strengthened their post at Regaf.

Meanwhile Emin and Jephson had retired to Tunguru on the Albert Nyanza, and on 18th January, 1889, Stanley arrived at the lake for the third time with the remains of {1889.}

his expedition, and was joined by Emin and Jephson in the beginning of February. Selim Bey, now commander of a portion of Emin's rebel troops at Wadelai, on being summoned by Emin, left Wadelai with 14 Egyptian officers for Tunguru, and on arrival expressed his contrition for the mutiny. A council held on the 18th determined that the evacuation should take place on the 10th April, and although Selim Bey, who had returned to Wadelai, where Fadl el Maula Bey was in command, wrote to say all would return with Emin to Egypt, they did not arrive in time, and, although every opportunity was given them of overtaking the expedition, no one appeared. The expedition, numbering about 600 men in all and 900 women and children, eventually arrived in Zanzibar at the end of the year 1889.

Emin returns to the coast.

The Emir Karamalla, after retiring from before Lado and Emin in 1885 to quash disaffections amongst his own Emirs against the Khalifa's succession, appears to have become disaffected himself. So the Khalifa, seeing the danger of trying to hold a huge province with insufficient forces, and fearing that Karamalla, being a Dongolawi, might revolt altogether, ordered the latter to evacuate the province and retire to Shakka and eventually to Omdurman. Thus the land returned to the semi-barbarous state it was in before the Egyptian occupation, and had peace from the Dervishes for some years, for the Mahdist operations were chiefly confined to the neighbourhood of the Nile, and had little effect in the direction of the Bahr el Arab and interior of the Bahr el Ghazal country.

Bahr el Ghazal evacuated by Dervishes.

In 1890 a rebellion against the Mahdists sprang up among the Shillûks, in the neighbourhood of Fashoda,* and the Emir of Gallabat, Zeki Tumal, was sent thither to quell it, with a force chiefly consisting of the Gallabat men who had fought so well against the Abyssinians in the spring of 1889.† During the whole of 1891 the war continued with varying fortunes, the Dervishes on more than one occasion being heavily defeated, and the communications between Omdurman and Bahr el Jebel being completely interrupted, much to the anxiety of the Khalifa. Alarmist reports continued to arrive in Omdurman during 1891 to the effect that Emin Pasha was at Dufile, advancing northwards with a large body of

1890. Shillûk war.

1891.

---

* *V.* p. 181.   † *V.* p. 191.

Germans, and reinforcements were sent to help Zeki and fight against the white invaders.*

Eventually Zeki got the upper hand of the Shillûks in the beginning of 1892, but the Dervish supremacy did not last long. In the summer of that year it was reported at Omdurman that the Italians were advancing westwards from Massawa. Zeki Tumal was therefore recalled with his army, and was thus obliged to evacuate Fashoda, leaving only a very small guard for the purpose of collecting taxes. *(margin: 1892.)*

He was then sent back to Gedaref and Galabat, to make headway against the Italians, but on reporting that it was impossible to invade Eritrea, as the Khalifa wished him to do, he was again recalled to Omdurman, treacherously seized, thrown into prison, and ultimately starved to death. *(margin: Fate of Zeki Tumal.)*

(For the movements of the remainder of Emin's men, and of the Congo expeditions, see "Précis of Events on the Upper Nile, 1878–1898," I.D.W.O. "Confidential.")

During 1892 reports reached Omdurman from the south of an European advance on Equatoria from the Zanzibar direction. At this period there was a small Dervish garrison at Regaf under Omar Saleh, and orders were sent to him to withdraw to Bor. This was effected, but the climate of Bor was so unhealthy, and the natives so difficult to manage, that Abu Girgeh, a powerful Emir whom the Khalifa was anxious to get rid of, was sent south in October with 250 men, with orders to send Omar Saleh to Omdurman. Abu Girgeh, who had got wind of the Khalifa's intentions, took the first opportunity of fighting the other Baggara Emirs who were with him, and absconding at Fashoda. *(margin: Abu Girgeh. October, 1892.)*

For several months he was supposed to have deserted the Khalifa and joined a serious movement in Kordofan which was led by a western saint, one Muzil el Muhan, and which aimed at the destruction of the Khalifa. The

---

* It is, perhaps, hardly necessary to say that these rumours were almost entirely devoid of foundation, for Emin, on his return to the interior, never went north of Kavalli's, having a lively recollection of his troubles (in 1888) on the Upper Nile. He was murdered at Kinena's, in the Congo Free State, on 26th October, 1892; this crime was owing to the petty jealousy of one Kibonge, who wished to show his rival, Munye Mohara, who had murdered several Belgians, that he too could kill a white man!

latter, by the way, had been much disturbed by this insurrection, and sent his cousin Ibrahim Khalil with 4,000 men to suppress it; but the movement died out by itself (*v.* p. 187).

1893. Abu Girgeh eventually arrived at Regaf in July, 1893. Probably fearing the Khalifa's wrath, and finding the station in a flourishing condition, he sent the Khalifa a present of ivory as a peace offering, this arriving in August, 1893. Not even a rumour of any fighting having taken place at either Regaf or Lado, least of all with any whites, seems to have reached Omdurman about this time.

On Omar Saleh arriving at Omdurman he assured the Khalifa that the district was not in danger, and that no Europeans had arrived there. The Khalifa thereupon **Ariba Wad** despatched his relative Arabi Wad Dafalla to take **Dafalla.** command, to transfer the garrison from Bor back to Regaf, and to place Abu Girgeh in chains (presumably for his misconduct at Fashoda).

It is more than likely that the above-mentioned rumours at Omdurman of a large Christian force in Equatoria did refer to Van Kerckhoven's Congo expedition, which had at that time (November, 1892), barely crossed the great watershed; but rumour, especially in the Sudan, is not to be trusted implicitly.

Arabi Wad Dafalla arrived in the autumn of 1893 from Omdurman, with 1,500 men, to supersede Abu Girgeh, the latter having another 1,500 at Regaf. Arabi on his arrival wrote to Fadl el Maula Bey, now in com- **Dervishes** mand of some of Emin's former men, inviting him to seize **and** **Congolese.** Baert* and his officers and to bring them to him, but Fadl had had enough of the Dervishes, and declined; 400, however, of Baert's 900 natives heard of this, and deserted *en masse* to the Dervishes, some of whom, under Abu Girgeh, were penetrating in a W.S.W. direction, and had arrived in the Makaraka country. Fadl el Maula then took service with Baert.

Baert does not appear to have actually come to blows with the Dervishes here, but with his thoughts intent on establishing Congolese posts on the Upper Nile, and even on the Albert Nyanza, at Kavalli's, he despatched four companies of Sudanese (400 men) under Fadl el Maula

---

* Successor to Van Kerckhoven.

to proceed to the Nile and there to establish posts in the interest of the Congo Free State. The exact route of this party is not known; they appear to have gone first towards the Nile in the direction of Regaf, but hearing the Dervishes had reoccupied that spot and were close at hand in force, they retreated to Makaraka and Wandi. Here they were overtaken and had a severe fight with the Dervishes, losing Fadl el Maula (killed—some say taken prisoner and executed) and about half their number, together with a large quantity of material of all sorts. After this defeat, which took place in January, 1894, the remaining 200 struck out for the Nile, and reached it about Muggi and Labore, but, finding little food, drifted towards Wadelai, and arrived there early in February.

Fight at Wandi.

1894.

To refer now to Uganda for a moment.

Colonel Colvile was appointed Chief Commissioner in 1893, and arrived there on the 16th November of that year. One of his first acts was to declare war against Kabarega, King of Unyoro, who had for some time been perpetually harassing Uganda, and on the second day of 1894 he occupied his capital. On the 2nd February Major Owen was despatched with a small party by boat to Wadelai, and on the 4th he arrived there, meeting at first with a hostile reception from the banks. He landed, however, hoisted the British flag, enlisted 50 natives (Luri) to protect it, and learnt from the natives that no white man had reached the place since Emin Pasha left it in 1888. The garrison had gone, he was informed, in April, 1893, to join the Dervishes. Hearing next day reports that a large body of "Dervishes" was approaching from the north, he retired, and arrived at Kibiro on the 11th.

Defeat of Kabarega.

Owen at Wadelai.

From subsequent events it appears that these "Dervishes" were none other than the remaining 200 of Fadl el Maula Bey's men, and had Owen remained another day, he would have been able, no doubt, to bring them back with him into British territory.

As it was, this event was only postponed for a short time, for Captain Thruston, who was sent to reconnoitre the western shores of the Albert Nyanza in March, found on the 23rd of that month the two Sudanese companies at Mahaji Sghir. To this spot they had drifted from Wadelai, not finding enough supplies at the latter place.

They were straightway enlisted by Thruston, and eventually brought back under the British flag to Uganda.

Events in the Bahr el Ghazal up to February, 1894.

We must now take a glance at the Bahr el Ghazal, and endeavour to bring the history of that province, for the present, up to the beginning of 1894.

1886.

The state of things in the Bahr el Ghazal since 1886 had been, on the whole, peaceable. On the death of Osman Ganu, Dervish commandant of Shakka, about 1888, the Emir Abu Mariam had succeeded him, and for three or four years little fighting had taken place. The country had relapsed into its original barbarous state of small native independent tribes, and Dervish influence, although nominally extending over the whole province, did not make itself felt in the direction of aggression.

1888. Abu Mariam.

Nothing worthy of record occurred until La Kéthulle appeared on the scene from the south. This officer had been ordered by Van Kerckhoven in 1891 to proceed to Rafai's, make friendly treaties with him, and obtain his assistance in furthering Van Kerckhoven's expedition. He left Bomokandi in February, 1892, and reached Rafai's early in April. Here he was received in a most friendly manner, and made a treaty with Rafai on the 7th April. During the remainder of the year he established Congo posts up to the 7th parallel of north latitude, such as Alewali and Bandassi. Rafai assisted him to the best of his ability, and from December, 1892, to April, 1893, accompanied him on an exploring tour *viâ* Yangu, Baraka, and the Upper Bali to Sango and back. La Kéthulle then returned to Yakoma, where a large expedition for the North was being organised by the Belgians, under Captain Nilis.

1891.

1892.

1893.

During this summer (1893), in consequence of some inter-tribal fighting, Abu Mariam advanced against the Dinka or Janghé tribe. A battle took place, in which Abu Mariam was killed and his force destroyed, whereupon the fugitive Dervishes took refuge in Shakka, leaving many of their rifles in the hands of the Janghé. On hearing of this, the Belgian Governor of Semio (Le Marinel) sent to Faki Ahmed and Adjerra, chiefs in the Dar Fertit, and unwilling allies of the Dervishes, asking them to make common cause with the Janghé against the Mahdists. At the same time he despatched an ally of Semio's, one Baudué, who appears to have been starting an expedition in the direction of Dem Bekr "to

Dinkas beat Dervishes.

conquer the Bahr el Ghazal" on his own account, to help them, and reinforced him by sending 2,000 men to Ombanga.

They were, however, not required. The Dervishes were too broken to renew the attack on the Janghé, and no further action appears to have taken place in this direction. Mahmud, chief Emir of Kordofan and the Bahr el Ghazal, was much incensed at Abu Mariam's defeat, and sent to Darfur for reinforcements; but the chiefs in Darfur refused to assist, or even to come and see him.

Mahmud.

By the beginning of 1894 the Congo Expedition for the North was ready, and in February Nilis, with La Kéthulle as second in command, five other whites (Lannoy, Gérard, Libois, Gonse Deschrymacker, and Sergeant Philippart), and a strong party, made a start for the North.

1894.

Recapitulating shortly, we see that by the end of February, 1894, the Dervishes based on Regaf were pressing the remains of the Kerckhoven expedition under Baert on the Congo-Nile watershed, but that in the rest of the Bahr el Ghazal their influence was practically nil, their only post of any importance, and that weakly held, being Shakka, to the north of the Bahr el Arab. The Congo forces had not succeeded in establishing posts on the Nile, whilst between the north-west of the Bahr el Ghazal and Semio's country they were busy cementing relations with the natives, who seemed not ill-disposed to receive them. Since the British Government had taken over Uganda on 1st April, 1893, fears had been expressed that the Dervishes would attack the colony from the north; but for this there appears to have been no justification, for the Khalifa had no intention of enlarging his dominions in this direction, and was content to keep Regaf as a penal settlement and as an outpost against the inroads of the whites.

The expedition under La Kéthulle (for Nilis's name disappears almost at once) penetrated *viâ* Sandu, up the Chinko River, Sango, back to Sandu, Bakuma, Kreish, Bandassi country (7° 30" north latitude), Upper Adda or Bahr el Arab (8° 40" north latitude), to the important town of Hofrat en Nahas (where there are valuable copper mines), being well received all along the route. At Hofrat en Nahas the natives are said to have offered to take La Kéthulle west along the caravan route to Lake

La Kéthulle.

Chad, but he declined, and himself returned along his own route to Rafai, where he arrived on 8th June, 1894, and at proceeded to Europe.

Re-occupation by Dervishes.
The Khalifa on hearing of the presence of Europeans in the Bahr el Ghazal and of their having communicated with the Emir of Shakka, sent orders to Mahmud to reoccupy the Bahr el Ghazal, and in consequence a force of 1,800 Sudanese riflemen and 2,000 spearmen, under the Emir Khatem Musa, was despatched from Shakka towards the Belgian posts in the summer of 1894; they were delayed some time by the rains, but eventually pushed forward. The Belgians, whose headquarters were at Liffi, with advanced post at Hofrat en Nahas, retired before Khatem Musa, who entered Faroga. Sheikh Hamed, finding himself deserted by the Belgians, sided with the Dervishes, and handed over the treaties; these, together with two letters written by Belgians at Liffi dated September, 1894, arrived at Omdurman in January, 1895.

The result of the Dervish victory over Fadl el Maula manifested itself at Omdurman in May, 1894, by a steamer from Regaf bringing back loot in the shape of many tarbûshes, two guns, ivory, five red standards with white stripes, and many breech-loading rifles and Congo Free State buttons, together with a report that a great victory had been gained over "the Turks." This produced at first considerable conjecture in Egypt as to the identity of those who had been defeated.

As regards Abu Girgeh, he was thrown into prison about the same time by Dafalla.

The Dervishes had meanwhile been losing ground in the west, and only retained garrisons at El Fasher, El Obeid, Nuhud, and Shakka, besides the penal settlement at Regaf.

During 1894 there were various disturbances and rumours of invasion by white men in general from the south-west, and by Rabeh Zubehr in particular. Although little is known about these western movements in Wadai, &c., it is worth noticing that much information, decidedly accurate on the whole, regarding movements of Europeans and their native troops on the Upper Nile trickled down to Omdurman and thence to the Egyptian Intelligence Department.

A rumour reached Omdurman in November, 1894, that the Regaf troops were being hard pressed (this must refer to the fights of the "Mahdists" with the Congolese), and eleven barges full of troops were sent as reinforcements. Numerous reports now reached Omdurman that the whites had beaten the Dervishes; this may refer to the victory by the Congolese at Egaru on the 23rd December, 1894. The Regaf garrison was now estimated at 1,500 riflemen and 3,000 spearmen, with two steamers.

In consequence of the Franco-Congolese treaty of 1894, Major Cunningham and Lieut. Vandeleur were sent from Uganda in the beginning of 1895 to Dufile, where they planted the British flag on the 15th January. A hostile reception was given them at Wadelai in consequence, it is believed, of the alliance of the chief of that place with Kabarega.

On the retreat of the Belgians in the Bahr el Ghazal, Khatem Musa retired towards Shakka, but famine and disease broke out in his camp, and most of his black Jehadieh deserted to Semio. The latter thereupon marched against Musa, who had but 800 left out of 4,000, and even these were mostly sick. Khatem Musa retreated towards Mahmud's force in Kordofan, Abu Khawata, the recently-appointed Emir of Shakka, accompanying him. The Bahr el Ghazal was thus left open to any Europeans who chose to enter (April, 1895).

1895.
Re-evacuation by Dervishes.

In June a frantic message arrived at Omdurman from Wad Dafalla, clamouring for reinforcements, as he was threatened by the speedy advance of an European force. He had therefore retired to Shambe.

This panic would seem to have been a false alarm, consequent, perhaps, on Congolese reinforcements having been sent to Dongu. However, numbers of men were collected and hastily sent upstream from Omdurman under one Hamadnalla, Emir of the Powder Factory at Khartum. Strengthened by these (4,000 in all) Wad Dafalla returned to Regaf, and sent Hamadnalla in the autumn to suppress an attack by the riverain tribes.

During 1896 Dafalla and his men appear to have been paralysed by the news of the Dongola campaign, and remained quiet.

1896.

Nothing further of interest occurred, as far as we know, until the attack and occupation of Regaf in 1897, by Chaltin.

Chaltin's column—part of a large force of Congo troops

under Baron Dhanis—composed of five white officers, four white non-commissioned officers, 806 trained riflemen, some guns, 250 porters, 50 Azande (Niam-Niam) riflemen, and 500 spearmen under their chiefs Renzi and Bafuka, arrived at Surrur at the end of the year, and left it on the 1st January. On the 14th February they reached the Nile at Beddên, and their scouts came into touch with the Dervishes. On the 17th they attacked the Dervish position near Regaf, held by about 2,000 men, and routed them with great loss; later in the day they had another small action, and occupied Regaf, the Dervishes bolting to the north. Chaltin lost one white officer (Sarolea) killed and a few men, and the enemy lost nine Emirs, 200 dead, three guns, 700 rifles, and a large stock of ammunition and provisions. Regaf was found to possess a good landing-place, and was strengthened by earthworks. Lado no longer existed.

1897.

Capture of Regaf by Chaltin, 14th February, 1897.

A report from the Congo (June, '97), states that there are now 15,000 (!?) Dervishes at Bor, and that they have three European prisoners, of whose identity nothing is certain.* Chaltin himself had then about 1,300 men with him, and was mostly at a spot called Loka, on high ground, four days' march west of Regaf. He reported the soil to be poor, and that there was little prospect of trade. Captain Hanolet has now succeeded him.

Marchand expedition.

As regards the French Expedition of over 400 men under Marchand and Liotard, which started from the French Congo in 1896 with a view to penetrating into the valley of the Upper Nile, it reached the Sue River, an affluent of the Bahr el Ghazal, last autumn, and began launching two 5-ton gunboats. It is probable that the members will experience considerable difficulty in their task, in consequence of insufficient water for navigation till July, the *sudd*, and the pronounced hostility of the natives.

1898.

The Dervish supremacy in the Bahr el Ghazal and regions bordering on the Upper Nile has now been greatly diminished owing to their severe defeat at Regaf, and also owing to the necessity of reinforcing their threatened centre about Omdurman.

---

* One is reported to be an Englishman, by name Hackiff.

APPENDIX I.

THE SUDD, AND METHODS FOR DEALING WITH IT.

Dr. Junker writes as follows:—

"Before leaving this watery domain, a few words may be acceptable regarding the formation of the *sudd* in the Upper Nile regions. How disastrous such obstructions may at times prove, was shown by the fatal issue of the voyage undertaken the same year by Gessi Pasha from Meshra er Rêq to Khartum. The steamer *Safia* had left Meshra on September 25th, 1880, taking in tow some boats with over 400 Arabs and officials, leaving the Bahr el Ghazal province after the war with Soliman, and the whole flotilla got completely hemmed in by a grass-barrier near the Ghaba Jer Dekka, some distance below the Bahr el Arab confluence. All efforts to get disentangled were in vain; provisions soon fell short; famine and typhus combined swept away over half of the men; the others lived on the flesh of the dead, and not one of them would have ever seen Khartum again had not Marno appeared with the steamer *Bordein* as an angel of deliverance on January 4th, 1881, bringing succour to the survivors after months of unspeakable horrors and misery.

"As regards the firmness of their texture, the grass-barriers show considerable diversity. Some are loose enough to be forced by a powerful steamer at the cost of much patience, toil, and help, while others resist all such efforts. The latter type is more easily developed in the Bahr el Jebel, which abounds far more than the Bahr el Ghazal in isolated or stagnant backwaters and lateral lagoons. Such tenacious masses are, in fact, more frequently formed in the Bahr el Jebel, while the looser kinds are more characteristic of the Bahr el Ghazal.

"It is abundantly evident that the vegetation itself does not spring up spontaneously on the spot where it becomes solid enough to dam up such a mighty river as the Upper Nile, whose breadth, depth, and current would necessarily prevent such a growth. Few rivers in the world have so slight a fall as the Upper Nile, and its western affluent, the Bahr el Ghazal. In its course across many degrees of latitude, the former traverses a uniform level region, and in many places the current is maintained merely by the pressure of the streams descending from the more elevated parts of the Bahr el Jebel basin.

" Through the periodical rise of the Nile, which differs considerably in volume from year to year, being determined by the amount of the rainfall in the tropics, the low-lying riverain tracts are flooded, and these consist in many places of flat depressions where the Nile waters lodge after the general subsidence. Such depressions often continue even at low water to communicate with the main stream, of which they form, as it were, so many inlets; or else they become transformed in the dry season to small lakes and ponds, which resume their connection with the Nile at each returning rise. These are the '*old*' or back waters, the *Maiyehs* of the Arab boatmen, which are constantly changing their level and assuming a different aspect with the rise and fall of the flood-waters. They form hundreds of *culs-de-sac* of all sizes, by which the difficulties of the navigation is greatly increased. Such conditions do not occur in the Sobat with its high and regular banks, but are partly found in the section between the Sobat and the Moqren el Bahūr, and especially on the Bahr el Jebel, as far as and beyond the station of Bor. Other conditions prevail in the Bahr el Ghazal, where the *Maiyehs* are doubtless rarer, but where broad flooded expanses are more frequent.

"The periodically replenished lateral lagoons and depressions naturally promote a rank growth of aquatic plants, and the *Maiyehs* are in fact the hot-beds and nurseries of all the grass islands which drift away to the main stream when the communications are re-opened. But at other times the same stagnant waters serve to retain the masses which, being rooted very lightly to the ground, gradually form floating islands. Such islands, continually growing in thickness and solidity, would in fact become stable, and in course of time fill up nearly the whole of the *Maiyeh*, but for the fact that at each periodical flooding they get detached from the bed of the depression and raised to the surface. Then they drift away before the high winds and reach the Nile in various states of development. During our detention at Fashoda, strong north winds had constantly prevailed, and under their action all the floating masses along the northern bends of the river would be inevitably driven into the main stream.

"In a word, the favourable conditions for the development of the *sudd* in the Upper Nile basin are:—

"1. A rise of the flood-waters above the normal level in order to bring the backwaters into free communication with the river, and at the same time detach and raise the floating masses to the surface.

"2. Favourable winds to further detach and drive these masses into the river, where they either drift harmlessly with the currents, or else coalesce together into formidable barriers. At the same time, the winds, as is obvious, may have a contrary effect, arresting as well as propelling the masses, breaking up as well as building up the barriers; hence the constant changes that these formations are subject to through the shifting of the winds, as well as from the varying character of the periodical floods.

"3. The growth of those innumerable little plants, which spring up in still and sheltered waters, and then drift away to enlarge or render more compact the tangle of the floating masses. Such are, for instance, the Azolla, Pistia, Aldrovanduà, Lemna, Ottelia, Ultricularia, Ceratophyllum, Potamogeton, Naias, Lagarosiphon, and others.

"But even under the most favourable conditions a protracted damming up of the Nile is of relatively rare occurrence, as, however deep the barrier may be, the current always flows underneath. In the opinion of long-experienced Arab boatmen, the prevailing relations in the forties and fifties were much the same as at present, though in those years the obstructions were never so compact as some of those occurring in recent times. The best known were those of 1863, at the time of Miss Tinné's visit; of 1870 and 1871, by which Sir Samuel Baker's expedition was delayed, and which was ultimately cleared away by the vigorous action of Ismaīl Eyub Pasha in 1874; of 1878, at my first excursion, when the Nile rose to an unusual height, and caused extensive floodings in the delta.

"It may be mentioned that in the lower reaches of the White Nile the current is too strong to allow of any accumulations. Here the smaller masses, breaking away from the southern barriers, are carried swiftly along to and beyond Khartum. But very little reaches Egypt itself, most of the floating growths being either arrested in the recesses along the banks, or else becoming waterlogged and sinking to the bottom, where they are slowly decomposed.

"In the composition of the *sudd*, the prevailing element, at least in the Bahr el Ghazal region, is the so-called Om-Suf, or 'Mother of Wool' (*Vossia procera*), an aquatic grass, which, to the unscientific eye, looks more like a reed. It is a favourite food of animals, and in its midst grow patches of papyrus, but very little ambatch, which generally shoots up from deep water and enters only casually into the composition of the sudd.

"The varying texture of these obstructions depends largely on the different conditions under which they have been brought together, on their age and general constituents. Their tenacity is at times so great that huge amphibia, such as the hippopotamus and crocodile that occasionally get entangled in their meshes, are unable to free themselves, and thus perish of hunger or want of air. As a rule they are more compact, and consequently present greater obstacles to navigation in the Bahr el Jebel and White Nile than in the Bahr el Ghazal. In this river we were generally able to force our way through such impediments, even though steaming against the current. But in the Bahr el Jebel the steamer alone is often helpless, and requires the aid of special apparatus to break through.

"In most cases the object aimed at is simply to get through, leaving the obstruction to close up again or not behind the steamer. But when systematic and continuous operations are undertaken to clear the waterway, the course adopted is to break up the masses piecemeal, and send the fragments into the current to prevent them from again coalescing, at least in the same place. Solid masses can be attacked successfully from the north side only, that is, operating against the current. In this case most of the work is in fact done by the stream itself, by carrying off the fragments as they get detached by the men at work on board the steamer. But were the steamer to force its way with the current into the tangle, the detached pieces could not drift away, and the ship would run the risk of being caught, as in the pack-ice of the Arctic regions, by the fragments closing in from behind. In November, 1878, Emin Bey was thus arrested with his steamer on the journey down to Khartum, and being unable to overcome the obstacle, had to return to Lado. To the same circumstance was due the already described disaster that befel Gessi and his people in the Bahr el Ghazal two years later.

"The usual plan is for the steamer to select a suitable point of attack, and go full speed into the elastic *sudd*, if possible through some opening between the shore and the barrier, where the elastic parts are generally more easily detached. Some of the crew help with long-forked poles, guiding all released masses sternwards, while others co-operate on the barrier itself just in front of the prow, pressing it down below the surface and thus facilitating the progress of the steamer. They work breast-deep, steadily moving forward or clambering up to get the higher parts under-water. During these operations the progress of the vessel is scarcely perceptible, although the paddles are continually kept going.

"But should all efforts fail, recourse is had to another process which, though tedious, aims at clearing the waterway to the utmost. As before, the steamer drives at full speed into the yielding tangle, in which, however, it soon gets hemmed in. Then all dead inflammable matter, such as dry papyrus stalks, is fired; and when consumed, two diverging cables are made fast to the floating mass at a distance of 30 to 50 yards from the prow. The ropes are secured by being wound round long stakes, which are driven right through the thick mass at an oblique angle to prevent them from yielding when the steamer begins to back off. After one or two efforts this manœuvre generally detaches a large floating island, which either at once drifts away down-stream, or else is taken in tow by another steamer, and sent adrift at any point where the current is strong enough to carry it down.

"Should even this method fail, then the whole mass is

broken up and torn away bit by bit by the steamer. Such operations are excessively tedious, and Marno was occupied from September, 1879, to April, 1880, with four steamers and several hundred men in clearing the Bahr el' Jebel.

"To these aquatic growths the White Nile, as well as many other sluggish streams of tropical Africa, owe their characteristic aspect. The White, which is the 'Clear,' is so named in contradistinction to the Blue, that is, the 'Dark' or 'Turbid' river, which contains a large proportion of inorganic matter kept constantly churned up by its rapid current and eddies. In the White Nile, on the contrary, as well as in its numerous affluents, the floating vegetation acts like a filter, purifying the troubled flood-waters of the rainy season, and sending them down in almost a limpid stream as far as and even beyond the Blue Nile confluence."

The miseries endured by people blocked in the *sudd* are graphically described by Dr. Felkiu :—

"Imagine then a space of clear water, 100 yards broad and 300 long, bounded on each side by tall grass and reeds, which grow to a height of 20 or 30 feet above the water, so that nothing but water, grass, and sky could be seen. The river was dark and dirty; supposing you called for a glass of water, you obtained a liquid mixture of mud and water; if a pinch of alum was added to clear it, the result was that about a quarter of an inch of mud was deposited at the bottom of the glass. The sickening smell of tropical plants and of the rotting vegetation oppressed us; now and then dead fish floated past, or at times we saw the decaying body of a native slowly borne down the stream. The air was alive with mosquitoes, whose attacks continued by day as well as by night. The steamer was so crowded that there was no room to walk about the deck, so that want of exercise told upon our health, in addition to the impure water and insufficient food: for all our fresh meat was soon finished, and our principal food was dhurra pancakes, and this was nearly exhausted before we were released, the sailors having to be put on short allowance long before. Nearly every day we had a terrible storm of wind and drenching rain, and the heat of Khartum having warped the decks, the cabins were not watertight; so that in a storm the driest place was sitting in the paddle-box, but I usually preferred the soaking deck to the smells and mosquitoes which congregated there. About sunset a cold dense fog arose from the river and hung like a pall over the steamer. Even night brought no alleviation to our misery: owing to the frequent storms we were obliged to sleep under cover, and the damp, hot atmosphere below turned the cabins into a vapour bath. Sleep was impossible; the hours passed in a semi-stupor, broken by frightful dreams and horrid nightmare, so that morning found us unrefreshed, and each day less able to contemplate with stoical indifference the outcome of our imprisonment. More than half the crew were down with fever, and the way in which the poor sailors had to work while trying to extricate the steamer was piteous in the extreme. In order to get wood they were obliged to drag the boat through the floating vegetation for nearly 3 miles, and then work up to their waists in water to reach the little wood procurable. One load of wood was their daily task, and 10 hours' work was required to obtain it; however, they never grumbled, but when unloading the boat at night might even be heard singing as they passed the wood up to the steamer." (September, 1878.)

Emin Pasha in November, 1878, steaming down the river from Lado, came across three blocks, the first two of which he successfully circumvented by lateral channels. The third stopped him completely, and he heard of a fourth, which would effectually have blocked any boat.

As it is likely that blocks will occur in the same places in bad years, the positions are given:—

First block, 9 miles north of Shambe (lateral channel, right bank).

Second block, 8 miles north of Hellet Nuer (lateral channel, left bank).

Third block, 30 miles south of Lake No.

Fourth block, 8 miles east of Lake No.

APPENDIX II.

GLOSSARY OF SOME SUDANESE TERMS.

Agaba	Rocky obstacle; bad going.
Alim (pl. Ulema)	Religious teacher; learned man.
Atmur	Desert, or desert route.
Arabi (pl. Orban)	Free Arab, as opposed to village or town Arabs.
Arbaïn, Darb el	40 days' desert road, from El Fasher (Darfur) to Assiut.
Baggára	Cattle-breeding tribes.
Bazinger	Former slaves, used as irregular troops by slave-traders.
Beit el Mal	Public warehouse; treasury.
Debba (pl. Dibab)	A small stony hill.
Dem	Camp of straw *tukls*.
Farukh	Traders' gun-boys; hence, irregulars.
Gala (pl. Galat)	Fort on a hill.
Gellab (pl. Gellabun)	Itinerant traders; hence, slave-traders.
Gharb, El	West; or left bank of Nile.
Ghazi	One who fights in the cause of Islam.
Gihat	Direction.
Goz (pl. Gizan)	Small sandy hill.
Hadendoa tribe	From *Hada* = chief, and *endoa* = people.
Hilla or Helle (pl. Haliai)	Village.
Hosh (pl. Hishan)	Enclosure.
Íd (pl. Adad)	Desert well.
Kherif	Rainy season (generally June to September).
Kufriat	Ruins.
Magdum (= Mokaddem)	Darfur name for chief of district.
Mahdi	"The Guided" in *hadaya* (= salvation).
Meshra	Strictly speaking, a watering-place on a river; hence, landing-place, ford, ferry.
Muwalled (pl. ín)	Native of mixed parentage (generally Turkish or Egyptian father and black mother).
Sayid, Sidi	Lord (not *said* = happy).
Safel, Es	North.
Said, Es	South.

GLOSSARY OF SOME SUDANESE TERMS—continued.

Sabah, Es	East.
Siat Ilbil	Camel-breeding tribes.
Sherg, Esh	East, right bank of Nile.
Shitta	Winter (October to March).
Sirsiwari	Lieut.-Colonel of Bashi Bazuks.
Seff	Dry season, Summer (April to June).
Tabia (pl. Tawabi)	Fort.
Tajer	Settled trader.
Tukl	Straw hut; conical or flat roof.
Takruri	Negro pilgrims from Wadai or Darfur, who settle in the Eastern Sudan; chiefly near Gallabat.
Turki	Hated oppressor, of any nationality.
Ushr	Tithe tax.
Wahabi	Moslem revivalists in Arabia, mostly crushed by Ismail Pasha.
Zeka	Dervish tax on animals and money.

APPENDIX III.

BONCHAMP'S JOURNEY TO THE UPPER SOBÂT, 1897-98.

The expedition of M. de Bonchamps, which left Addis Abbaba (Abyssinia) for the Nile in 1897, is reported to have worked from Goré (8° 5′ N. lat. and 36° 40′ E. long.) down the Baro River, along its left bank, crossing the Gelo and Alworn Rivers, on to a huge desolate marshy plain, which it traversed for 125 miles.

Twenty-five miles further on, the junction of the Baro with the Juba (or Upper Sobât) was reached. The Juba was here 150 yards wide, deep, with a strong current, and full of crocodiles. Not being able to cross it the expedition returned (Christmas, 1897) to Abyssinia.

www.ingramcontent.com/pod-product-compliance
Lightning Source LLC
Chambersburg PA
CBHW021830230426
43669CB00008B/926